THE PROGRESSIVE ERA

Recent Titles in the Guides to Historical Events in America
Randall M. Miller, Series Editor

McCarthyism and the Red Scare: A Reference Guide
William T. Walker

The Underground Railroad: A Reference Guide
Kerry Walters

Lincoln, the Rise of the Republicans, and the Coming of the Civil War:
A Reference Guide
Vera Kerry Walters

America in the Cold War: A Reference Guide
William T. Walker

Andrew Jackson and the Rise of the Democrats: A Reference Guide
Mark R. Cheathem

THE PROGRESSIVE ERA

A REFERENCE GUIDE

Francis J. Sicius

Guides to Historic Events in America
Randall M. Miller, Series Editor

 ABC-CLIO™

An Imprint of ABC-CLIO, LLC
Santa Barbara, California • Denver, Colorado

2972421

APR 2 2 2016

Copyright © 2015 by ABC-CLIO, LLC

Library of Congress Cataloging-in-Publication Data

Sicius, Francis J.
  The Progressive Era : a reference guide / Francis J. Sicius.
    pages cm. — (Guides to historic events in America)
  Includes bibliographical references and index.
  ISBN 978–1–61069–447–6 (cloth : alk. paper) — ISBN 978–1–61069–448–3 (ebook)
    1. United States—History—1865–1921. 2. United States—Politics and government—1865–1933. 3. Progressivism (United States politics) I. Title.
E661.S555 2015
973.8—dc23   2015001376

ISBN: 978–1–61069–447–6
EISBN: 978–1–61069–448–3

19 18 17 16 15   1 2 3 4 5

This book is also available on the World Wide Web as an eBook.
Visit www.abc-clio.com for details.

ABC-CLIO, LLC
130 Cremona Drive, P.O. Box 1911
Santa Barbara, California 93116-1911

This book is printed on acid-free paper ∞

Manufactured in the United States of America

To the memory of William D Miller

CONTENTS

LIST OF ILLUSTRATIONS

SERIES FOREWORD

Perhaps no people have been more difficult to comprehend than the Americans. As J. Hector St. Jean de Crèvecoeur asked during the American Revolution, countless others have echoed ever after —"What then is this American, this new man?" What, indeed? Americans then and after have been, and remain, a people in the process of becoming. They have been, and are, a people in motion, whether coming from a distant shore, crossing the mighty Mississippi, or packing off to the suburbs, and all the while following the promise of an American dream of realizing life, liberty, and happiness. The directions of such movement have changed, and sometimes the trajectory has taken a downward arc in terms of civil war and economic depression, but always the process has continued.

Making sense of that American experience demands attention to critical moments—events—that reflected and affected American ideas and identities. Although Americans have constructed an almost linear narrative of progress from the days of George Washington to today in relating their common history, they also have marked that history by recognizing particular events as pivotal in explaining who and why they believed and acted as they did at particular times and over time. Such events have forced Americans to consider closely their true interests. They also have challenged their commitment to professed beliefs of freedom and liberty, equality and opportunity, tolerance and generosity. Whether fighting for independence or empire, drafting and implementing a frame of government, reconstructing a nation divided by civil war, struggling for basic rights and the franchise, creating a mass-mediated culture, standing up for capitalism and democracy and against communism, to name several critical developments, Americans have understood that historic events are more than just moments. They are processes of change made clear through particular events but not bound to a single moment or instance. Such thinking about the character and consequence of American history informs this new series of Guides to Historic Events in America.

Drawing on the latest and best literature, and bringing together narrative overviews and critical chapters of important historic events, the books in the series function as both reference guides and informed analyses to critical events that have shaped American life, culture, society, economy, and politics and fixed America's place in the world. The books do not promise a comprehensive reading and rendering of American history. Such is not yet, if ever, possible for any single work or series. Nor do they chart a single interpretive line, though they share common concerns and methods of inquiry. Each book stands alone, resting on the expertise of the author and the strength of the evidence. At the same time, taken together the books in this new series will provide a dynamic portrait of that on-going work-in-progress, America itself.

Each book follows a common format, with a chronology, historical overview, topical chapters on aspects of the historical event under examination, a set of biographies of key figures, selected essential primary documents, and an annotated bibliography. As such, each book holds many uses for students, teachers, and the general public wanting and needing to know the principal issues and the pertinent arguments and evidence on significant events in American history. The combination of historical description and analysis, biographies, and primary documents also moves readers to approach each historic event from multiple perspectives and with a critical eye. Each book in its structure and content invites students and teachers, in and out of the classroom, to consider and debate the character and consequence(s) of the historic event in question. Such debate invariably will bring readers back to that most critical and never-ending question of what was/is "the American" and what does, and must, "America" mean.

Randall M. Miller
Saint Joseph's University, Philadelphia

PREFACE

The Progressive Era—roughly the period that stretches from 1890 through 1920—represents one of the great turning points in American history. In broadest terms, it marks the collective response to the newly emerging industrial world, which presented challenges to every aspect of traditional American life including attitudes toward the natural environment, gender roles, class discrimination, and race relations. By the end of the nineteenth century, it had become clear that new forces such as urban growth, corporate trusts, the transcontinental railroad, and mass migration were radically changing the fabric of life. Rugged individualism, which had become the hallmark of the American character in earlier centuries, seemed impotent against these new dynamics, but people believed that their government, honestly administered and guided by experts of the new social sciences, could bring order and security to their personal and public lives. Secure in this faith, citizens empowered their public officials at various levels to keep their water supplies safe, regulate utility prices, defend workers, supervise education, protect their food supply, guard their natural environment, and regulate capitalism. Those who supported this aggressive public policy called themselves "Progressives" and gave their name to an entire historical era. Although historians have relegated this "era" to a specific period of time, the progressive impulse continues to endure and remains a potent theme in American political thought.

The significant impact of the Progressivism has evoked various interpretations by historians. To some, the movement was energized by a middle-class urge to control forces that threatened to destroy an idyllic world created from their imagined past. To others, it represented a desire to alleviate working-class unrest, which could—and sometimes did—explode into violence. Other historians have defined Progressivism as an attempt to order the newly emerging forces of industrialization with a modern administrative system based on science, especially the newly discovered social sciences. Wherever the truth lies, the reality is that the Progressive impulse that energized the country at the turn of the century changed forever the nature of American government and its relation to its people and made the Progressive Era one of the great watersheds of American history.

As every other important period, the Progressive age should be revisited by historians from time to time. New syntheses should be written in order to understand and reevaluate the era's significance and lessons for the present. A new perspective is particularly poignant at this time in history when some are heralding the demise of the Progressive impulse in American politics. This text combines a topically organized narrative, short profiles of events and people, historic analysis—based on recent scholarly interpretations of major issues—and an appendix of primary sources. It is the hope of the author that this readable narrative supported by useful tools of the trade will enable students to practice the art of history and to decide for themselves the significance of the Progressive movement, both in the past and the present.

ACKNOWLEDGMENTS

The idea for this book came to me while I was a Fulbright scholar in Chile in 2012. Presenting the history of your country in another language to another culture can stimulate new perspectives; I am grateful to my fellow scholars at the Center for Social and Cultural Research (CISOC) at the University Alberto Hurtado in Santiago, Gabriel Valdivieso, Herminia Gonsalves, Luis Bahamondes, Pedro Guell, Carmen Silva, Javier Romero Ocampo, and Martina Yopo Diaz, for their observations, ideas, and reflections they shared with me. I would also like to thank Antonio Campaña, director of the Fulbright Commission in Chile for his hospitality and support while I was a guest in his country. At my home institution St. Thomas University, I can always count on my colleagues Joe Holland and Richard Raleigh to provide comments or insights that help clarify my own thoughts. Once the idea for this book began to take form in print, the sage advice of Randall Miller in guiding the manuscript through various revisions is immeasurable. He is not only a meticulous editor (which I am not) but he knows the Progressive Era well and was able to ask questions and make observations that made this a much better book than it would have been without his inputs. I am also grateful to Senior Editor Michael Millman and his staff at ABC-CLIO, who guided this history of the Progressive Era through the process that transformed my manuscript into a book. Thanks also to my Dean Scott Zeman and Associate Dean Jim Conley, who kept my administrative and committee responsibilities to a minimum, which allowed me time to work on this manuscript. Finally, thanks to my wife Isabel Valenzuela, who is always there to lend counsel, patience, good humor, and love, which kept this project going through some trying times.

CHRONOLOGY

1890

June 2

The 1890 census indicates a population in the United States of 62,979,766, an increase of 25.5 percent since the 1880 census.

December 29

At Wounded Knee, South Dakota, the last major battle between United States troops and Indians ends. Hundreds of Indian men, women, and children are slain, along with 29 soldiers.

1892

January 1

Ellis Island, in New York Harbor, opens as the main East Coast immigration center. Before it closes in 1954, it will receive more than 12 million immigrants.

June 7

Republicans convene in Minneapolis, Minnesota, and nominate President Benjamin Harrison as their standard bearer.

June 21

Democrats convene in Chicago, Illinois, and nominate former president Grover Cleveland.

July 5

Populists from around the country convene in Omaha, Nebraska, to create a third party, the People's Party. They nominate former Civil War general and U.S. congressman James B. Weaver as their presidential candidate.

November 8   With his victory over incumbent Benjamin Harrison and People's Party candidate James B. Weaver, Grover Cleveland becomes the first person to return to the presidency after being defeated in a previous election.

1893

May 1   Chicago World Columbian Exposition opens to the public. The world's fair hosted 50 nations and 26 colonies and over 25 million people visited it.

May 5   The New York Stock Exchange collapses, starting the financial panic of 1893.

November 7   Women in Colorado are granted the right to vote.

1894

June 25   After a wildcat strike over wages broke out at the Pullman factory outside of Chicago, Illinois, Eugene Debs, president of the American Railway Union, calls for a boycott. Within four days, 125,000 workers on 29 railroads had "walked off" the job rather than handle Pullman cars.

1896

May 18   The *Plessy vs. Ferguson* decision by the Supreme Court upholds the principle of "separate but equal."

June 18   Republicans meet in St. Louis, Missouri, and nominate William McKinley as their standard bearer.

July 7   Democrats open their National Convention in Chicago, where they nominated the youthful William Jennings Bryan after being moved by his famous "Cross of Gold" speech.

November 3   Republican William McKinley claims victory in the presidential election over Democrat William Jennings Bryan.

1897

September 1   The era of the subway begins when the first underground public transportation in North America opens in Boston, Massachusetts.

1898

February 15   The U.S. battleship *Maine* explodes and sinks under unknown causes in Havana harbor, Cuba, killing 216 sailors.

April 22   The blockade of Cuba begins when the U.S. Navy aids independent forces within Cuba. Several days later, the United States declare war on Spain.

May 1   The U.S. Navy destroys the Spanish fleet in the Philippines.

May 12   San Juan, Puerto Rico, is bombed by the U.S. Navy under the command of Rear Admiral William T. Sampson.

December 10   The peace treaty ending the Spanish-American War is signed in Paris. The Spanish government agrees to grant independence to Cuba and cede Puerto Rico, Guam, and the Philippines to the United States.

April 29   After leading a march of 500 unemployed workers into Washington, D.C. that had begun on March 25 in Massillon, Ohio, James S. Coxey, head of "Coxey's Army," is arrested for treason.

1900

January 29   The American League is organized in Philadelphia with teams from Buffalo, Chicago, Cleveland, Detroit, Indianapolis, Kansas City, Milwaukee, and Minneapolis.

February 1   The first of the famous Brownie cameras is introduced. It sells for $1 and uses film that sells for 15 cents a roll. For the first time, the hobby of photography is within financial reach of almost everyone.

April 30	Hawaii is organized as a territory.
August 23	Booker T. Washington forms the National Negro Business League.
November 3	The first automobile show in the United States opens in Madison Square Garden in New York City under the auspices of the American Automobile Club of America.
November 6	Republican president William McKinley is reelected, defeating Democrat William Jennings Bryan, who had also been his opponent in 1896.

1901

February 25	U.S. Steel Incorporated.
March 1	The Pan American Exposition opens in Buffalo, New York.
March 4	William McKinley is inaugurated president for the second time.
April 25	New York becomes the first state to require automobile licenses. The fee is $1.
September 6	Anarchist Leon Czolgosz shoots President McKinley while the president is attending the Pan American Exposition in Buffalo, New York.
September 14	McKinley dies and Theodore Roosevelt becomes the 26th president of the United States.
October 16	President Theodore Roosevelt invites black leader Booker T. Washington to the White House.
November 16	A cartoon appears in the *Washington Star* prompting the Teddy Bear craze, which started when President "Teddy" Roosevelt refused to kill a captive bear tied up for him to shoot during a hunting trip to Mississippi.

1902

January 1	The first Rose Bowl game is held in Pasadena, California, with the University of Michigan defeating Stanford University 49-0.
March 4	The American Automobile Association is founded in Chicago.
March 29	Thirty-eight-year-old Henry Ford leaves the Detroit Automobile Company and begins his search for backers for his new Ford Motor Company.
April 14	James Cash Penny (J. C. Penny) opens his first Golden Rule Store for clothes, shoes, and dry goods in Kemmerer, Wyoming.
May 12	Over 100,000 coal miners in Pennsylvania call a strike and keep the mines closed all summer.
June 8	The first automat restaurant opens in Philadelphia, Pennsylvania, at 818 Chestnut Street.
November 18	Brooklyn, New York, toymaker Morris Michton creates the teddy bear after President Roosevelt.

1903

January	*McClure's Magazine* that had begun in June 1893 introduced its new format of investigative reporting and launched the muckraking era in American journalism.
July 23	The Ford Motor Company sells its first automobile.
October 1	By a score of 7-3, the Pittsburgh Pirates defeat the home team Boston Pilgrims (later renamed Red Sox) in the first modern World Series game. Boston, however, goes on to win the series, five games to three.
December 1	*The Great Train Robbery*, the first western and narrative film, is released.
December 17	The first airplane flight occurs at Kitty Hawk, North Carolina. The Wright brothers Flyer I flies for 12 seconds.

1904

February 23	The United States acquires control of the Panama Canal Zone for $10 million.
April 30	President Theodore Roosevelt officially opens the St. Louis World's Fair.
May 14	The first Olympic games to be held in the United States begin in St. Louis.
August 16	New York City begins building Grand Central Station.
November 8	Theodore Roosevelt defeats Democrat Alton B. Parker to win the presidency in his own right.

1905

February 7	Congress grants statehood to Oklahoma, which becomes the 46th state to enter the union.
February 23	The Rotary Club is founded in Chicago.
March 3	The U.S. Forest Service is created.
September 22	Race riots in Atlanta, Georgia, kill 10 blacks and 2 whites.
December 16	The U.S. entertainment trade publication *Variety* publishes its first weekly issue.

1906

April 18	At 5:12 a.m., San Francisco is devastated by an 8.2 earthquake.
June 29	President Theodore Roosevelt signs a bill creating Mesa Verde National Park in southwestern Colorado.
June 30	President Roosevelt signs into law the Pure Food and Drug Act and the Meat Inspection Act.
August 13	At Fort Brown, Texas, some 10–20 armed white men attack an all black army unit; the attack results in a shooting rampage that leaves one townsperson dead and one police officer wounded.

August 22	The first Victor Victrola is manufactured.
December 10	President Theodore Roosevelt becomes the first American to be awarded the Nobel Peace Prize.

1907

July18	Florenz Ziegfeld's "Follies of 1907" premiers in New York City.
August 28	Two Seattle teenagers begin a telephone message service that grows to become United Parcel Service (UPS).
September 29	The foundation stone is laid for the Washington National Cathedral.
October 27	Union Station opens in Washington, D.C.
December 6	The worst mining disaster in U.S. history occurs as 362 men and boys die in a coal mining explosion in Monongah, West Virginia.
December 7	The first Christmas Seals are sold in Wilmington, Delaware, to help the fight against tuberculosis.
December 31	For the first time a ball is dropped in New York City's Times Square to signal the arrival of the new year.

1908

February 18	The first U.S. postage stamps in rolls are issued.
March 4	The New York State Board of Education bans the act of whipping students in its schools.
October 1	The Ford Model T, the first car for millions of Americans, hits the market at a cost of $825.
November 3	Republican nominee William Howard Taft defeats Democratic candidate William Jennings Bryan for the presidency of the United States.
December 25	Jack Johnson knocks out Tommy Burns to become the first black heavyweight champion of the world.

1909

February 12	The National Association for the Advancement of Colored People (NAACP) is founded.
February 16	The first subway car with sliding doors goes into service in New York City.
March 4	In a blustery storm that left 10 inches of snow on the ground, President William Howard Taft is inaugurated as the twenty-seventh president of the United States.
May 31	The NAACP holds its first conference at New York City's Henry Street Settlement House.
August 2	The first Lincoln head pennies are minted.

1910

February 8	The Boy Scouts of America, modeled on the Boy Scout Association, established by Baden-Powell in Britain in 1908, is incorporated in Washington, D.C.
March 17	The Camp Fire Girls organization is formed in Sebago Lake, near South Casco, Maine.
March 23	The first auto race occurs in Los Angeles, California.
April 3	Alaska's Mt. McKinley, the highest mountain in North America, is climbed.
April 21	Author Mark Twain, born Samuel Langhorne Clemens, dies at the age of 74 in Redding, Connecticut.
May 18	Earth passes through the tail of Halley's Comet with no consequences, although astronomer Camille Flammarion claimed that gas from the tail would possibly snuff out all life on the planet. His pronouncement led to panicked buying of gas masks and quack "anti-comet pills" and "anti-comet umbrellas" by the public.
June 16	The first Father's Day is celebrated in Spokane, Washington, by Bruce Dodd. In 1924 President Calvin Coolidge will declare it a national holiday.

June 25	Congress establishes a postal savings system.
July 4	African American boxer and world heavyweight champion Jack Johnson knocks out J. J. Jeffries, ending the racist call for a "Great White Hope" to recapture the crown. Johnson would retain the title until 1915.
July 24	James McGillivray publishes the first account of the mythical lumberjack Paul Bunyan.
August 20–21	The Great Idaho fire kills 86 people and destroys three million acres of timber in Idaho and Montana.
October 1	A bomb set by anarchists explodes at the *Los Angeles Times* building, leaving 21 dead and several injured.
November 12	In the first movie stunt, a man jumps into the Hudson River from a burning balloon.

1911

March 11	Charles Kettering creates the first successful electric starter for Cadillac.
March 18	Former president Theodore Roosevelt opens Roosevelt Dam in Phoenix, Arizona—the largest dam ever built in the United States to date.
March 25	In New York City, the Triangle Shirtwaist Factory fire kills over 140 women workers, many of them immigrants. Thirteen girls survive the fire that breaks out on the top three floors of the Asch building as the work day is ending.
May 15	The U.S. Supreme Court orders the dissolution of Standard Oil Company, ruling it violates the Sherman Antitrust Act.
August 15	Proctor and Gamble Company unveils its Crisco shortening.

1912

January 6	New Mexico enters the Union as the 47th state.

January 10   The world's first flying-boat airplane, designed by Glenn Curtiss, makes its maiden flight at Hammondsport, New York. Curtiss is the first licensed pilot and Orville Wright is the second.

January 12   In Lawrence, Massachusetts, over 20,000 textile workers go on strike to protest wage cuts.

February 3   New U.S. football rules are set. The field is shortened to 100 yards, touchdowns earn six points instead of five, four downs to make a first down are allowed instead of three, and the kickoff is moved back from midfield to the 40 yard line.

February 14   Arizona becomes the 48th state to enter the Union.

March 27   The first cherry blossom trees, a gift from Japan, are planted in Washington, D.C.

April 14   The luxury liner *Titanic* strikes an iceberg in the North Atlantic and sinks with the loss of 1,500 lives.

August 7   The Progressive Party nominates Theodore Roosevelt as their candidate for president.

October 14   Theodore Roosevelt, former president and Progressive Party candidate, is shot at close range by an anarchist in Milwaukee, Wisconsin. Although wounded, Roosevelt continues with his speech.

November 5   Woodrow Wilson becomes the first Democrat to win the presidency since 1892 when he defeated Republican William Howard Taft and Progressive candidate Theodore Roosevelt.

1913

January 1   U.S. Parcel Post Service begins delivering packages under 50 pounds.

January 15   The first telephone line between New York and Berlin is inaugurated.

February 3   The Sixteenth Amendment to the U.S. Constitution providing for a federal income tax is ratified.

March 15	President Woodrow Wilson holds the first open presidential news conference.
April 8	The Seventeenth Amendment to the U.S. Constitution requiring direct election of senators is ratified.
April 26	Thirteen-year-old Mary Phagan is killed at an Atlanta pencil factory. She had stopped to pick up her check on her way to Peachtree Street to watch a Confederate Memorial Day Parade. Leo Frank, a Jewish factory manager, is accused of raping and murdering the young working-class girl, and he is later lynched.
September 10	The Lincoln Highway (U.S. 30) opens as the first paved coast to coast highway.
October 7	Henry Ford adapts the assembly line method to automobile manufacturing, which reduces production time from 12 hours to 93 minutes. Output doubles and the price of the Model T Commercial Roadster (the least expensive model) drops from $900 to $595.
October 10	The Panama Canal is completed when President Woodrow Wilson presses a button in the White House that triggers a blast in Panama that explodes the Gamboa Dike.
December 23	President Wilson signs the Owens Glass Bill better known as the Federal Reserve Act, which establishes a decentralized, government-controlled banking system in the United States.

1914

January 1	The St. Petersburg-Tampa Airboat Line became the world's first scheduled passenger airline service, operating between St. Petersburg and Tampa, Florida. The service lasted only four months.
January 5	Henry Ford announces that he will pay a minimum of $5 a day and share the $10 million profit from the previous year with his employees.

April 4	*The Perils of Pauline*, a film series shown in weekly installments, is shown for the first time in Los Angeles.
April 20	The Ludlow Massacre occurs as soldiers kill 45 strikers during a mine strike in Ludlow, Colorado. Colorado militiamen called in by John D. Rockefeller Jr. to settle the strike torch a tent camp of 1,200 striking mine workers.
May 1	President Wilson issues a proclamation declaring the second Sunday in May as national Mother's Day.
July 11	Babe Ruth signs with the Boston Red Sox; he earns $2,900 in his rookie year.
July 15	Vaudevillian Henry Fox introduces the fox-trot at the Ziegfeld Follies.
July 28	Austria-Hungary declares war on Serbia, thereby initiating World War I in Europe.
August 5	Cleveland, Ohio, installs the first electric traffic lights.
December 8	*Watch Your Step*, the first musical revue to feature a score composed entirely by Irving Berlin, opens in New York City.
December 21	The first feature-length silent comedy, *Tillie's Punctured Romance*, is released.

1915

January 12	The U.S. Congress establishes Rocky Mountain National Park.
January 21	The first Kiwanis Club is formally founded in Detroit, Michigan.
February 8	D. W. Griffith's movie epic about the Civil War, *The Birth of a Nation*, premiers at Cline's Auditorium in Los Angeles.
February 2	President Wilson opens the Panama-Pacific Expo in San Francisco to celebrate the opening of the Panama Canal.

April 5	African American boxer Jack Johnson (1878–1946), the heavyweight champion since 1908, loses the title in Cuba to Jess Willard in the 26th round.
May 1	The luxury liner *Lusitania* leaves New York Harbor for a voyage to Europe. Despite the fact that warnings are published in the travel section of the *New York Times* and other papers by the German Embassy that it regards the liner as a battle target, hundreds of Americans board the ship.
May 6	Babe Ruth makes his pitching debut with the Boston Red Sox and also hits his first home run, but Boston loses to New York in 15 innings.
May 7	Almost 1,200 passengers die including 123 Americans when the British liner *Lusitania* is torpedoed by a German submarine off the coast of Ireland. The event sparks an outburst of anti-German sentiment in the United States.
May 17	The National Baptist Convention is chartered.
May 28	John B. Gruelle patents the Raggedy Ann doll.
July 28	Ten thousand blacks march down Fifth Avenue in New York to protest lynching.
August 17	Leo Frank, a Jewish factory manager is lynched by a mob of anti-Semites in Cobb County, Georgia, after Georgia governor John Slaton, believing Frank is innocent had commuted his death sentence to life imprisonment.
September 22	Southern Methodist University in Dallas, Texas, holds its first class, and Xavier University, the first African American black Catholic college opens its doors in New Orleans, Louisiana.
October 4	Dinosaur National Monument in Colorado and Utah is established.
October 9	President Wilson becomes the first president to attend a World Series game.

October 12   Ford Motor Company manufactures its one millionth Model T automobile.

October 23   Twenty-five thousand women march in New York City to demand the right to vote.

November 19   Joe Hill, a labor leader and songwriter, is executed for murder.

December 4   The Ku Klux Klan receives a charter from Fulton County, Georgia.

1916

January 28   Louis D. Brandeis, a private practice attorney and leader in the U.S. Zionist movement, is appointed by President Wilson to the Supreme Court, thus becoming the first Jewish Supreme Court justice.

February 5   Enrico Caruso records "O Solo Mio" for the Victor Talking Machine Company.

March 9   The forces of Mexican revolutionary General Francisco Pancho Villa raid Columbia, New Mexico.

April 20   Wrigley Field in Chicago opens.

June 1   The National Defense Act increases the strength of the U.S. National Guard by 450,000 men.

June 15   President Wilson signs a bill incorporating the Boy Scouts of America.

June 17   American troops under the command of General Jack Pershing march into Mexico in order to lead a punitive expedition against Pancho Villa.

July 4   Nathan's Famous hot dogs opens a stand at Brooklyn's Coney Island and holds a hot dog eating contest that becomes an annual event.

September 11   The "Star Spangled Banner" is sung at the beginning of a baseball game for the first time in Cooperstown, New York.

October 27   The first published reference to "jazz" appears in *Variety*.

November 7	President Wilson is reelected over Republican challenger Charles Evans Hughes, but the race is so close that the results are not known until November 11. Meanwhile, Montana elects Jeannette Rankin, a lifelong feminist and pacifist, as the first female member of Congress.

1917

January	The film *The Spirit of '76* produced by Robert Goldstein opens in Los Angeles. Goldstein is later arrested and convicted under the Espionage Act for producing a film that placed an ally—Great Britain—in an unfavorable light.
January 19	The Zimmerman Note, a coded message sent to Germany's minister in Mexico, proposes an alliance with Mexico in the event of war with the United States. Intercepted by the British and made public, the note hastens the U.S. involvement in the war against Germany.
April 2	President Wilson delivers his war message to Congress and recommends that a state of war be declared between the United States and the Imperial German government.
May 30	The five-member white Dixie Jazz Band from New Orleans led by Nick LaRocca cuts its first record —"Dark Town Stutters Ball" and "Indiana"—for Columbia records in New York City.
June 15	Congress passes the Espionage Act, which makes it illegal to interfere with the operation or success of the U.S. military, to denounce the war, or to promote the success of the enemies of the Unites States.
July 20	The U.S. draft lottery for World War I begins.
October 21	American troops fire their first shots in battle in Europe.

October 24   The Bolshevik revolution begins in Russia.

December 26   President Wilson places railroads under government
                    control for the duration of the war. He names Secre-
                    tary of War William McAdoo as director.

1918

January 8   President Wilson delivers his "Fourteen Points"
                    address, which outlines the war aims of the United
                    States, including the proposal to create a League of
                    Nations. Mississippi becomes the first state to ratify
                    the Eighteenth Amendment prohibiting the sale,
                    manufacture, or transport of liquor in the United
                    States.

January 27   *Tarzan of the Apes*, the first Tarzan film, premiers at
                    the Broadway Theater in New York City.

March   A flu epidemic, which is part of a world pandemic
                    that will eventually kill almost 200,000 Americans,
                    breaks out at Fort Riley, Kansas, where 48 men die.
                    It plagued the country until the winter of 1920

May 14   The U.S. Post Office and the U.S. Army begin regu-
                    larly scheduled airmail service between Washington
                    and New York through Philadelphia.

June 28   The U.S. Marines take Bois de Belleau in fighting on
                    the western front in Europe.

September 11   The Boston Red Sox beat the Chicago Cubs in six
                    games to win the World Series.

October   In a deadly month over 200,000 Americans die in the
                    worst global epidemic of the century. Some cities like
                    Baltimore and Washington, D.C., run out of coffins.

October 8   Sergeant Alvin York single handedly eliminates
                    35 machine guns, kills more than 20 Germans, and
                    takes 132 members of the Prussian Guard prisoner.
                    A modest man, York shrugs off his heroic actions say-
                    ing, "It's over. Let's forget it."

November 11	A truce is signed ending World War I, the so-called war to end all wars.
December 1	President Wilson orders all U.S. breweries to shut down to save grain for the war effort.

1919

January 16	Nebraska, Wyoming, and Missouri become the 36th, 37th, and 38th states to ratify the Eighteenth Amendment, the Prohibition amendment.
January 18	The Versailles Peace Conference opens in France and President Wilson attends.
February 6–11	A five-day general work stoppage by more than 65,000 workers breaks out in Seattle, Washington. It is one of the largest of numerous strikes that year as dissatisfied workers in several unions strike to gain higher wages after two years of World War I wage controls.
March 15–17	The American Legion is founded in Paris by members of the American Expeditionary Force.
June 14	The U.S. Congress passes the Nineteenth Amendment granting suffrage to women.
July 24	A race riot in Washington, D.C., leaves 6 dead and 100 wounded.
July 27	A race riot in Chicago leaves 15 whites and 23 blacks dead and over 500 injured.
August 23	The "Gasoline Alley" cartoon strip begins in the *Chicago Tribune*.
September 9	Boston police officers go on strike seeking recognition for their trade union and improvements in wages and working conditions.
October 1	The Chicago White Sox intentionally throw the World Series to Cincinnati in what will become known as the "Black Sox Scandal."

October 2	President Wilson suffers a stroke that will leave him partially paralyzed.
October 8	The senate and the House pass the Volstead Act that will prohibit the sale or consumption of alcoholic beverages.
October 17	The Radio Corporation of America (RCA) is established.
November 10	The American Legion holds its first national convention in Minneapolis, Minnesota.

1920

January 2	Some 2,700 arrests are made in raids in 33 cities as part of a campaign against political radicals and labor agitators, spearheaded by the Department of Justice and Attorney General A. Mitchell Palmer.
January 3	The Red Sox sell Babe Ruth to the New York Yankees for $100,000.
January 4	The Negro National League, the first black baseball league, is organized by Rube Foster.
February 14	The League of Women Voters is founded in Chicago to encourage greater participation by women in government.
June 12	Republicans meeting in Chicago nominate Warren G. Harding for president and Calvin Coolidge for vice president.
June 13	The U.S. Post Office rules that children may not be sent by parcel post, a practice that had begun after 1913 when the post office declared it would begin delivering packages of less than 50 pounds.
July 6	Democrats end their convention in San Francisco by nominating James Cox as their presidential candidate and Franklin Roosevelt as their vice presidential candidate.

August 2	Marcus Garvey presents his "Back to Africa" program in New York City.
August 18	Tennessee becomes the 36th state to ratify the Nineteenth Amendment that gives women the right to vote.
November 2	Republican Warren G. Harding defeats James Cox decisively to become the 29th president of the United States. Promising to return the country to "normalcy," his election seemingly closes the door on Progressive politics for a decade. Results of the election are broadcast from the Westinghouse Company rooftop in Pittsburgh on station KDKA.
November 20	The Nobel Peace Prize is awarded to President Woodrow Wilson.
November 25	Radio station WTAW in College Station, Texas, broadcasts the first play-by-play description of a football game, a Thanksgiving contest between the University of Texas and Texas A&M. On the same day in Philadelphia the first Thanksgiving Day Parade is held.

CHAPTER 1

INTRODUCTION: THE PROGRESSIVE ERA

> The scope of a modern government in what it can and ought to accomplish for its people has been widened far beyond the principles laid down by the old "laissez faire" school of political writers, and this widening has met popular approval.
>
> —William Howard Taft[1]

When calamity of either natural or human origins disrupts the rhythms of everyday life, people often look to the government —usually the federal government—for help. This has not always been the case. There was a time when the federal government was considered at best an indifferent observer to the events that might upset the lives of its citizens. This perception changed radically at the turn of the twentieth century when a group of reformers collectively known as Progressives took control of the national political agenda. Although one could say that political and social reformers had existed since the beginning of the Republic, Progressivism took the national spotlight in September of 1901 when an assassin killed President William McKinley, and Teddy Roosevelt became the 26th president of the United States. Those who had championed Progressive reform in government, business, family life, labor, conditions of women, and the environment rejoiced that one of their own—who had been a reform governor of New York—was in the White House.

Since the term *Progressivism* first entered the American political vocabulary in the mid-1890s, a facile and conclusive definition of these reformers whose agendas crossed geographic, political, educational, gender, class, and racial lines has been elusive. Women contributed significantly to the movement, but most Progressives were not feminists. And although it has been described as largely a middle-class movement, captains of industry as well as laborers joined their ranks. W. E. B. Du Bois, the leading black intellectual of the time, could be called a Progressive, yet racism motivated the agenda of many Progressives.

Despite the eclectic origins of their motives, Progressives had much that drew them together. First of all, most shared a manner of thinking, which philosopher William James defined as *pragmatism*. James saw ideas as organic and therefore subject to Darwinian principles of natural selection and survival. Those theoretical designs that proved functional survived; those that did not died. Pragmatism determined that the central question of an idea was not, "is it true?" but rather, "does it work?" Second, the Progressives accepted a psychological theory called behaviorism that asserted that environment shaped (or as some even argued determined) behavior. Sustained by these theories, Progressives believed that a government empowered by scientific expertise and the political will could attack and solve any social, economic, or political challenge the country might face. Once in control, Progressives at every level of government championed laws that regulated every aspect of American life from the dinner table to the workplace, thus changing permanently the relationship of American citizens to their government. The Progressive impulse that began with the new twentieth century expanded over the ensuing decades and despite challenges in recent years, it remains tightly woven into the country's political fabric in the twenty-first century.

In the national conversation over government's role in society, two contrapuntal ideas as old as the country's founding have dominated the discourse. On one hand, Americans have embraced the myth of rugged individualism. This idea, as old as the original settlements, celebrates the self-motivated frontiersman, who—free from the restraints of regulation or even tradition—blazes his own path and place in the wilderness. The most recent political manifestation of this belief finds expression in proponents of free market economy and limited government. The counterpoint to the "rugged individual" is the vision of community and mutual assistance proclaimed by John Winthrop in 1634 and cited by every president in recent times at least since president-elect John Kennedy's address to the Massachusetts legislature. Winthrop admonished his fellow citizens to

> be knitt together in this worke as one man, wee must entertaine each other
> in brotherly Affeccion, wee must be willing to abridge our selves of our

superfluities, for the supply of others necessities, wee must uphold a familiar Commerce together in all meekenes, gentlenes, patience and liberallity, wee must delight in eache other, make others Condicions our owne rejoyce together, mourne together, labour, and suffer together, allwayes haveing before our eyes our Commission and Community in the worke, our Community as members of the same body.[2]

In modern political discourse, this view is well summarized by Sandra Opdycke who wrote

our proudest national achievements have been accomplished through government action. When there are wars to be fought, highways to be built rivers to be spanned, diseases to be conquered, or disasters to be overcome, private efforts often lacked the scope and resources to do the job. From the First Continental Congress to Medicare we have repeatedly chosen to tackle our biggest challenges by working together through public institutions.[3]

Through the nineteenth century, the new markets and economic opportunities created by the expanding frontier, the opportunities for enterprise created by revolutionary discoveries that replaced water, animal, and human power with steam, electricity, and finally petroleum-based energy, and supported by the philosophy of social Darwinists, who preached the doctrine of the survival of the fittest, the myth of the rugged individual dominated the political discourse. By the end of the century, forces that had emerged during the preceding years of geographic, commercial, and industrial growth, had become so overwhelming that many Americans turned to government for help. Reaction began in the agricultural plains states where farmers organized politically to regulate railroads and banks. It then moved to the cities, where reformers took control of their local governments, threw corrupt city bosses out of power, and enlisted responsible government agents to "scientifically" manage housing, water, sewage, public space, and every other aspect of life that they deemed could be improved by proper vigilance. With these collective actions, the political pendulum began to swing away from the myth of individualism toward that of community.

Propelled by two world wars and the Great Depression, the Progressive idea, which hailed the need for big government to face big challenges, dominated the political conversation for much of the twentieth century.

But by the end of the century, some had become disillusioned with government's ability to draw the community together for collective and positive action, and many could agree with President Reagan who quipped, "The most terrifying words in the English language are: I am from the government and I am here to help." And in a more serious context in his first inaugural address Reagan declared, "Government is not the solution to our problem; government is the problem." For a generation now, President Reagan's words have resonated among many. And in the first decades of the twenty-first century, the American people are once again in a fierce, often divisive, debate over the role of the government. In the midst of the current political conversation, this book attempts to contribute to an understanding of what gave rise to the Progressive impulse in American politics in the early twentieth-century movement. It attempts to explain why it began, who championed its cause, and what its results were.

Although the very word they used to describe themselves implied forward looking, nostalgia motivated many Progressives. This group, primarily middle class, imagined a past where family farms, small towns, and local businesses defined the political, social, and economic landscape. They shared a collective memory of a world where elections were honest, most people treated each other fairly, and the immutable laws of supply and demand guaranteed fair prices and wages. According to these believers, that idyllic world had been disrupted in the post-Civil War era by the rise of large corporations that created monopolies that manipulated laws of supply and demand, by immigrants unlearned in the intricacies of democracy who sold their vote to corrupt officials, and by angry and often violent workers who rebelled to the point of revolution against exploitation of large corporations. These middle-class reformers genuinely felt in the "middle," crushed between large corporations on one side and the angry masses on the other. Unable to control these new economic forces, they hoped to enlist the power of government on their side to neutralize that which threatened to consume them. This sentiment, nurtured by many writers who dramatized the excesses of corporations and the eroding quality of life, solidified the Progressive movement nationally.

The Progressive movement of the early twentieth century was multifaceted and complex; allies on one issue could be opponents on another. The varied contingents that propelled the Progressive impulse are the subject of this book. Although some common themes can be noted, specific motives cannot be universalized. This book will treat each aspect of Progressivism as carefully and independently as possible in chapters dedicated to the various aspects of the movement. What holds the chapters and the book together is the common strand of hope expressed by all these groups that the world would progress if their ideas could somehow be linked to the collective will through the government.

Like most political movements, Progressivism began with economic issues and therefore this book begins with a discussion of the economic forces that brought people to the realization that the time had come for political change. Farmers and workers were the first to suffer from the economic realities of the post-Civil War industrial era. Although not defined as "Progressives," they were the first to call for a new political order, which Progressives would later champion. Farmers in the Midwest organized to enlist government on their side against railroad corporations, whose monopolistic control over transportation allowed them to charge exploitative rates. Industrial workers initially turned to unions in their struggle against what they perceived as unjust wage and workplace policies. When that failed, they resorted to violence and then finally to politics. Eventually these two groups, workers and farmers, recognized that they had a common adversary and despite differences of culture, history, and economic interests, they united politically. The highpoint of this alliance came in 1896 when William Jennings Bryan challenged the Republican defender of big business, William McKinley, for the presidency. The national political alliance of workers and farmers waned after Bryan's 1896 defeat but it remained powerful at the state level, especially in the Midwest. But more importantly, the political will that stimulated the movement survived and grew, and in the ensuing decade politicians, who embraced much of what the farmer-labor alliance had stood for, came to power at the state and local level under the banner of Progressivism.

Across the nation, at the turn of the century, Progressive reform dominated the political agenda, and the next chapter of this book turns its attention to the reform governments that were elected in various regions of the country. Progressives such as Gifford Pinchot, in Pennsylvania, Hiram Johnson in California, and Robert La Follette in Wisconsin won governorships, and state legislatures with Progressive majorities passed laws designed to improve social and economic conditions. Many of these states pressed for common goals: control of monopolies, which distorted the eternal laws of supply and demand; education for all children, especially the immigrants, so that they might learn to be good Americans; reform of local government; antivice laws; workman's compensation; and labor protection, especially for women and children. True to their belief in environmental determinism, they also battled for minimum housing standards, universal access to clean water, and new sewage and waste control in the urban centers of the country. They lobbied for pasteurized milk for children, mass inoculation campaigns, and for extermination of the hookworm in the South. They also fought for more open space in the cities and expansion of the national park system.

Like most political movements, there were excesses and abuses. For example in the South, good government and honest elections became an excuse for disenfranchising black voters. And in other parts of the nation, in name of good government, city bosses were driven from offices. Although many were corrupt, in an era devoid of social services, urban politicians maintained their power by providing services and a voice to immigrants. A bag of groceries or a sack of coal from a ward heeler might represent a bought vote, but for an unemployed worker it also meant a meal and warmth in lean times. Without the city boss, this social cushion—meager as it was—disappeared for many.

Progressivism came to fruition in the city, which is the focus of the next chapter of this book. In the post-Civil War decades, the unregulated rise of factories in urban neighborhoods, the largest immigration the country had ever experienced—and the crisis in housing, public service, and governance it created—made the word "city" a metaphor for corruption, excess, social decline, and all else that was wrong—in the eyes of reformers—with the world on the threshold of the new twentieth century. But despite its deficiencies, the city with its theaters, vaudeville, baseball parks, and varieties of life was rapidly making urban life the focal point of American culture. The rapidly expanding cultural and commercial life of the cities at the end of the century accelerated the ever widening gap between country and city life in the United States.

Conditions in the city also gave rise to a newly emerging group of professionals, known as social workers, who played an important role in moving the Progressive agenda that was primarily concerned with "social" issues. These specialists—many of whom were women—saw firsthand the consequences of overcrowding, poverty, and ignorance in the slums of rapidly growing cities. They advocated minimum housing and educational standards regulated by government officials as well as workplace regulations to "acculturate" and protect the poor—mostly immigrants—from avaricious landlords and bosses. Aided by the camera skills of Jacob Riis, who published an exposé of slums accompanied by pictures, these social experts introduced Middle America to a world of extreme poverty, degradation, and brutality. The implication inherent in the message was that unless the tide was turned, Middle America's idealized view of life would soon be gone. Awakened to the horrible conditions in the slums and tenement houses, women took the lead in creating a political platform with a social agenda and soon issues related to housing, education, and the workplace began to enter the political conversation at state and local levels.

As women organized and demonstrated in the name of the poor, they began to gain political strength, which they eventually harnessed to their own long-running struggle for equality. The next chapter of this book will explore how women reformers transformed causes of social concern for the downtrodden to their own causes more relevant to gender than class. This chapter will explore the efforts of Victoria Woodhull, who in 1872 became the first woman to run for president of the United States. It will trace the growth of the seed she planted to its fruition, the Nineteenth Amendment, which gave women the right to vote. The story of women in the Progressive Era also includes Margaret Sanger, who connected poverty among immigrants to the large economically unsupportable families they produced. She introduced "birth control" to the Progressive dialogue and the assertion that women had a right to control their own bodies to the feminist narrative. Carrie Nation, who championed the cause of Prohibition in the name of protecting women and the family, can also be included in this eclectic group known collectively as Progressives. Her individual campaign to end what she considered the diabolic plague of alcoholism was part of a larger political movement that under the leadership of Wayne Wheeler's Anti Saloon League became by the second decade of the twentieth century the most powerful lobbying group in the country. Their actions culminated in the passage of the Eighteenth Amendment, which made legislation possible that was designed to end consumption of alcoholic beverages in the United States.

This book next turns to African Americans who at the turn of the century realized that—with government approbation—their social and economic condition had deteriorated over the 40 years since the end of the Civil War to a position little better than slavery. Consequently, they began to organize and in turn align themselves with the Progressive movement. Their actions represented the first organized attempt since the end of Reconstruction to establish racial justice in the United States. Unfortunately, by the turn of the century, racial barriers were so firmly in place that it would require more political will and energy to tear them down than the Progressives possessed. But the Progressive Era did witness the testimony of Ida Wells, the intellectual power of W. E. B. Du Bois, and the political savvy of Booker T. Washington. The Progressive movement also coincided with the founding of the National Association of the Advancement of Colored People (NAACP) and with it the beginning of the modern Civil Rights movement.

The next chapter dedicates itself to writers and journalists who played an important role in informing, motivating, and defining Progressives. It includes popular novelists, journalists, socialist, and utopian writers like Upton Sinclair (*The Jungle*, 1906), Edward Bellamy (*Looking Backward*, 1887), Henry George (*Progress and Poverty*, 1879), Henry Demarest Lloyd (*Wealth Against Commonwealth*, 1894), and others. These writers informed and some also emboldened Progressives to explore more radical solutions to social and economic inequality. These writers did more than expose abuses in industry and government. In many cases, they also proposed solutions. Although some (like Bellamy) simply created utopian visions of the future, others like Sinclair—who was summoned by Roosevelt to address a congressional hearing that resulted in the creation of the Meat Inspection Act—actually contributed to the development of a new political reality.

The principal objects of censure by many social writers were the newly emerging corporations and the "robber barons" who directed them. The meteoric growth of industry and capital in the post-Civil War years gave rise to a need for a new order to manage the large industrial conglomerations particularly in iron, steel, oil, and the railroads. These organizers of trusts, monopolies, and interlocking directorates brought great wealth to themselves and those around them and they were critically—sometimes enviously—referred to as "robber barons." The next chapter of this book turns to these industrial giants. It will explore the origins of the companies such as Standard Oil, the conditions in which they were created, their accomplishments, as well as their abuses, the latter of which made them the central focus of many Progressive reformers.

This chapter also addresses the Progressive response to the harm that unregulated industrial and economic expansion had done to the nation's natural environment, which is the focus of the book's next chapter. Throughout the nineteenth century, millions of acres of public land had been given or sold at a pittance to various industries, particularly railroads and mineral corporations. These concessions led to exorbitant private gain at public expense. Progressives, such as Gifford Pinchot, attacked the process that had allowed the country's natural resources to fall into the hands of a few powerful interests with little concern for the land or posterity, other than extracting all the monetary rewards possible. Coining the word *Conservation* to define their movement, they argued for stronger legislation to protect the public interest in the country's natural resources. The Conservation movement was, according to one historian, a tribute to the group of men whose concept of public responsibility for conservation demonstrated a faith in democracy and a social concern that became characteristic of the Progressive tradition.[4]

Religion also influenced the social consciousness of the Progressive movement. The next chapter will tell the story of Baltimore's archbishop James Cardinal Gibbons, who unlike his counterparts in the Church hierarchy of Europe championed the cause of labor and even contributed to Pope Leo XIII's encyclical "Rerum Novarum" that defended the workers' rights to organize in order to demand a living wage, thereby reversing a traditional papal opposition to labor unions. Gibbons warned the Pope that the American Catholic Church, made up almost entirely of immigrant workers, could not survive a worker exodus that the European Church suffered in the nineteenth century when it condemned all labor movements and advocated a paternalistic solution to the social inequalities created by the industrial revolution.

Protestant ministers contributed much to the emerging social consciousness of the late nineteenth century as many began to turn their flocks away from the idea that poverty was the result of personal depravity and toward the concept that to follow Christ's example meant they should work to bring the kingdom of God to Earth, which demanded bringing social justice to everyone. This view soon became known as the "Social

Gospel" movement and was preached by important Protestant scholars such as Walter Rauschenbusch, who from his ministry in the Hell's Kitchen section of New York, convinced many fellow Christians that the gospels called them to service to the poor. His powerful and morally persuasive voice intertwined the "Sermon on the Mount" with the Progressive political agenda.

The final chapter of this book deals with Progressive foreign policy, which culminated in the Great War. For some historians, World War I marks the end of the Progressive movement, but in the view of others it represented the flowering of Progressivism. Under the aegis of war some of the greatest dreams of the Progressives were realized, as almost the entire economy was bought under government control. Laws were passed that controlled the daily lives of Americans, even determining—through the Lever Act—what they ate and drank. When the war—and the regulations it generated—ended, a majority of the country discharged a collective sigh of relief that government regulation was on the wane. They elected Warren Harding as the president, and he promised to return the country to "normalcy" and away—with the exception of Prohibition—from the social experiments of the previous two decades. For many historians, Harding's election marked the end of the Progressive Era, but other historians argue that the Progressive impulse survived and reemerged in full force in the 1930s with the New Deal and in the 1960s with Lyndon Johnson's "Great Society" and remains today in the likes of the EPA, FEMA, and the Affordable Care Act. All these are expressions of a Progressive vision that has its modern roots in the turn of the century alliances and coalitions of people that decided that government should be a democratic voice in defense of the interests common to all and not a defender of the interests of a few.

NOTES

1. William Howard Taft, Inaugural Address March 4, 1909.

2. https://www.mtholyoke.edu/acad/intrel/winthrop.htm (January 22, 2013).

3. Sandra Opdycke, *No One Was Turned Away: The Role of Public Hospitals in New York City Since 1900* (New York: Oxford University Press, 1999), 3–4.

4. J. Leonard Bates, "Fulfilling American Democracy: The Conservation Movement, 1907–1921," *The Mississippi Valley Historic Review* 44, no. 1 (June 1957): 29–57.

CHAPTER 2

FARMERS AND WORKERS STRUGGLE FOR JUSTICE

> The value of labor cannot be measured with money. A strong man's intellect moves as easily as a blacksmith's arm. . . . If the Republic is to endure we must encourage the average man.
> —Senator William Alfred Peffer, of Kansas[1]

F armers always need to borrow money and by the end of the nineteenth century, because of currency deflation, that practice had become increasingly costly. In 1890, the farmer who had borrowed $1,000 10 years prior had to pay back the equivalent of $1,250 plus interest. And because of that same currency deflation, a bushel of wheat that sold for $1.10 in 1880 brought only 85 cents in 1890. No wonder the farmers were angry. They knew somebody was getting rich because of the devaluation of currency, but it was not them. Faced with economic crisis, despite myriad causes—mechanization, expansion of arable land, and series of years with bumper crops to name a few—the farmers sought a simple explainable reason for their economic plight at the end of the century and they found it in exploitative railroads and monetary policy created and directed for and by northeastern bankers.

They channeled their anger into politics. After a number of local victories in the late 1870s and 1880s that saw the creation of the Interstate Commerce Commission that regulated railroads and laws that called for limited control over state banks, the farmers of the Midwest, the plains states, and the South by 1892 had created the strongest third-party movement the country had ever seen. Rooted in various regional coalitions such as the "Farmers Alliance," the "Farm Labor Party," and the "Southern Alliance," nationally they became known as the "People's Party" or "Populists." Common wisdom told them that steadily decreasing prices over the past two decades resulted from what they referred to as the "Crime of 73," a federal law passed in 1873 that took silver out of circulation, which had the effect of deflating the currency and hurting western mining interests. Therefore, free coinage of silver became the banner under which they marched. They organized national conventions first in St. Louis, then in Ocala, Florida, and finally in Omaha, Nebraska, where in 1892 they adopted a national platform for the Populist Party and nominated James B. Weaver—Civil War veteran, lawyer, politician, and son of a farmer—as their candidate for the president of the United States. In addition to their position on silver, the platform advocated government ownership and management of all services used by the public including railroads, steamship lines, telephone, and telegraph companies. Senator Alfred Peffer of Kansas reflected common populist wisdom when he declared that, "the people would be served, more equitably and at greatly reduced expense, by public agents working on fixed salaries, than by private persons who use their business for personal gain." They also called for a federal reserve to regulate currency, a graduated income tax on the wealthiest Americans and corporations, and the direct election of senators.[2]

The Populists united under the belief that bimetallism was the solution to the economic woes of the farmer. In a book entitled *Coin's Financial School*, Harvey Coin argued that bimetallism would end poverty. (*Coin's Financial School*, p. 212)

Weaver obtained 1,041,028 votes and won four states, the best perfor-
mance of any third-party candidate in the history of American elections
up to that time. Although the Populists have been dismissed by some
mid-twentieth century Progressive historians as being traditionalist and
antimodern, it cannot be denied that many issues first addressed in the
Populist platform, such as a graduated income tax, price support for farmers, direct election of U.S. senators, the eight-hour workday, and universally accessible public education, became law under the Progressives and
New Deal leaders they preceded and many of their proposals anticipated
the regulatory state that emerged in the Progressive Era.

Although their movement was rooted in rural politics, Populists recognized their common struggle with urban labor. Their platform—written
while urban workers were engaged in an epic struggle with the steel industry—declared, "We sympathize with the just demands of labor of every
grade, and recognize that many of the evils from which the farming community suffers [also] oppress universal labor, and that therefore producers
should unite in a demand for the reform of unjust systems and the repeal
of laws that bear unequally upon the people." This unprecedented alliance
of urban and rural workers emerged from their recognition of a common
adversary, the rapidly expanding industries and monopolies that seemed
to be dominating the country's economy, and in the process crushing economic life out of the average worker whether on the farm or in the factory.

The rapid expansion of industry and banking that had disrupted the life
of the farmer in the post-Civil War decades had also been catastrophic for
the new class of industrial workers that filled the factories springing up
across the urban landscape. From 1860 to 1900, industrial production
had increased tenfold and the number of industrial workers had grown
from 1 to 5½ million. At the same time, corporate ownership had consolidated to the point where 2 percent of the country's manufacturers produced over 50 percent of the nation's products. This concentration gave
manufacturers power to control not only prices of their products but wages
paid to produce them. The condition of wage earners at the end of the
century reflected this economic dynamic of the post-Civil War decades.
Despite the enormous gains enjoyed by entrepreneurs in the late nineteenth century, both farmers and industrial workers saw real wages and
living conditions decline. In many ways, the urban environment left factory workers in far more desperate conditions than their rural counterparts.

They not only labored in demoralizing and dangerous factories but also had to house their families in poor, overcrowded, and often unsafe tenements.

Conditions at the Carnegie Steelworks illustrated the challenges faced by most workers. The plants employed 14,359 common laborers who earned less than $12.50 a week at a time when a family needed $15 for a minimum subsistence. Nearly 25 percent of the recent immigrants employed at the Carnegie Steel Works were injured or killed each year between 1907 and 1910; 3,723 in all.[3] And manufacturers remained indifferent to the workers' plight. Not uncommon was the comment of a Connecticut textile mill owner who justified the 12-hour day and the six-day week because it kept "workmen and children" from "vicious amusements."[4] A New Jersey manufacturer of hats and caps boasted that he finally had "4 and 20 good, permanent workmen," not one infected with "the brutal leprosy of blue Monday habits and the moral gangrene of 'trades union' principles."[5]

Unlike the farmers who organized politically and effectively, most industrial workers eschewed politics. Those workers who did react to the injustices of management chose direct action against employers through strikes, as for example, the Molly Maguires who organized in the coalfields of Pennsylvania. But a decidedly larger number of laborers had left families in Europe and intended to work hard in the United States for a few years, save enough money to return to their home, and buy a farm or set themselves up in a small business. For example, between 1908 and 1910, for every 100 southern and eastern European immigrants who arrived in the United States, 44 returned to their homeland.[6] Those who maintained such dreams avoided the distraction of fighting to improve conditions of labor in their temporary workplace. On the other hand, local craft unions fortified primarily by native-born workers multiplied in the last decades of the nineteenth century. Inspiring speakers like Mother Jones crisscrossed the country urging workers to organize. And brave lesser known men of color in the South like George Williams labored under threats of violence to organize workers in the textile mills. "I do beleave [sic] that we are treated worse than any humans on earth," Williams wrote, "to call our selfs [sic] free men we have to leave home to go to work before daylight & it is black dar [sic] when we get home again, we have to work from daylight to twelve o'clock & we only get a half of an hour for dinner & then we go to work at half past twelve & work till dark & we only get from 90 cts to $1.25 per day." B. W. Scott, another black organizer for the Knights of Labor (K of L) in the South, complained to Terence Powderly, the K of L union president, that the Georgia militia was not used "for the purpose for which it is intended but for pol. purposes & to intimidate Labor as has just been demonstrated in the late Strike here on Sugar Plants. When K of L were shot down [sic]." There was never an attempt to stop labor violence he pointed out, "so long as nothing but K of L were shot."[7] As a result of the organizing skills of brave men like Williams and Scott, in the 1880s, the number of black workers in the K of L exceeded 70,000 or 10 percent of its membership and became one of the few institutions in the South where the color line was broken. In 1886 when the Noble Order of the K of L, which had begun in 1869 with 20,000 members, could boast over 800,000 strong, workers finally believed that they could present a united national front to protest their conditions.

Although at its peak, the nation's largest and most powerful union at the time represented only about 20 percent of the working class; the unions and the issues they protested provide insight into the conditions under which labor suffered in the post-Civil War era of industrial expansion.[8] In addition to the labor war that erupted between mine workers and owners in Cripple Creek, Colorado, in 1894, the Haymarket riots in 1886 instigated by a strike against the McCormick farm equipment company in Chicago, the Homestead Strike against Carnegie Steel in 1892, and the Pullman Strike against the railroad carriage company of the same name in 1893 drew national attention to the injustices suffered by labor at the hands of the newly emerging corporations.

In the nineteenth century many industrial workers were paid by the day, which was considered to be 12 hours. In most industries, manufacturers expected workers to be on the job at the predawn hour of 5:00 a.m. and to remain at their work until the sun began to set at 5:00 p.m. The long day was broken by a half hour allotted for lunch. The following excerpt of a contract between the Florida East Coast Railroad and the workers was typical:

> Train Crews will report for duty at 5:00 A.M. and from 5:00 A.M. until 5:00 P.M. will constitute a day's work.
> Brakemen and flagmen $1.75 per day of twelve hours

Wipers and watchmen $1.35 per day of twelve hours
Time worked in excess of twelve hours will be paid at the following rates:
First half hour no overtime, after first half hour
Brakemen and flagmen 17½ cents an hour
Wipers and Watchmen 13½ cents an hour[9]

In the spring of 1886, workers at the McCormick plant in Chicago walked off the job to demand that 8 hours should comprise a work day, not 12. During the previous year, there had been an outbreak of strikes across the nation demanding the same. Following normal practice at the time, management simply ignored the strikers and replaced them with others. On May 3, frustrated by the lack of impact their action had, a number of strikers attacked the replacement workers as they were leaving the factory. A riot broke out, police were called, and in the ensuing struggle a striking worker was killed. Several others were severely wounded. August Spies witnessed what he saw as a police action not designed to restore order but to punish and break the striking workers. Spies was a leader of the anarchist movement in Chicago and published a weekly paper: the *Arbeiter Zeitgung*. Following the events at the McCormick plant, Spies distributed a circular denouncing police brutality, calling for revenge, and announcing a meeting the following evening at Haymarket Square. Spies and his anarchist allies saw the events at the McCormick plant as an opportunity to rally aroused and angry workers to their cause of anarchism.

The majority of workers probably did not support the anarchist goals of "destruction of the existing class rule by all means ..." But they did want to express solidarity and anger at what had occurred in front of the McCormick plant the previous day, and therefore, they showed up at the rally 1,400 strong. They gathered where Randolph Street met Des Plaines Boulevard and formed a plaza known as the "Old Haymarket." Rain drove half the crowd away but the rest remained to listen to anarchist speakers rail against the capitalist system. The peaceful, if not boring, gathering ended when Sam Fielden mounted the wagon and launched into a fiery tirade that brought the crowd alive. A police inspector sent as an observer from his precinct became unnerved at the spectacle and fearing the outbreak of a riot returned to his barracks where he organized an army of 60 armed police and returned to the Haymarket. Shortly after their arrival, a bomb exploded, and the anxious police began shooting randomly into the panicking masses. Many in the crowd were prepared for battle and they returned the fire. When the smoke and dust had settled, seven policemen lay dead and 60 were wounded. The number of dead and injured workers was not reported but it was much higher.

The news of the riot shook the nation. "Rioting and Bloodshed in the Streets of Chicago," screamed a *New York Times* headline, as readers the next morning learned that, "The villainous teachings of the anarchists drew bloody fruit in Chicago."[10] In editorial cartoons and certainly in the average American's mind, the wild-eyed, long-coated, bearded, bomb thrower now replaced the previous image of the flamboyant, exaggerated, and almost comic ranting anarchist. Across the country, demands to crush the anarchist menace arose. Chicago abided. They tried and hung seven anarchist leaders for the Haymarket murders, even though many were not even at the rally that night. The Haymarket riot became a useful tool for manufactures who conveniently tied the anarchist movement to the labor movement, thus crippling the growing K of L and stifling union growth across the country. And the 12-hour-workday remained entrenched in the American business model until the second decade of the twentieth century.

Skirmishes between workers and police broke out frequently over the next decade as organized labor struggled against intransient manufacturers over control of the workplace. In 1892 while the Populist Party was organizing for a run at the presidency, worker unrest once again captured national headlines when a strike at Carnegie Steel's plant at Homestead, Pennsylvania, turned into one of the most violent episodes in American labor history. On July 1, union members took possession of the factory in order to prevent replacement workers from taking their jobs, and when the sheriff ordered the men to disperse, he was driven away.

Angered by the worker's disdain for the law, Carnegie Steel Chairman, Henry Frick—who directed the company's strike strategy while Carnegie vacationed in Scotland—hired 300 armed watchmen from the Pinkerton Detective agency to reinforce the sheriff's office. To avoid angry strikers and sympathetic townspeople, the Pinkerton forces planned to arrive at the steel mill on barges through the plant's river entrance. But the striking workers and sympathetic locals were not deceived, and as Frick's mercenaries approached the river entrance to the factory, they were confronted by an angry militia of 7,000 angry workers and local citizens. Stepping out from the crowd, William Foy, a member of the Amalgamated Union shouted to the Pinkertons urging them to return home. In response, a gunshot rang out from the barge, and William Foy fell dead. In angry response, the crowd rained a barrage of bullets on the surrounded barges. Outgunned and outnumbered, the hired guards were pinned in cross fire from both banks of the river and had no escape. They tried to surrender, but their pleas were ignored. The battle raged throughout the day. Attempts were made to sink the barges and then to fire them, all to no avail. Finally at the urging of union leader Hugh O'Donnell, the besieged guards were allowed to surrender. Armed workers and townspeople marched the Pinkertons to the sheriff's office. On the way, they had to walk a gauntlet of angry townspeople, mostly women, who pummeled them with broomsticks and ax handles. They also hurled bricks and insults and demanded that Frick's hired army be tried for murder. The sheriff released the exhausted and vanquished guards when they promised to leave town and they returned to their homes thankful to be alive. The next day across the country Americans read headlines similar to the one in the *New York Evening World*, which declared "AT WAR: Pinkertons and Workers Fight at Homestead."

The next day General George Snowden arrived with 700 state militia men who encamped on the banks of the river and on Carnegie hill overlooking the factory. But the citizens of Homestead remained steadfast. After a week standoff, a truce was declared and General Snowden and the army took control of the factory. Now, with the armed forces of the government behind him, Henry Frick announced the next day that the strikers would be invited back to work. But if they refused, replacements under protection of the state militia would fire up the steel works. Some returned, but the majority, although disheartened, continued their protest.[11] As the strike lingered on and morale declined, in New York City, anarchist Alexander Berkman and his lover Emma Goldman—neither of whom had any connection to the Amalgamated Steel Workers Union—hatched a plot to murder Frick in retaliation for the death of several workers and to rejuvenate the strike. Neither had the money necessary to travel to Homestead or purchase the necessary weapon, so Emma decided to prostitute herself for the money. On the street, she met a sympathetic man who refused her services but gave her $50 and urged her to seek another profession. Goldman took the money, bought a gun, a suit of clothes, and ticket for Berkman, and sent him off to Homestead.[12] After waiting in Frick's outer office for hours posing as a salesman, Berkman finally gained admission. He entered the office and with grim determination, opened his briefcase took out a gun and fired at Frick. Three of his bullets hit their mark, but with Frick still alive, Berkman stabbed him with a knife several times before being subdued and beaten unconscious by office workers. Berkman had injured Frick severely but not fatally. The failed murder attempt by an anarchist shifted public sympathy away from the strikers and soon after the defeated workers returned to the factory. Some workers were prosecuted for various offenses, but the western Pennsylvania juries refused to convict them.

Less than a year later, in a small company town on the southern border of Chicago another strike attracted national attention. It began as a wildcat protest against the Pullman Company, which had become in the last decades of the nineteenth century one of the major manufacturing companies in the country. Beginning in 1867 with a cash value of around $10 million, the Pullman Company, by 1893, had successfully destroyed all its competition and its sleeping and parlor cars covered over three-fourths of the country's railroad lines. The founder and head of this corporation, George Mortimer Pullman, although raised in poverty himself, remained unsympathetic to workers' protests and was especially antagonistic toward labor unions. He believed that he understood the working class and their needs far better than any union leader and set out to prove his theories when he purchased land on the outskirts of southern Chicago and built his new factory that included a planned community for his workers. He built homes that varied in size from two-room flats to spacious three-floor homes. He also constructed a number of public buildings including a hotel, a public school, church, library, and theater. There were public parks that provided spacious areas of fresh air and sunlight, and well-lit streets. His town also provided clean water and a safe sewage system. The city reflected the collective wisdom of nineteenth-century urban planners, and visitors from all over the world came to marvel at George Pullman's creation and to commend his response to labor strife of the late nineteenth century.[13]

But his goal to provide affordable, comfortable living facilities for his workers came crashing down with the depression of 1893, when Pullman in the interest of not laying any workers off dropped wages by about

25 percent. Unfortunately, he did not do likewise with his rents that workers still had to pay at predepression rates. Costs for food in the local stores, gas, and sewage likewise remained unchanged. In May of 1894 when workers could no longer endure the economic strain of reduced wages, they walked off the job. Many of the wildcat strikers belonged to Eugene V. Debs's American Railroad Workers Union, so union members all along the line refused to handle Pullman cars. When the union men were threatened with dismissal for refusing to service Pullman cars, Debs called for a strike, and by the end of June, 50,000 railroad men had walked off the job and threatened to cripple the national rail system. Soon there were no trains moving west of Chicago. Railroad company lawyers convinced U.S. attorney general Richard Olney that the strike was illegal because it prevented the movement of the U.S. mail, and he issued a federal injunction against the strikers. When the union refused to obey the injunction, President Grover Cleveland ordered federal troops to the railroad yards to facilitate movement of the trains and to protect replacement workers from violence. Once again, government chose the side of the corporations, and enraged workers reacted. They began stopping trains, smashing switches, and setting fire to stations and railcars. Government troops responded with force. When a mob tried to stop federal soldiers escorting a train through Chicago, the soldiers fired on the crowd killing several demonstrators and wounding many more. On July 10, 1894, Debs and three other union leaders were arrested for interfering with U.S. mail. They were released within a few hours, but Debs realized with federal troops entering the fray that the strike had become a lost cause and continuing it would be useless. Most railroad workers resumed their old jobs and received the same wages as before. Some workers were put on a blacklist, which meant that no railroad in the United States would hire them. On July 17, 1894, Debs was sent back to jail and served a term of six months. The union he had created no longer existed when he got out of jail.

The interference of by the federal government in the Pullman strike altered the strategic map of union organizers. Olney's decision to approve an injunction, citing the Sherman Anti-Trust Act as the legal basis to do so, had dragged industrial relations into the political arena, where corporations held considerable power. Defeated union leaders understood that job action alone was not going to be an effective weapon in the fight for justice for workers. They were going to have to become political if they hoped to effect change. They were also influenced by the Independent Labor Party Movement in Great Britain, which had effectively brought the voice of labor into the political conversation in that country.

Populist leaders observed with growing interest the politicization of the labor movement, and by the end of 1894 two years before the next presidential elections, the alliance between workers and farmers began to solidify. After events at Homestead and the obvious political implications of the Pullman strike, Populists leaders stepped up their campaign to attract urban workers to their movement by courting the unemployed and aiding Jacob Coxey's army of disgruntled workers on their long trek to Washington to demand that the government create jobs through public works. Henry D. Lloyd, a labor advocate who had defended the Haymarket anarchists and in 1894 had written a scathing condemnation of Standard Oil, helped seal the alliance between urban labor and rural farmer by running for Congress in 1894 on the Populist ticket.[14]

The urban–rural worker alliance remained a difficult one and ran counter to the entire political history of the country, which since the time of Jefferson had defined politics in terms of a division between urban and rural interests. Historians have pointed out that although the Populists had incorporated a demand for government ownership of railroads and telegraphs in their Omaha platform of 1892, neither they nor the Farmers' Alliance members were doctrinaire socialists. They were, rather, angry agrarian capitalists who found themselves unprotected by government from exploitation by the railroads. Many urban workers on the other hand were not married to industrial capitalism and were strongly influenced by socialist orators who often appeared at labor rallies.

The railroads provided the catalyst for this uncertain amalgamation of urban and agrarian political interests. Although many farmers were uneasy with the prospect of government ownership of the railroad, they accepted this proposal into their platform, which drew them closer to the urban workers who were much more comfortable with the implied socialist politics.[15] While anger at the new corporations in general and at the railroads in particular moved farmers and urban workers toward an alliance, silver solidified the new coalition. The Bland Allison Act of 1878, which authorized the government to coin silver at a fixed ratio, had temporarily ended the silver debate, but it reentered the political dialogue in the1890s when indebted farmers in the plains states and the South hoping to inflate the currency advocated the free coinage of silver. They were supported in their efforts by mining interests in Nevada where new veins of the metal were being discovered. Money lenders particularly in the Northeast and businessmen who preferred a gold standard opposed the movement toward what they called "cheap money." In 1890, responding to demands of miners and farmers, Congress passed the Sherman Silver Purchase Act, which would allowed those who owed money to pay their debts with cheaper dollars. But fearful of runaway inflation, President Cleveland successfully pushed for its repeal in 1893. That same year the country fell into the worst depression in its history with 19 percent unemployed, and silver once again entered the conversation. It seemed like a logical way to allow farmers to pay their debts and purchase products that would pull the country out of depression. Urban workers believing that an inflated currency would put more money in circulation and eventually more money in their wages rallied to the silver banner.

The Republican Party dominated by business and banking interests in the Northeast saw things differently. At its convention that opened on June 16, the party platform declared itself "unreservedly for sound money" and opposed to the free coinage of silver, "except by international agreement with the leading commercial nations of the earth." The Republican platform declared the party unequivocally the party of big business and made the election of 1896 the first election to be divided on class lines. The platform even shocked the most loyal of voters, their black constituency. One African American voter lamented, "I am a colored man and a Republican and have been for seventeen years; but be it thoroughly understood that I am not married to any party that will dodge from justice to the people and yield to the few who want to enslave the country by a single gold standard law." He advised, "Every Negro voter to stop going around howling, 'straight Republican ticket.'"[16]

With a Democratic president who had led the repeal of the Sherman Silver Act and a Republican platform that had endorsed the gold standard, Populists were certain that they had found an issue that would solidify the worker-farmer alliance and bring them victory in November. But a revolution in the Democratic Party foiled their plans. It began when pro-silver Democrats seeing an opportunity to take control of the party created a sudden and unexpected insurgency. "The Democratic movement toward silver," one historian wrote, "was like an avalanche: a mere whisper at first, then ... suddenly a roar, a crash, [and] an irresistible cataclysm." The gold Democrats led by President Cleveland were overwhelmed by the new passion for silver within the party. The insurgents seemed to have taken up the challenge of class warfare instigated by the Republican platform. One gold Democrat remarked, "For the first time I can understand the scenes of the French Revolution."[17]

On July 7, 1896, outside on the streets of Chicago, the day was sunny, cool, and agreeable, but inside the Democratic national convention the temperature was boiling hot. A grand upheaval was brewing. The political storm brewing within the convention hall had begun the previous year, when a few Democratic members of Congress asserted that the money question was the paramount issue and that supporters of free coinage of silver should organize and take control of the Democratic Party. The silver insurgents waited in anxious anticipation as their chief spokesman, William Jennings Bryan, mounted the podium. Bryan rode the tide of the Democratic insurgence to its crest. In the oratorical style of a preacher, he called on the party to nominate a new Andrew Jackson, one who would once again crush the avaricious bankers who were strangling the economic life out of the working man. And to those Republicans—and others—who demand a gold standard, the Democratic Party should with one loud voice declare that, "you shall not press down upon the brow of labor this crown of thorns. You shall not crucify mankind upon a cross of gold." The *New York Times* called the rhetoric "revolutionary." When Bryan finished, the convention erupted into a half hour of demonstration. He was lifted on the shoulders of supporters but soon his great girth became unsupportable, so he stood on a chair saluting well wishers. Caught up in the greatest explosion of passion the party had experienced since the nomination of James Garfield, delegates could do nothing else but nominate Bryan as their standard bearer. In addition to calling for the free coinage of silver, the Democratic platform denounced Cleveland's action in the Pullman boycott and described "government by injunction as a new and highly dangerous form of oppression. ..."[18] The platform also demanded stricter federal regulation of the railways, an end to national banknotes, a tariff for revenue only (after the money question was settled), an income tax, the protection of American labor by prevention of the "importation of foreign pauper labor," and stricter enforcement of antitrust legislation.[19] Gold Democrats could do nothing more than shake their heads and get on their trains back East, hoping for the best but expecting the worst. Some proposed splitting the party, while others vowed to abandon their party and—for the sake of the country—support the Republican platform of "sound money."

Most Populists following events in Chicago were at first perplexed but later ecstatic as they contemplated a Populist-Democratic coalition that would certainly secure the alliance with labor and assure victory in November. There were a number of protests from some who from the beginning declared "principle over party," and worried that the Democrats would consume their party, but their voices were drowned out by the din of exuberance and enthusiasm of the moment. In the end, the Populists supported William Jennings Bryan, the Democratic presidential candidate. With Populists and organized labor in the Democratic camp and industrial and finance capitalists clearly in control of the Republican Party, the campaign of 1896, as a number of historians have pointed out, "provided vent for an expression of class antagonisms such as the country had never before known."[20]

Bryan, at 36 the youngest man ever nominated for the presidency, waged an energetic, passionate, and precedent-breaking campaign. Prior to 1896, it was perceived as unseemly for a presidential candidate to campaign personally. The accepted policy was for the nominee to stay at home and give speeches from his front porch to reporters who gathered at the appointed time. Bryan changed all this. He traveled to 27 states and gave over 600 speeches. Part of this was innovation, part necessity. The Republican Party had collected over 3.5 million dollars for its campaign trust or five times what Bryan had collected. McKinley remained at his home in Ohio while 1,500 surrogates crisscrossed the country. Prominent Republicans including Teddy Roosevelt warned Americans that Bryan was a dangerous radical whose policies would destroy the country. Although described at the time and by future historians as an election of class warfare, Republicans effectively argued a counterpoint to the silver proposal. Republicans warned workers that Bryan's plan to inflate the currency would reduce the value of their hard-earned dollars and cents. This argument, along with threats from their employers that Bryan's election would force them to close their factories, resonated with many urban workers who returned to the Republican fold.

With accusations of Democratic radicalism planted in the minds of voters, the Republican campaign culminated on November 2, which they designated as "Flag Day." They called for all those who supported the principles of good sound American government to display their flags on that day and march in favor of the Republicans. The message was clear: "True Americans vote Republican." McKinley defeated Bryan soundly by a popular vote margin of 51 to 47 percent and an electoral college margin of 271 to 176. Bryan won the rural traditional Populist vote but the hope for coalition with labor never materialized. He was unable to win a majority of urban worker votes in the Northeast. And the political coalition formed by the Republicans dominated national politics for the next 30 years.

The urban labor and rural farmers' political alliance could not endure. The grievances that brought them together were symptoms of economic and social changes in the country that went beyond their ability to grasp. Despite their failure, Populists mark an important turning point in American political history and provide a preface, if not an introductory chapter, to the story of Progressivism. They were the first to wage a collective response to the challenges created by the post-Civil War demographic, economic, and industrial convolutions that transformed the country. And many of their proposals including an income tax, direct election of senators, protection for workers, and government regulatory agencies, would in the ensuing decades become law under Progressive political persuasion. Although they correctly identified the emerging challenges of the late nineteenth century, farmers and labor were inept at defining an effective strategy. The facile policies of reducing politics to single issues such as silver versus gold were over. The new complexities of social and economic life demanded a more sophisticated political view. The newly emerging middle class—urbane, rational, and educated—collectively known as Progressives, began to formulate solutions to the myriad problems that Populists had begun to identify, but failed to solve.

NOTES

1. William Alfred Peffer, "The Mission of the Populist Party," *The North American Review* 157, no. 445 (December 1893): 678.

2. Peffer, p. 666.

3. Herbert G. Gutman, "Work, Culture, and Society in Industrializing America, 1815–1919," *The American Historical Review* 78, no. 3 (June 1973): 553.

4. Ibid., p. 544.

5. Ibid., p. 545.

6. Ibid., p. 554.

7. Philip S. Foner, W. H. Sims, George H. Williams, Andrew McCormack, C. C. Mehurin, M. I. Mattox, and B. W. Scott, "The Knights of Labor," *The Journal of Negro History* 53, no. 1 (January 1968): 72–73.

8. Gutman, p. 555.

9. Florida East Coast Papers, File Number 11957, Flagler Museum, Palm Beach, Florida.

10. *New York Times* (May 5, 1886), 1.

11. *New York Times* (July 5, July 12), 1.

12. Emma Goldman, *Living My Life* (Minneola, New York: Dover Publications, 1971), 91–93.

13. Lindsey Almont, "Paternalism and the Pullman Strike," *The American Historical Review* 44, no. 2 (January 1939), 272–3.

14. Chester Destler, "The Consummation of a Labor-Populist Alliance in Illinois, 1894," *The Mississippi Valley Historical Review* 27, no. 4 (March 1941): 593–6.

15. Robert F. Durden, "The 'Cow-bird' Grounded: The Populist Nomination of Bryan and Tom Watson in 1896," *The Mississippi Valley Historical Review* 50, no. 3 (December 1963): 398.

16. Ibid., pp. 405–6.

17. Ibid.

18. Ibid., p. 407.

19. Ibid.

20. Arthur M. Schlesinger, *The Rise of the City, 1878–1898* (New York: Macmillan and Co., 1933), 427.

CHAPTER 3

PROGRESSIVE POLITICS

I do not by any means believe the initiative, the referendum, and the recall are the panacea for all our political ills, yet they do give to the electorate the power of action when desired, and they do place in the hands of the people the means by which they may protect themselves.

—Hiram Johnson[1]

P rogressives who believed in rationally ordered, honestly run systems, based on scientifically collected social data, found the antithesis of their theories in the political reality of late nineteenth-century politics. Faced with the appalling level of graft, corruption, incompetence, and apparent indifference to the common good that seemed rampant throughout the country, Progressives began to organize politically, and when an assassin's bullet put Theodore Roosevelt in the White House in 1901, it marked the zenith of a Progressive political movement that had begun a decade earlier in the trench warfare of local and state politics.

Progressive politics had largely urban roots. In the post-Civil War years, mass migration from rural America and Europe along with the meteoric growth of banks and industries transformed American cities into modern centers of life, culture, and economics. By 1890, the metropolitan area of New York and Brooklyn contained nearly 2½ million people, and Chicago and Philadelphia were not far behind with a million apiece. Even southern cities like Memphis, which grew from 23,000 people in the postwar decade to over 100,000 at the turn of the century, and Atlanta whose metropolitan area population exploded from 21,000 in 1870 to half a million in 1910 experienced the post-Civil War urban population boom. The people who populated the city for the most part had come from towns, villages, and farms and were accustomed to a humble yet harmonious life centered on family, tradition, religion, and common economic activity. They were unprepared for the social cacophony and economic complexity of the new urban reality.

The increasing tension of city life was reflected in a variety of ways. A New York doctor, for example, in 1881, described the effects on "the human organism of the heightened speed of movement, the constant struggle for survival, the discordant sounds of the streets, and the ceaseless mental excitements and endless distractions."[2] The political structure of the city also suffered from the seismic undulations of the postwar urban landscape. Historically rooted in a far less complex antebellum world, local government lacked the means to address the challenges brought about by the late nineteenth-century city's explosion of industry and humanity.

In order to fill the organizational vacuum, a new political animal, the urban boss, emerged. Typical of this new species was Tammany Hall organizer George Washington Plunkett, who bragged, "I saw my opportunities and I took em, ..." The cogs in the wheels of the new political machines were the new immigrants, who arrived with great hope for a better life, but often little else. Dizzied by the whirl of industrial urban life, the new arrivals welcomed the stability provided by the political boss or his lieutenant who would often greet a lonely new arrival at the port of entry and find him a place to stay, some groceries, often a job, and sometimes even a companion from the homeland to ease his loneliness. In return, the grateful immigrant would remember the politician on Election Day and return favors given for the favor of his vote. In this way, piece by piece, person by person, the great urban political machines were built. As Plunkett said:

> If there's a family in my district in want, I know it before the charitable societies do, and me and my men are first on the ground. I have a special corps to look up such cases. The consequence is that the poor look up to George W. Plunkett as a father, come to him in trouble—and don't forget him on Election Day. Another thing, I can always get a job for a deservin' man. I make it a point to keep on the track of jobs, and it seldom happens that I don't have a few up my sleeve ready for use. I know every big employer in the district and in the whole city, for that matter, and they ain't in the habit of sayin' no to me when I ask them for a job.[3]

For the political bosses who distributed these favors, the rewards were unlimited. Kickbacks for granting franchises to the new telephone, gas, electric, and water utilities that were cropping up in cities and inside information on property that the city needed for a new park or road provided a cornucopia of wealth for political bosses.[4]

Progressives found a political kingdom built on favors and corruption anathema to their political universe, which was based on the belief of honest democratic institutions honestly created. Progressive writer Ray Stannard Baker condemned "government of the bosses, by the bosses, and distinctly for the bosses . . . [who are] the very disease of democracy."[5] Progressives acknowledged their own loss of power to these new political entrepreneurs. But they maintained their faith in the democratic process and soon formed political organizations of their own to battle the urban bosses. They framed the contest in terms of good versus evil and intended to wage war against those whose actions corrupted democracy. With missionary zeal, reformers like Judge Ben Lindsey affirmed, "ideal democracy was the cure for universal evil."[6] To the Progressives, the personification of evil was the urban boss and their battle cry was "Reform!" The political organizations created by Progressives often included the words *improvement* or *reform*, which to them meant wresting control of the city from the urban bosses through political activism.

Many sociologists and some historians have explained that the city boss emerged in response to the needs of the vast majority of the population who were immigrants and underpaid urban workers. They argued that the city political machine—although often corrupt—provided an adequate safety net in an era when government social programs did not exist and the better off neglected or abandoned their civic responsibilities. There is validity in this assessment. For the most part, urban welfare in the nineteenth century was rooted in a system of colonial era poor houses and charitable institutions, which could hardly provide relief for the masses of humanity that populated the late nineteenth-century city. Aside from the private philanthropy and volunteerism of those who organized settlement houses, the only viable alternative for the desperately poor was the urban political machine that created systems of informal aid, which stretched into every working-class neighborhood of the city.

Systems designed by the urban bosses to aid poor workers and immigrants may, in many cases, have proved adequate but modern cities also needed an infrastructure of roads, water, sewage, and communication. Urban bosses, who concentrated on the microcosm of individual human needs, lacked the political will or ability to manage these greater, more complicated challenges of urban growth. While corrupt politicians lined their pockets with graft, the cities they were elected to manage deteriorated. In Chicago's first ward known as the "Levee," for example, prostitution and gambling flourished under the protective eye of ward leaders "Hinky Dink" McKenna and "Bathhouse John" Coughlin, who took in thousands in kickbacks from the local merchants of vice, while the streets and sidewalks in Chicago remained in constant disrepair, and the public utilities provided abysmal service. While immigrants and the poor received some small considerations that bought their vote, the sewer and garbage collection and disposal systems could not handle the volume of waste produced every day in the city; the public school system was overcrowded, understaffed, and underfunded; the smoke, fumes, and waste from industrial plants polluted the air and ground; a large percentage of the populace lived in crowded, rickety, unsanitary tenement houses that flourished in the face of minimal building regulations; and the city's police force neither controlled crime nor kept the peace.[7]

According to Lincoln Steffens, who wrote a series of articles in *McClure's Magazine* on corruption in local government at the turn of the century, the cities of St. Louis, Minneapolis, San Francisco, Philadelphia, and numerous other communities all suffered from inept or corrupt city officials. In the opinion of Andrew White, Cornell University's first president, the city governments of the United States with very few exceptions were the "worst in Christendom—the most expensive, the most inefficient, and the most corrupt."[8] To address these problems, men and women—mostly middle class and educated—of cities affected by political incompetence and corruption organized reform associations such as the "City Club of Chicago." In their statements of purpose, they decried "the political, social, and economic conditions of the community in which we live . . ." and pledged to aid in "improving civic conditions and to assist in arousing an increased sense of social responsibility, and to promote the public welfare."[9] In New York, Progressives formed the "People's Municipal League" and the "Citizens' Union" that declared similar goals.

A belief common to all these groups was that a modern city demanded a well-organized management system based on scientifically collected data to replace the clumsy and inept boss system. Drawing analogies between successful business and effective government, they applied the principles of expert management proven effective in business corporations to complex urban communities. They advocated new forms of urban government such as the "city-manager" plan that turned the daily functions of the city over to a team of experts in urban affairs.[10] And they proposed taking power from city council members who ran their sections of the city as private fiefdoms by creating a centralized governing system under a strong mayor. Local reformers met with mild success in most large cities where scientific formulas of urban management could be applied. In the ensuing decades, over 450 municipalities adopted the city management form of government.

The city management system along with a strong centralized mayor's office remain an important victory and lasting legacy of local progressive leaders, and most cities continue to be governed in this manner. But urban bosses adapted to the demands of reformers and learned to accommodate themselves to the urban management system making the political success of Progressives in local government fleeting. From time to time reform mayors could be elected, but their term of office was often short and soon the political machines were back in control. In Philadelphia, for example, Rudolph Blankenburg, a German Quaker and wealthy retired businessman, helped form the "Keystone Democratic Party" to fight Republican corruption and ran successfully on that ticket in 1911 as a reformer. He took control of the police force out of the hands of the ward leaders, reorganized the civil service system, and based city hiring and promotion on a merit system. He also persuaded the legislature to pass a bill that enabled the city to develop subway and transit lines under municipal control. Despite improvements that Blankenburg brought to Philadelphia, in 1915 the Republican machine defeated him and regained control of the city. Blankenburg's defeat proved New York machine politician George Plunkett's axiom: "Reformers can't last in politics."

> He can make a show for a while, but he always comes down like a rocket. Politics is as much a regular business as the grocery or the dry-goods or the drug business. You've got to be trained up to it or you're sure to fail. Suppose a man who knew nothing about the grocery trade suddenly went into the business and tried to conduct it according to his own ideas. Wouldn't he make a mess of it? He might make a splurge for a while, as long as his money lasted, but his store would soon be empty. It's just the same with a reformer. He hasn't been brought up in the difficult business of politics and he makes a mess of it every time. That was what was said after the throw downs in

1894 and 1901. But it didn't happen, did it? Not one big Tammany man deserted, and today the organization is stronger than ever.

Despite their inability to wrest permanent control of the city from the urban bosses, Progressives made their mark on local politics and the word *reform* became embedded in the political vocabulary of both Progressives and entrenched political bosses like Matt Quay, who restored the power of his Pennsylvania machine under the banner of reform. The lasting imprint of Progressive influence on urban politics is the bureaucratic army of experts that now populate most city halls, where they administer the budget and manage services such as public health, utilities, education, and public security.

Progressive reformers also took control of various state governments across the country and instituted much-needed and long-lasting reform. Among the most important accomplishments at the state level were establishment of a minimum age for workers, an eight-hour work day, protection of women in the workplace, workers' compensation for injuries sustained on the job, protection of natural resources, public health, standardized licensing requirements for professionals, and educational reform.

In the West, Californian Hiram Johnson typified the vision and the accomplishments of Progressive governors nationwide. In 1910, Johnson won the gubernatorial election as a member of the Lincoln-Roosevelt League, a liberal Republican movement running on an anti-Southern Pacific Railroad platform, and promised to wrest control of the state from corporate giants. He carried his message into the governor's office where he spearheaded legislation that called for the popular election of U.S. senators, women's suffrage, and initiative, referendum, and recall. His election reforms took control of government out of the hands of special interests and gave Californians unprecedented participatory power in their state government. He also established a railroad commission that reined in the power of the Southern Pacific Railroad.

In the Midwest, another Progressive, Bob La Follette of Wisconsin, became governor of that state in 1900 by promising a program of tax reform, regulation of corporations, and an extension of political democracy. Demonstrating the Progressive faith in experts of the new social sciences, La Follette employed a staff from the University of Wisconsin to draft bills and administer the laws that he introduced. "I made it a policy," he wrote in his autobiography "to bring all the reserves of knowledge and inspiration of the university to the service of the people, to appoint experts from the university wherever possible upon the important boards of the state— the civil service commission, the railroad commission and so on—a relationship ... by which the state has greatly profited."[11]

Progressives were fascinated with technology and science. They wanted to apply the social sciences to better government, but they were also fascinated with practical science and the engineering miracles of the late nineteenth century; Florida's governor Napoleon Bonaparte Broward, for example, in addition to creating a Progressive workman's compensation program and a systemized process for developing higher education in the state, including the establishment of a college for women and one for backs, also spearheaded a plan to drain the Everglades through the scientific application of canals throughout the wetlands of South Florida. The project promised to be a great boom to farming and growth in unpopulated South Florida became in the latter part of the century an ecological disaster that the state was still trying to repair.

In the East, both Theodore Roosevelt and Woodrow Wilson, governors of New York and New Jersey, respectively, won the presidency, thus bringing the Progressive policies hatched in state government to the White House. Their presidential terms—Roosevelt began his in 1901 and Wilson ended his in 1921—marked the beginning and the end of what historians define as the Progressive movement. Roosevelt gained notoriety as a reformer when in 1895 he was elected president of the Board of the New York City Police Commission. In the ensuing two years he brought much needed change to the police department, which at that time was described as the most corrupt in the country. Roosevelt established civil service examinations, tested the physical qualifications of the police, and insisted on intense training of officers including in the use of firearms. Often, Roosevelt walked the streets himself, police baton in hand, to assure that officers were at their assigned posts doing their duty and order prevailed.

In 1896, he crisscrossed the county in support of William McKinley and after McKinley's election joined the new administration as assistant secretary of the navy. A year later, he joined the struggle against Spain in Cuba. Upon his return as a war hero, he was elected governor of New York where he continued his efforts at political reform. Roosevelt's crusade in Albany made political bosses so uncomfortable that New York Republican leader

Thomas Platt urged McKinley to put him on the ticket as vice president in 1900 in order to get him out of New York politics, where his reforms were disrupting old alliances. At that time, the vice presidency was a politically flaccid position that historically had been a career-ending appointment. From the historical perspective of 1900, after the postrevolutionary era triumvirate of Presidents Washington, Adams, and Jefferson, only one man, Martin Van Buren, had been elected to the presidency after serving as vice president. But three had entered the office as a result of the death of their predecessor, and Roosevelt would be the fourth.

When Roosevelt took office after McKinley's assassination in 1901, political boss Mark Hanna lamented, "Now look that damned cowboy is president!" But Theodore Roosevelt was much more than a "damned cowboy." He was "Everyman." To the intellectual, he was a prolific writer and the author of a definitive history of the West; to the sportsman, he was a hunter and an amateur boxer. To the common man, he was a person who had overcome childhood illness to become a war hero. To the naturalist, he was a birdwatcher; to the Westerner, he was a rugged frontier cattle rancher. To the northeastern establishment, he was a member of one of the oldest families in the United States. He was also a Mason and a devout Christian. Roosevelt embraced the presidency as he had every one of his life's endeavors—with enthusiasm and gusto.

Declaring that the country will not be a good place for anyone until it is a good place for everyone, Roosevelt promised a "Square Deal for the American people" that would create an economic system that gave each man the opportunity to be the best that he could possibly be. Like most Progressives, Roosevelt envisioned a powerful federal government that acted in the public interest with no alliance to any of the power brokers that seemed to control the American economy. Mark Hanna had warned the often impetuous TR to go slowly. But this man who now added the presidency to his conquests that included cattle rustlers in the West, young toughs on the streets of New York, and enemy Spaniards on San Juan Hill, saw little virtue in a policy of caution.

But without a Progressive mandate and a balky conservative Congress, he had to choose his crusades carefully. He had no fight with big business per se and indeed thought that a well-managed corporation was the natural product of capitalism's development. But as a moralist, Roosevelt also believed that leaders of big business should act responsibly. He felt the same about leaders of the newly emerging labor unions who were struggling for power. Failing to do so threatened the general public whose only recourse was a strong and impartial government that acted fairly. Following the pragmatic model of the age, Roosevelt's ideas evolved in response to conditions.

Using the political capital provided by his personal popularity, which he referred to as his own "bully pulpit," Roosevelt transformed the presidency into a powerful force that set the Progressive political agenda for eight years. Under his leadership, the federal government created and enforced laws that protected the natural environment, consumers, and workers. He even took on corporations through antitrust suits to control corporations he felt were threatening the "Square Deal" that every American deserved. The bully pulpit was also utilized when he knew that direct political action would be useless. He knew, for example, that given the Southern Democratic power in the senate and House that any legislation directed at ending the unjust system of segregation in the South would fail. Roosevelt did, however, host a well-publicized luncheon with black educator Booker T. Washington in the White House to let his feelings on integration be known to the South as well as the rest of the country. The simple act of breaking bread set off a firestorm of protest across the South including several lynchings and threats against Washington's life.

Roosevelt's energy carried beyond the country's borders, where he forged a new direction in foreign policy. The Spanish War, which his predecessor waged, may have opened the door to the Caribbean, but it was TR who went barging in. Proclaiming that the United States had "international police power" in the Caribbean, Roosevelt used the military to fill the power vacuum left by the Spanish departure. During his term of office, in order to prevent a French military invasion in the service of European bankers, he sent troops and financial experts to seize the customs office of the Dominican Republic and manage that country's fiscal affairs. He also sent Marines into Honduras and Cuba. But the most flamboyant act of all was his seizure of the Isthmus of Panama from Colombia in order to enable the construction of a canal connecting the Atlantic and the Pacific Oceans.

Having fulfilled most of the promises of his Progressive agenda, Roosevelt announced he would not run for the presidency in 1908, and he turned the reins of government over to his handpicked successor

William Howard Taft. The new president continued with the agenda established by Roosevelt and the Progressive wing of the party. In 1909, he proposed an amendment to the constitution that would permit the collection of an income tax; he worked to reduce the tariff and launched over 40 antitrust lawsuits against corporate giants including Standard Oil that was dissolved in 1911. He also issued an injunction against western railroads preventing them from raising their rates, launched a postal savings bank, and created a Childs Bureau headed by Julia Lathrop making her the highest ranking woman in the federal government. He signed a bill creating the eight-hour work day for all employees in the federal government or working for companies with federal contracts, and he vetoed a bill calling for literacy tests for immigrants. Despite these accomplishments, after four years, Taft found himself alienated from the Progressive wing of the party. Some thought he had not pushed the Progressive cause with sufficient enthusiasm, and others charged he had become too cozy with big business and the conservative wing of the party. For example, he replaced Roosevelt's aggressive foreign policy with what he called "Dollar Diplomacy" that invited big business into a foreign relations partnership with the government. Finally, Taft's own more moderate views of Progressivism must have frustrated many. In a letter to his brother, Taft complained that the country would need to rewrite the constitution in order to carry out Roosevelt's agenda. The final straw came when he fired Director of the Division of Forestry Gifford Pinchot for making a disagreement with Secretary of Interior Richard Ballinger over western land use public. Pinchot was the man most responsible for Theodore Roosevelt's conservationist legacy and with this final act Taft threw down the gauntlet between himself and the most liberal wing of the Republican Party. It is also certain that the energetic and popular Roosevelt was simply too hard an act to follow. In 1909, Taft took off on a cross-country speaking tour, and an observer in Winona, Minnesota, commented, "I knew he was good natured but I never dreamed he was so dull."

Disillusioned with Taft, Progressive Republicans rallied around a rejuvenated Teddy Roosevelt, who in 1910 gave the most radical speech of his career. Declaring that only a powerful federal government could regulate the economy and guarantee social justice, he announced a plan he described as the "New Nationalism." He demanded an end to the unholy alliance between big business and corrupt government officials. He called for a new government that would establish a national health insurance plan, social security, a minimum wage law for women, workman's compensation, an inheritance tax, a federal income tax, farm relief, direct election of senators, and women's suffrage. Roosevelt's speech energized the disheartened Progressive wing of the Republican Party. Fighting Bob La Follette of Wisconsin announced his candidacy for president and soon Roosevelt himself threw his hat in the ring. Although Taft had championed the Progressive cause, it was clear from the enthusiasm demonstrated for Roosevelt's "New Nationalism" that Progressives had gone well beyond Taft's political universe. Taft still held control of the party and in the end he would capture the Republican nomination. But it was a Pyrrhic victory. The Progressives bolted the party and nominated Theodore Roosevelt and Hiram Johnson of California as candidates for president and vice president of their newly formed Progressive Party.

The Democrats also chose the progressive path and nominated Woodrow Wilson, former governor of New Jersey and former university president of Princeton to carry their banner. The Democrats won the election over a fractured Republican Party. Wilson garnered 48 percent of the vote to easily beat Roosevelt's 28 percent, while Taft came in a distant third. Although the Republicans Progressive standard bearer lost, historians note that when Eugene Debs's 900,000 or 6 percent are included it means that 82 percent of the voters in 1912 had chosen a Progressive candidate. Clearly, 1912 was a high water mark for Progressivism, and it marks a time when the great majority of Americans supported the Progressive agenda that called for bigger government to help bring order to a world that appeared to be spinning out of control.

Wilson entered the presidency with an army of hopeful followers eager to complete the Progressive agenda, which Wilson called "the New Freedom" that called for an attack on what he described as the triple wall of privilege: the tariff, the banks, and trusts. Contrary to Roosevelt's view of strong government regulating large corporations, Wilson's Progressivism envisioned a Jeffersonian world of limited-sized manufacturers and farmers engaged in healthy competition. In 1913, his Progressive majority in Congress, believing that high tariffs were strengthening the large corporations at the expense of the average American, passed the largest tariff reduction since the Civil War. They also passed a graduated income tax on corporations and the wealthiest Americans. Wilson completed his fiscal

Imprisoned for speaking out against World War I, Eugene Debs was nominated for president by the Socialist Party in 1920, while still serving his sentence. (AP Photo)

reform legislation by creating the Federal Reserve Board, which would determine the amount of money circulating in the economy. Taken together these three pieces of legislation marked a major watershed in the economic history of the United States. As a result of this legislation, the cost of government would no longer be paid by tariffs and land sales but rather by wealthy Americans and corporations. Second, control of the country's monetary policy would be in the hands of the federal government not private bankers. Other progressive legislation champ-ioned by Wilson included a new antitrust act to break price-fixing by large corporations, a Child Labor Act, an eight-hour day for railroad workers, and low-cost loans to farmers. He also used his influence to establish the Federal Trade Commission, which created a bipartisan executive agency to oversee big business. At the end of his first two years in office, many Americans agreed that Wilson was well on his way to completing the task begun by Teddy Roosevelt.

Wilson's continued domestic plan to rein in the power of corporations and to pursue other pieces of social legislation soon became distracted by foreign affairs. From his first days in office, he had been carefully observing events in Mexico, where Victor Huerta had murdered the popular revolutionary leader Francisco Madero and seized control of the government. Most of world accepted the action as a fait accompli and recognized the government of Huerta, but Wilson refused to recognize the credentials of a government he described as a "band of murderers" led by a "butcher." He then proceeded to implement a course of action designed to disrupt and eventually overthrow the Huerta government. Initially, Wilson supported the anti-Huerta Venustano Carranza but he quickly ended this relationship when Carranza, much to Wilson's surprise, demonstrated national pride and more political sagacity than Wilson and rejected the president's overtures. In response to the rejection, for a short time, Wilson lent aid to the bandit revolutionaries Pancho Villa and Emilio Zapata but soon abandoned this tactic. Finally, he decided on Carranza as the only legitimate alternative. This decision angered Villa who launched a series of raids on the U.S. border, which brought him in conflict with American troops already stationed there by Taft when the revolution had originally broken out in 1910. When the smoke settled, it was clear that Wilson had ushered in an era of relations with Mexico that were the lowest they had been since war had broken out between the two countries seven decades prior. One might have expected more from a former professor of political science.

Wilson's attention to foreign affairs became more focused after 1914 when Europe became embroiled in what their generation called the "Great War." Although at first Wilson urged Americans to remain neutral in thought and deed and asserted that the United States was "too proud to fight," the country eventually became drawn into the war. Many historians say that the war ended the Progressive movement in the United States. But during the years of the conflict, Wilson's war policy helped Progressives realize their dream of regulating and controlling the entire national economy. Using his war powers, Wilson created agencies to oversee, regulate, and in some cases, manage the entire economy. He appointed Wall Street wizard Bernard Baruch to head up the War Industries Board, which coordinated production, allocated materials, set up work rules, and organized purchasing and distribution systems across the country. He created a Food Administration Board under Herbert Hoover that mobilized both the production and consumption of food. A Fuel Administration Board was also created to develop and implement energy conservation and a Public Information Committee was established to sell both government control of the economy and the war itself to the American people. Sedition laws were passed to punish those who disagreed too loudly. Thus, the war helped Progressive politicians realize their ultimate goal of a responsive government in control of the economy for the social well-being of its citizens.

But the war changed the entire political landscape. When it ended, the American people, who had overwhelmingly approved of the Progressive agenda just eight years prior, decided they had had enough of government interference in their lives. They elected a conservative Republican Warren Harding, who promised to return the country to "normalcy." After a decade and a half of head-spinning political change, the Progressives' political hegemony came to an end. But Progressives left a legacy that changed the perception and nature of government forever, by fixing in the collective political psyche of the American people the idea that the federal government is an active player not an indifferent observer of the economic life of its citizens.

NOTES

1. Hiram Johnson, Second Inaugural Address—January 5, 1915. TO THE SENATE AND ASSEMBLY OF THE STATE OF CALIFORNIA.

2. Arthur M. Schlesinger, "The City in American History," *The Mississippi Valley Historical Review* 27, no. 1 (June 1940): 57–60.

3. William L. Riordan, *Plunkitt of Tammany Hall* (reprint, New York: E. P. Dutton, 1905, 1963): 52–53.

4. Ibid., pp. 3–6.

5. Stanley Schultz, "The Morality of Politics: The Muckrakers' Vision of Democracy," *Journal of American History* 52, no. 3 (December 1965): 542.

6. Ibid., p. 528.

7. Maureen A. Flanagan, "Gender and Urban Political Reform: The City Club and the Woman's City Club of Chicago in the Progressive Era," *The American Historical Review* 95, no. 4 (October 1990): 1034.

8. Schlesinger, p. 59.

9. Flanagan, p. 1034.

10. Schlesinger, p. 64.

11. Robert La Follette, *Robert La Follette's Autobiography: A Personal Narrative of Political Experiences* (Madison, WI: The Robert M. La Follette Co., 1911, 1913), 31.

CHAPTER 4

THE CHANGING CITY

In the country one sees only nature's fair works, and one's soul is not saddened by the cruel struggle for mere existence that goes on in the crowded city.

—Helen Keller[1]

From the end of the Civil War to the turn of the century, the population of American cities increased sevenfold and in the process radically transformed family, religious, social, and economic life in the United States.[2] The city, propelled into a whirl of rapid expansion by industrial and demographic growth, did not absorb the transformations easily. Noisy, crowded, and malodorous thoroughfares dominated the terrain. Houses and apartment buildings crowded against each other competing for limited space. Rivers that once provided refreshment and drinkable water became sewage drains carrying the waste of the city out to the ocean or to larger bodies of water where officials assumed it would dissipate. Factory smoke filled the lungs, watered the eyes, and blurred the vision. The very concept of time itself changed. Because the factories and trains, which drove the city demanded timely schedules, life no longer moved to celestial rhythms but rather to the steady beat of the clock. Money became the measure of progress, and factory whistles beckoned workers as church bells had once called the faithful to an earlier form of worship.

But the city also brought pleasures. Theaters—both traditional and newly contrived—blossomed; museums brought the wonders of the world to within reach of the masses. Steam and then later electric trains bustled through or above city streets carrying people—beyond distances they normally walked—to the new suburban amusement parks, countryside recreation areas and beaches. City life became the great new adventure of the early twentieth century.

The population explosion that created the great cities was not so much the result of a fecund but rather of a newly mobile people. In the post-Civil

War years as frontiers diminished, technology reduced the need for labor on the land, and at the same time, created new technological attractions in the cities and the means—through steamship and locomotive—to get there. With promises of success on the land declining, people were drawn to the city. The movement of the native population was dramatically augmented by the wave of immigrants arriving from Europe. European migration was not a new phenomenon. Most Americans traced their ancestors there, but the new immigrants came from parts of Europe previously unrepresented. According to Senator William Dillingham's congressional committee, 78 percent of the European immigration in 1910 had come from southern and eastern Europe. This fact did not go unnoticed and frequent references—and contrasts—were made to the old immigrants of "good stock" from northern Europe and the less desirable new immigrants from southern and eastern Europe. More than 70 percent of the new immigrants settled in cities. In 1893, Chicago contained the third largest central European community in the world and ranked only behind Warsaw and Lodz in the number of poles living within its boundaries. And according to the 1890 census, 80 percent of those living in New York had either been born abroad or were of foreign parentage.[3]

Immigrant groups tended to identify particular areas within the city as their own. They created their own space—in the least expensive neighborhoods—where they could maintain some semblance of cultural tradition among their compatriots. Consequently, the cities became a cacophony of subcultures marked by boundaries of language, foodways, and other aspects of social and religious identity. Jacob Riis in his book, *How the Other Half Lives*, wrote,

> A map of the city colored to designate nationalities would show more stripes than a zebra and more colors than any rainbow. The city in such a map would fall into great halves green for the Irish prevailing in the West side tenement districts and blue for the Germans on the east side. But intermingled with these ground colors would be an odd variety of tints that would give the whole the appearance of an extraordinary crazy quilt.
>
> The red of the Italian would be seen forcing its way northward along Mulberry Street to the quarter of the French purple on Bleeker Street ... On the West side the red would be seen overrunning the old Africa of Thompson Street pushing the black of the negro rapidly up town against querulous but unavailing protests.[4]

New York City's Mulberry Street, also known as "Little Italy" was one of the many of New York's Immigrant neighborhoods that arose in the nineteenth century. (Library of Congress)

No matter what neighborhood they settled into, most immigrants lived in limited space, which they rented on a weekly or monthly basis. In New York City, in 1890, in the poorer wards, over 90 percent of the people rented, and in other cities the numbers were almost as high. These areas of the city teemed with humanity. In 1890, 7 of the 10 largest cities had population densities of more than 100 persons per acre in their poorer areas.[5] These conditions left those who lived there at the mercy of greedy landlords, who unhindered by restrictive building codes that were nonexistent in some areas and unenforced in others, squeezed as much profit as possible out of their buildings. As wealthy families moved to the more comfortable outer limits of the city or into exclusive areas within cities, speculators bought their single-family mansions and chopped them up into multiple dwellings.

As populations continued to grow, New York landlords and builders faced with masses of immigrants developed new methods for squeezing large numbers into limited spaces. They began to tear down the large mansions that had been converted to multiple dwelling spaces and replaced them with a new structure called the "tenement" house. Initially, the word *tenement* was used to apply to any multiple family rental building. Eventually, the word evolved to mean any residential building in a slum.[6]

One of the first New York tenements had been built just prior to the Civil War, and civic leaders praised the new builders for creating economical living space that would allow people to move out of the garages, cellars, and broken down houses in which they had been living. Economy of space dominated the design of these early tenements and little thought was given to the livability of what were cramped and often dark living spaces. In the late 1870s, sociologists and architects teamed up to create a new and what they considered a more humane building they called a "dumbbell," a by-product of the Tenement Housing Law of 1879, which required that each bedroom in any newly constructed building have at least one window. The building had an indentation at its midpoint, hence the name "dumbbell." Given this design, even when it abutted another similarly shaped building, it created an open shaft of about five feet width, which allowed for some light and a measure of air to pass by interior windows. It was usually built to a height of five or six stories and housed four families on each floor. Each block contained 10 tenements, which meant that a block of dumbbell apartments might house up to 4,000 people.[7] By 1900, New York had over 42,000 tenement buildings that housed over a million and a half people. Similar but not as drastic overcrowding had also occurred in other large cities such as Cincinnati, Boston, Cleveland, and Chicago. Stephen Crane in his novel *Maggie, Girl of the Streets* (1896) provided his middle-class reading public with a glimpse of life within these urban infernos.

> Eventually they entered into a dark region where, from a careening building, a dozen gruesome doorways gave up loads of babies to the street and the gutter. A wind of early autumn raised yellow dust from cobbles and swirled it against a hundred windows. Long streamers of garments fluttered from fire-escapes. In all unhandy places there were buckets, brooms, rags and bottles. In the street infants played or fought with other infants or sat stupidly in the way of vehicles. Formidable women, with uncombed hair and disordered dress, gossiped while leaning on railings, or screamed in frantic quarrels. Withered persons, in curious postures of submission to something, sat smoking pipes in obscure corners. A thousand odors of cooking

food came forth to the street. The building quivered and creaked from the weight of humanity stamping about in its bowels.

Not everyone in the city lived in tenements, and those with steady work were able to move into more compatible housing that—thanks to the newly emerging public transportation systems—began to stretch away from the original city boundaries into places of more pleasant air and surroundings. Also after the turn of the century with Progressive and reform-minded political leaders taking control of many city governments, more stringent housing codes were put into place and conditions improved for everyone. Urban housing varied throughout the country based on local topography and custom. In Philadelphia and Baltimore, for example, where home ownership had been a long-standing tradition, row houses were common and extended throughout the city to the suburbs. Boston and Newark utilized the four-story "three decker" that derived its name from the three wooden galleries or decks built one above the other in the front of the building. Chicago and St. Louis built two and three deckers in solid rows that extended the length of a city block.[8]

Black migration also contributed to the radical changes in the demographic landscape of northern cities as thousands of blacks began leaving the South for better jobs, less oppression, and greater freedom that black-owned publications such as the *Chicago Defender* and the *Pittsburgh Courier* promised they would find in the North. Individuals, families, and sometimes entire communities, led by a pastor or a barber shop proprietor, moved North and settled into cities such as Chicago, Detroit, Cleveland, New York, and Philadelphia. When they arrived they often found that conditions were not as favorable as promised but, on the other hand, not as bad as conditions they had left. Although they were forced into the lowest paying factory jobs and their choice of neighborhood was not merely restricted by economics but also by racism, they could still celebrate their escape from under the boot of white southern oppression. The salaries, although meager, were better than they had received in the South, their children in most cases had decent schools to attend, and best of all, they could vote. Within a generation, black voting blocs formed and for the first time since the end of Reconstruction blacks had a voice in Congress. By the 1890s, in the South, most black Americans had either been barred from or had abandoned electoral politics in frustration. With minimal voter participation, the voice advocating black issues was silenced. After North Carolina Representative George White's departure from the House of Representatives in March 1901, no African American served in the U.S. Congress for nearly three decades. With his election to the U.S. House of Representatives from a Chicago district in 1928, Oscar De Priest of Illinois became the first African American to serve in Congress since White's departure. But while the victory symbolized renewed hope for African Americans struggling to regain a foothold in national politics, it was only the beginning of an arduous journey.

Blacks also brought their music from the South. When the rhythms of the southern juke joints came to the city, a new art form developed that would evolve into blues, ragtime, jazz, swing, bebop, and rock and roll and in the process created a genuine American music art form, which much of the rest of the world heard and imitated. Urban blacks also produced a new genre in American literature. Spearheaded by writers in Harlem, black communities all over the newly populated urban north created small pockets of writers and artists that brought a new style to the American literary scene.

Most blacks came from the impoverished South in a condition that reflected their origins, but many did not stay in that situation for long. Within the urban black community, an influential and prosperous middle class soon emerged. As Elise Johnson MacDougall pointed out at the time, there were black professionals and businessmen and women who lived in well-appointed homes, joined clubs, and took vacations to California and Europe. By 1916, there were sufficient number of black tennis clubs in American cities to form *The American Tennis Association*, the first black sports organization in the United States.

Many urban immigrants regardless of color or nationality found temporary refuge thanks to the work of middle-class Americans who were moved to action when they were awakened to the plight of the masses of urban poor living in the inner cities. By the mid-1880s, earnest young Americans began to establish residences in some of the poorest city neighborhoods. These houses, called "settlements," provided a refuge—especially for young—from the daily life in the ramshackle tenements of the inner city. These volunteers provided baths, food, basic schooling, citizenship classes, job information, and child care. Every city had them, but the most famous was the one founded by Jane Addams and her friend Ellen Gates in

Chicago in 1889. They established their settlement house in a mid-nineteenth-century mansion and named it Hull-House, after a former owner. By 1906, interest and donations had grown to the point where the women had expanded the old house into a complex of buildings that covered a city block and included a gym, a theater, a nursery, classrooms for their social and educational programs, and a cooperative living facility for working women.

Universities also responded to the challenges of the newly discovered urban poverty. In the spirit of late nineteenth-century scholarship, they established faculties and areas of study designed to identify and solve the problem. Women, who were beginning to enter college in larger numbers than ever before, were especially attracted to the new area of social studies, since it provided entry into another of the so-called nurturing professions—like teaching and nursing—which at the time seemed most appropriate to their gender. With pencil and pad in hand, this new mostly female army of social workers marched into neighborhoods of the urban poor and recorded the data, which provided the statistical arguments supporting social legislation of the Progressives, who believed that there was no social problem that a well-constructed law could not resolve.

Church leaders also joined the campaign to eradicate urban poverty. In the last decade of the nineteenth century, the prevailing mood of Christians on the plight of the poor could be best summarized by the views of Andrew Carnegie and Russell Conwell. Multimillionaire Andrew Carnegie acknowledged that the new rich, who had benefitted from the expansion of industrial capitalism, had an obligation to help those less fortunate. But he warned in his article "Gospel of Wealth," (1889) that the rich needed to be vigilant in order to make sure that donations did not fall into the hands of "the slothful, the drunkard, the unworthy." Distinctions had to be made, he advised, between the "deserving" and "undeserving" poor. Russell Conwell—like Carnegie a "rags to riches millionaire"—wrote in *Acres of Diamonds* (1891) "that the number of poor who are to be sympathized with is very small. To sympathize with a man whom God has punished for his sins . . . is to do wrong. . . . Let us remember there is not a poor person in the United States who was not made poor by his own shortcomings." He suggested that it was dangerous, even unchristian, to intervene in behalf of the poor of flawed character since it would encourage only their slothful and evil ways that had been the cause of their downfall.

A new group of ministers countered this argument with a theology they called the "social gospel." Walter Rauschenbusch in *Christianity and the Social Crisis* (1907) wrote that "whoever uncouples the religious and the social life has not understood Jesus. Whoever sets any bounds for the reconstructive power of the religious life over the social relations and institutions of men, to that extent denies the faith of the Master." Advocates of the new social gospel took their campaign out of the pulpits and into the streets. They conducted studies into the root causes of poverty and published their findings. They also turned to politics. As a social gospel preacher in Buffalo asserted, "If [you] cared to save the people who languish in squalor poverty and degradation . . . you must put your finger on legislation."[9]

Catholics, who comprised a majority of the urban poor, found an advocate in James Gibbons, the archbishop of Baltimore who championed the cause of the industrial worker. In the face of official Vatican policy that condemned labor unions and prohibited Catholics from joining them, Gibbons wrote, "It is the right of laboring classes to protect themselves, and the duty of the whole people to find a remedy against avarice, oppression, and corruption." He defended the Knights of Labor, the largest industrial union at the time, and—after securing papal permission—urged his flock to join the Knights of Labor.

The Americanization movement also aligned itself with the efforts to rescue the poor—comprised mostly of immigrants—from the clutches of poverty. This movement was a loosely connected group of varied and diverse associations. They included the daughters of the American Revolution, who sought to inculcate patriotism, ethnic clubs that demanded their members learn English before joining, the United Mine Workers that established citizenship schools, and settlement houses that held English and hygiene classes for immigrants. Progressives embraced these ideas and soon legislation began to appear in various states that mandated Americanization classes such as civics and hygiene classes and the recitation of the Pledge of Allegiance to begin each school day. The lasting effects of this movement can still be seen in many public schools where civics continues to be a required subject and the Pledge of Allegiance remains a daily ritual.

While it is true that the urban poor comprised a vast number, the burgeoning industrial cities also contained a thriving middle class. Of course, as the older urban neighborhoods became denser, the middle class escaped to the outer reaches of the city, which provided cleaner air, fresher streams, and more open space. Urban transit systems, which had been developing in some cities since the mid-nineteenth century, made it possible to live in areas beyond walking distance to work. Beginning with the horse railways, which were in general use by the 1850s, over the latter half of the century public transportation expanded allowing the middle class to escape the deteriorating condition of the urban centers. By 1870, New York had a steam-powered elevated line, and by 1881, the New York "EL's" composed of two lines were carrying 175,000 passengers a day. Over the next few decades, Kansas City, Chicago, Philadelphia, and Brooklyn had sophisticated streetcar lines that carried middle-class office workers from bustling central business districts to the sedate surroundings of their suburban homes. By the end of the nineteenth century, a commuting culture was in full throttle.[10]

The major technological breakthrough in urban transportation came with the advent of electric-powered streetcars, also known as trolleys. This cleaner, safer form of transportation replaced the noisier and dirtier horse-drawn or steam-powered cars and spread rapidly. By 1902, 97 percent of trolleys in over 50 cities ran by electricity.[11] As a result of this cleaner and more efficient mode of transportation, residential neighborhoods away from the congested areas blossomed, but thanks to the centripetal force of the trolley lines these new neighborhoods did not wholly fragment into distinct urban areas, though it did create a segmented city in that residential, industrial, financial, and commercial activities were increasingly concentrated in particular areas, which were at the same time linked by the radial rail lines connecting the various parts of the modern city. Although the city expanded its boundaries, it maintained its functional identity. Often, the architecture in these new middle-class urban neighborhoods tended to be dull and monotonous in design. Nevertheless, families were glad to be in neighborhoods where the air was cleaner, healthier, and brighter. There were green spaces for children and families had the comfort of knowing that by living among those of similar education, class, and income, the values learned at home would be reinforced in the neighborhood. These middle-class neighborhoods became symbols of material success for those who lived there and a source of envy and aspiration for those who did not. It reinforced the capitalist notion that through hard work one could achieve these symbols of comfort and success that a new home in the streetcar suburbs represented.[12]

Typical of suburban growth of the era was the area west of the original river boundary of Philadelphia known simply as "West Philadelphia." This area's population grew from 13,265 in 1850 to 129,110 by 1900.[13] Horse-drawn omnibuses propelled growth in the immediate post-Civil War era, but by the 1890s electric trolleys replaced horses on the urban railway tracks and ushered in the next stage in commuting and residential dispersion. Although the great majority of these "suburbanites within a city" could afford the added expense of private residences and the costs of commuting, their demand for services created possibilities for people from all walks of life to live in the area. While businessmen, doctors, lawyers, and other professionals and members of the middle class claimed West Philadelphia as their home, so did craftsmen, shopkeepers, and lesser skilled workers who served them. A small community of 36 African Americans families (with their own church) had even emerged by the 1850s in Hamilton Village district near 40th Street and the African American presence in West Philadelphia grew to 7,137 by 1900.[14]

The middle class were also the principal supporters and beneficiaries of the growing entertainment industries in Philadelphia and other rapidly expanding cities. Early on in the post-Civil War era, minstrel shows, "dime museums," and vaudeville comprised the principal forms of paid urban entertainment. Beginning in the 1840s in New York, blackface minstrelsy emerged as a major form of urban entertainment in the United States. It began in 1842 when songwriter Daniel Decatur Emmett and three associates blackened their faces and sang and danced to the accompaniment of banjos and tambourines. The show was an instant success. Blackface minstrelsy reached the height of its popularity in 1870 and declined rapidly after that. Not surprisingly, blacks thought the form especially offensive. Frederick Douglass decried it as the product of ". . . the filthy scum of white society, who have stolen from us a complexion denied them by nature, in which to make money, and pander to the corrupt taste of their white fellow citizens." Other entertainments also competed with blackface minstrelsy and eventually displaced it. Popular between 1841 and 1900, the "dime museum" marketed an eclectic range of entertainment, including freak shows, wax displays, melodramas, and pseudoscientific exhibits, to a diverse audience. Even more serious museums that focused on such subjects as natural history and the sciences frequently included entertainment to draw more people in to see their collections and attend lectures.[15]

More than any other popular entertainment, vaudeville manifested the characteristics of the new economic age of mass markets, consumerism, and corporations. The development of vaudeville marked the beginning of popular entertainment as big business, dependent on the organizational efforts of a growing number of white-collar workers and the increased leisure time, spending power, and changing tastes of an urban middle-class audience. Business-savvy showmen utilized improved transportation and communication technologies, creating and controlling vast networks of theater circuits standardizing, professionalizing, and institutionalizing American popular entertainment. Benjamin Franklin Keith, a dime museum owner opened the first vaudeville in his hometown of Boston in 1883. The success of his museum that featured Baby Alice the Midget Wonder, allowed him to build the "Bijou," a grand theater in baroque style that became the standard for the industry. Unlike the risqué extravaganzas that would spring up in the wake of his success, Keith established a "fixed policy of cleanliness and order," and strictly forbade the use of vulgarity or coarse material in his acts.[16] In order to assure middle-class support, Keith established moral standards for his shows that paid due respect to the Victorian values of the newly emerging middle class. He ruled with an iron fist, censoring performers whose acts fell below his standards of decency. Keith posted signs backstage, ordering performers to eliminate "vulgarity and suggestiveness in words, action, and costume" while performing in his theater "under fine of instant discharged."[17] He cultivated the support of civic leaders and organizations concerned with improving urban life including Boston's powerful Catholic Church. Along with his partner the playwright, Edward Albee, Keith built theaters in other Northeastern cities with the help of the Catholic Church, which funded the expansion of the Keith enterprise on the promise of more clean entertainment.[18] Keith also developed the policy of the continuous performances. Keith's idea revolutionized variety entertainment and tailored it perfectly to the conditions of life in the surrounding metropolis. A continuous 12 hours of performances opened vaudeville to wider audiences than previously possible.

Within a few short years, imitators sprung up around the country. Following the lead of Keith and Albee, entertainment entrepreneurs like

S. Z. Poli, Klaw and Erlanger, F. F. Proctor, Marcus Loew, and Martin Beck began their own profitable enterprises. By the 1890s, vast theater circuits spanned the country, and in the same vein as the captains of industry who dominated the American economy, Keith and Albee consolidated their control of vaudeville, first through the United Booking Artists and later through the establishment of the Vaudeville Manager's Association. Vaudeville theaters, often known as "palaces," fiercely competed, trying to outdistance each other in luxury, elegance, and grandiosity. Vaudeville theaters adapted the excessive and opulent architectural styles of southern European palaces to create buildings with few precedents in American cities. From the elaborate hand-painted ceiling to "the finest toilet and retiring rooms in the country," the theater owners ignored no imaginable luxury. Unlike their industrial counterparts, owners of vaudeville palaces offered entertainment, rather than strictly consumer goods per se, but they did contribute to the new age of consumerism by encouraging customers to purchase concessions and they derived added income by selling advertising that appeared in their theater programs.[19] Driven by competition, many vaudeville owners abandoned the moral code established by Keith and began offering shows that featured young women such as the Barrison sisters who were advertised as *The Wickedest Girls in the World.* They introduced a variation to the traditional vaudeville known as "Blue Vaudeville," which glorified the female form. Women were not expected to display talent, only their bodies. Although it may have been decried as a gross exploitation of women, "Blue Vaudeville" can also be seen as part of a larger trend of the era that—in an escape from Victorian morality—began to admire the human body both masculine and feminine for its form and grace. Magazine drawings of the Gibson girls in bathing suits and the mildly homoerotic drawings of well-formed, scantily clad men like the strongman Eugene Sandow in Richard Kyle Fox's *Police Gazette* were just two manifestations of this newly found admiration of the human form.[20]

Vaudeville prospered because it responded to a new urban public that reveled in the "spectacular:" And of all the city spectacles, historian Alan Trachtenburg writes that none surpassed the giant department store, the emporium of consumption born and nurtured in these years. Along with this growth came the arrival of giant emporiums that sold a wide array of merchandise. Department stores like Gimble's, Macy's, Lord and Taylor,

Marshall Field, Strawbridge's, and Wanamaker's that were well known in their geographic niche nurtured loyal customers who made weekly pilgrimages to their elegant shrines to consumerism. Customers were encouraged to come in, inspect the wares, browse and linger, and, of course, spend their money. Built with palatial elegance, the stores boasted glorious window displays that captivated passersby. The stores—paying particular attention to their female clientele—included tea rooms where customers could eat delicate cucumber sandwiches or chicken salad served with cream cheese, chopped dates, and olives. The department store defined a way of life for Americans. It was a compelling and vital establishment that made Americans believe that beauty was important and life was good. It also taught people how to adapt to urban life. The department stores advertised in newspapers, provided advice columns, and set up displays to show the proper wear and fare for the seasons. One could learn to be "modern" just by window shopping. The stores also catered to all classes. The rich had their salons, the middle class the main floors, and the poorer customers the "bargain basement."[21]

Middle-class women did not confine their activities to shopping and maintaining the home. Although they had not yet obtained the right to vote in most states, women did become involved in city politics and were particularly active in reform movements. For example, The Women's City Club of Chicago dedicated its activities to

> promoting the welfare of the city; to coordinate and render more effective the scattered social and civic activities in which they are engaged; to extend a knowledge of public affairs; to aid in improving civic conditions and to assist in arousing an increased sense of social responsibility for the safeguarding of the home, the maintenance of good government, and the ennobling of that larger home of all—the city.

According to historian Maureen Flanagan, women tended to operate independently and often more radically than their Progressive husbands. For example, in Chicago, the Women's City Club aligned with the Chicago Federation of Labor, the Chicago Federation of Teachers, the Women's Trade Union League, the Woman's Party, and the Socialist Party of Illinois in sponsoring a talk in Chicago by Congressman David L. Lewis advocating government ownership of the telephones. Women's organizations also aligned themselves with Church groups to press for the closing of brothels and red light districts.[22]

For many urban males, the counterpoint to the department store "tea room" remained the local tavern. Until Prohibition closed them down in 1920, the tavern remained a male domain. It was where men—especially single and working-class men—found masculine camaraderie. There they engaged in conversation and organized local political, sporting, and social events. Often working-class men received their mail at the bar and found out about available jobs in the neighborhood. It was a male-dominated public space where the only women present were those who were paid to service or entertain the men. And while middle- and upper-class urban men had their newly formed sporting clubs where they enjoyed the new preoccupation with exercise and also organized rowing, baseball, bicycle, and golf clubs, the working class bowled in the bar's alley way or basement and enjoyed less seemly sports like cock fighting and rat baiting in the cellars of their local bar.

Spectator and participant sports wove indelible patterns into the fabric of life in the industrial city and for the most part they reflected the emerging class distinctions of the era. Golf, rowing, tennis, bicycling, and even football became identified as sports of the elite. Bowling, cockfighting, dice, and boxing were recognized as sports of the lower classes. The exception to this was baseball, which transcended class and despite its pastoral claims became the great urban game of the era. Baseball thrived in the combination of industry, consumerism, and even politics that emerged in the city at the turn of the last century. And with its association of owners who had complete control of players' salaries and where they played, and control of all team schedules and ticket prices, showed that they shared the monopolistic skills of their counterparts in the industrial world. In the post-Civil War years, interest in baseball spread rapidly, especially in the cities. Boys and young men played baseball on every available lot in the city, and every city—large and small—put together a team of its best players and challenged nearby communities to a game that would be followed by a picnic festivities and bragging rights until the next contest. By the 1880s, the major cities of the country—eight in all—had formed a professional league of baseball players. And by the turn of the century, there were two leagues, the American and the National, playing in every major city north and west of St. Louis.[23] Teams brought a diverse urban population together. For a time, during the game at least, divisions of race, origins, income, class, and even gender dissolved in the communal ritual of rallying for the home team. Even newly arrived immigrants enjoyed an instant sense of community partaking in the completely American experience known as baseball.

As the country moved in time from the nineteenth to the twentieth century, the developing cities foreshadowed the future character of the country. Small towns would endure throughout the twentieth century where most who lived there laid claim to Anglo Saxon, Protestant values and traditions. But during the Progressive Era, the modern city emerged with its multicultural and economically stratified population, unique politics, new forms of popular entertainment, mobility, and living conditions. That city also became the focus and forum for Progressive reforms and politics that defined the age.

NOTES

1. Helen Keller, *The Story of My Life* (New York: Grosset and Dunlop, 1905), 124.

2. Charles Glaab and A. Theodore Brown, *A History of Urban America* (New York: MacMillan Co., 1967), 133.

3. Ibid., pp. 138–9.

4. Jacob August Riis, *How the Other Half Lives: Studies among the Tenements of New York* (New York: Scribner's, 1914), 25.

5. Glaab and Brown, p. 159.

6. Ibid., p. 161.

7. Ibid., p. 162.

8. Ibid.

9. Glaab and Brown, p. 239.

10. Ibid., p. 149.

11. Ibid., pp. 150–2.

12. Ibid., pp. 155–7.

13. Mark Frazier Lloyd, "Notes on the historical development of population in West Philadelphia," University of Pennsylvania Archives, http://www.archives.upenn.edu/histy/features/wphila/stats/census_lloyd.html

14. Miller and Siry, pp. 106–7; Lloyd, "Notes."

15. Andrea Stulman Dennet, *The Weird & the Wonderful: The Dime Store Museum in America* (New York: New York University Press, 1997), 134–7.

16. *National Magazine* 9 (November 1898): 146–53. As it appears in the University of Virginia website: "Vaudeville: A Dazzling, Display of Heterogeneous Splendor Designed to Educate, Edify, Amaze and Uplift" http://xroads.virginia .edu/~ma02/easton/vaudeville/vaudevillemain.html (2013).

17. University of Virginia website, op. cit.

18. Ibid.

19. Ibid.

20. Elliot Gorn and Warren Goldstein, *A Brief History of American Sports* (Chicago: University of Illinois Press, 2004), 113, 118.

21. Cindi Pierce, "The History of Department Stores," http://www .catalogs.com/info/history/history-of-department-stores.html (2013).

22. Maureen A. Flanagan, "Gender and Urban Political Reform: The City Club and the Woman's City Club of Chicago in the Progressive Era," *American Historical Review* 95 (October 1990): 1034.

23. Gorn and Goldstein, pp. 124–6, 170–5.

CHAPTER 5

Women Raise Their Political Voice

Men—their rights and nothing more; Women—their rights and nothing less.

—Susan B. Anthony[1]

"The American man is a failure! You are all failures!" Or so Henry Adams admonished his distinguished dinner guests that included President Teddy Roosevelt, Senator Henry Cabot Lodge, and his brother Brooks, a railroad baron. "Has not my sister here more sense than my brother Brooks? Wouldn't we all elect Mrs. Lodge Senator against Cabot? Would the President have a ghost of a chance if Mrs. Roosevelt ran against him?" Adams had faith that feminine wisdom would bring a new vision of unity to the rapidly fragmenting new century.

During the latter half of the nineteenth century, the wonders of invention and its effects—factories, cities, rapid transportation, and faith in material progress—had slowly but incessantly eroded the traditional family, over which women had reigned. Now, Adams lamented, in the "new age of invention and industry the woman had no refuge except such as the man created for himself." Many women rebelled against the cold, sexless, and statistic-driven world men had created. That story was not new, Adams noted. "For thousands of years women had rebelled. They had made a fortress of religion, had buried themselves in the cloister, in self-sacrifice, in good works ... " But in the new twentieth century, the field of good works—where women found their footing—was narrower than in the twelfth century. But acknowledging that he owed more to the American woman than to all the American men he ever heard of, Adams concluded that men might remain confused as to the direction of the new century but he was confident that women would embrace the challenges and exert a great influence on the history of the next hundred years.[2]

The same forces that had—according to Adams's lament—dislocated the home from the center of the moral universe, freed women to pursue domestic harmony in the public sphere. Across the nation women formed clubs and federations designed to address problems created by mass immigration, industrialization, urbanization, and other social convulsions of the latter half of the nineteenth century. Among those most active in the women's associations, many were supported financially by their husbands and others came from families of considerable wealth accumulated from the meteoric growth of the economy in the post-Civil War era. By the end of the nineteenth century, groups that had begun locally within a short time organized nationally and their numbers multiplied. The *General Federation of Women's Clubs*, for example, formed in 1890 with 500,000 members, boasted over 1 million members by 1905. In addition, associated charities, civic clubs, auxiliaries to fraternal orders, and suffrage associations added to the increasingly greater army of women bent on reform at the beginning of the twentieth century.

These new groups founded and directed by women added a domestic dimension to formerly male-dominated reform movements. As one historian has pointed out, women brought the benefits of motherhood to the public sphere. They set up libraries, trade schools for girls, and university extension courses. They also introduced home economics courses, improved the physical environment of schools, and elected women to school boards.[3] Women also joined campaigns designed to end white slavery and to clean out bordello districts in their cities. Most famously, women reformers sought to clean up the Levee in Chicago where the Eveleigh sisters entertained mayors, senators, the giants of industry and commerce, and even European princes in their world-renowned house with its luxurious theme-designed salons that transported their guests visually and sensually to Japan, Paris, India, and other exotic and erotic destinations of the world. The Eveleigh sisters closed their house under pressure from reformers in 1914 and retired to a Park Avenue apartment in New York. Their closure was one of many victories reform-minded women claimed in the Progressive Era.[4]

Although middle- and upper-class women dominated the narrative of women's reform movements in this era, working-class women also claimed a role in the campaign. In cities throughout the country, wherever young women worked in factories or offices, they organized "Working Girl Clubs" that championed the principles of "cooperation, self-government, and self-reliance." The working women paid an initiation fee and monthly dues, assumed leadership positions, participated in club government, voted on all club projects, and contributed to club committees. Class conscious, but not rebellious, they protested against disparaging articles printed about working women in local journals and actively campaigned to change their "public image" in hopes that the term *working girl* should someday come to "be applied in a manner both respectful and considerate [instead of] with indifference and oftentimes contempt."[5] Unlike their middle-class counterparts, the women in working-class clubs strove to improve their own condition rather than that of others. They instituted classes to teach the traditional female skills, such as sewing and cooking, as well as newer income-increasing ones such as typewriting and bookkeeping. The clubs also established savings plans and mutual benefit associations for protection against sickness and unemployment. In Chicago, Boston, and Philadelphia, the clubs started lunch programs, which provided nutritious meals in a safe environment, away from the glare of male workers.[6] By 1897, the "Working Girls Clubs" had grown to the point where they could establish a National League of Women Workers, which survived until at least 1914, and represented 100 clubs from six states with a total membership of 14,000.[7]

Working-class women also joined in the burgeoning union movement. In the city, with the rise of the factory and the department store, and the invention of the telephone and the typewriter, numerous new opportunities arose for paid female labor. The number of female factory workers doubled between 1850 and 1880, and then doubled again between 1880 and 1900. By the turn of the century, there were 5.3 million women working from necessity rather than choice. Women often started work at a tender age with little education and dismal prospects for the future and little sophistication to negotiate for improved conditions.[8] In 1888, the Bureau of Labor, under Commissioner Carroll D. Wright, published a survey that documented the hazardous nature of factory work for young girls. They cited frequent injuries that often resulted in "the loss of joints or fingers, the hand, or sometimes the whole arm." These dangers were compounded by the hot, oppressive, close quarters of the average workshop. They also reported "inadequate sanitary facilities," where sometimes "a hundred workers depended on a single closet or sink that [was] too often out of order." To combat these conditions, young working women began to organize.

In 1903, Mary Dreier, Rheta Childe Dorr, Leonora O'Reilly, and others in an alliance that transcended class division formed the Women's Trade Union League of New York, an organization dedicated to unionization for working-class women and to the decidedly middle- and upper-class issue of woman's suffrage. In that same year, they allied with the fledgling International Lady Garment Workers, which had been recently established in New York. Although led by males, the union rank and file, which had energized the great strikes of 1909 and 1910, was predominantly female. The first large-scale strike in 1909, known as "the Uprising of 20,000," began as a spontaneous walkout at the Triangle Shirtwaist Company factory. When the factory responded with a lockout of workers, word spread throughout the garment workers district and a rally was called. After listening to a group of distinguished, but passionless, men from the American Federation of Labor urging worker solidarity, Clara Lemlich, a factory worker, in a clear loud voice decried the conditions of women in the factories. She demanded an end to talks and called for an immediate general strike. Over the next few days, 20,000 of the 32,000 factory workers in the district walked off the job in support of the Triangle Shirtwaist strikers. Adopting the slogan, "We'd rather starve quick than starve slow," the female workers, mostly immigrants, defied the collective wisdom of those who insisted that women—especially immigrant women—could not be organized. But those who doubted the women's resolve failed to measure the depth of bitterness they held for the sweatshop owners. The strike quickly turned violent as police arrested picketers for petty offenses and looked the other way while local thugs beat strikers with clubs.

During the strike, gender trumped class as a large group of middle- and upper-class women supported the striking factory girls. They lent financial support and their heavy political clout. J. P. Morgan's daughter Anne played a leading role as well as Alva Belomont, former wife of William Vanderbilt. Mrs. Belomont in a powerful expression of gender solidarity called for an all-women's strike as she urged school teachers of New York to join the walkout. The women solicited donations to provide food and shelter for the strikers. They even joined the strike line as observers in an attempt to reduce the number of false arrests and physical attacks on the striking women. Introducing an innovation to strike tactics, they brought their automobiles—still a symbol of status—to the sites and created a pro-cession of automobiles from one picket line to another to allow for greater vigilance over police and factory-hired thugs. Women students from Vassar, Barnard, and Columbia also joined in the strike. As a *New York Times* reporter observed, "It was sort of a 'you a girl me a girl' spirit" that started it.[9] Among the students was Frances Perkins, a political science graduate student at Columbia who would become Franklin Roosevelt's secretary of labor in 1933.

On Christmas Eve, Eva McDonough Valesh, the chairperson of the committee organized to collect financial aid for the striking women, shamed a group of wealthy donors into giving to the cause by pointing out that on Christmas Day thanks to the city's generosity "every homeless man may have turkey ... But there will be no turkey tomorrow for the shirtwaist makers," she informed them, since "there is no organization in [the] city that provides a Christmas meal for women."[10]

Through the winter, the young women faced starvation, eviction, jail time, and brutality, but they endured, and in February they negotiated a settlement with the factory owners who accepted their demands of a modest wage increase, fewer working hours, and better working condi-tions. But the victory was far from complete since the owners refused union recognition, and a number of companies, including the Triangle Shirtwaist Company, refused to sign the agreement. Still, the partial suc-cess of the strike encouraged more workers in the industry to take action to improve their conditions and brought public attention to the sweatshop conditions. Encouraged by the results of the shirtwaist dressmaker's walk-out, the ILGWU led an even larger strike a few months later. Newspapers dubbed it the "The Great Revolt" when 60,000 cloak makers, men and women, walked off the job in New York and other major cities. The strike ended in another partial victory for the ILGWU and an agreement between employers and factory owners that in the future owners and employees would settle grievances through arbitration before resorting to strikes.

Satisfaction for the small victory over management soon turned to anguish when barely a year after the strike ended, on March 25, 1911, at the end of a tiring 12-hour day, a fire engulfed the Triangle Shirt-waist Company factory and 143 workers died. The factory operated on the top three floors of a building that sat on the edge of Washington Park.

Nearly all the workers were teenaged girls, mostly immigrants who did not speak English, which added to the confusion that day. There were four elevators with access to the factory floors, but when the fire broke out, only one was fully operational and in order to reach it the workers had to file down a long, narrow corridor, while flames raged around them. There were two stairways down to the street, but they were locked from the outside to prevent stealing. Within 18 minutes, it was all over. Forty-nine workers had burned to death or been suffocated by smoke, 36 were dead in the elevator shaft, and 58 girls who did not make it to the stairwells or the elevator died when in a panic to escape the flames they jumped from broken windows. In one case, a life net was unfurled to catch the jumpers, but three girls jumped at the same time, ripping the net. The event became more tragic after investigators revealed that most of the deaths were preventable. Fire Chief Edward Croker blamed the high casualty count on insufficient fire escapes and stairways, a lack of sprinklers, and the fact that doors had been sealed shut. "This calamity is just what I have been predicting," he said. "I have been advocating and agitating that fire escapes be put on buildings just such as this. This large loss of life is due to this neglect."[11] The factory owners were indicted on charges of negligence but a jury failed to convict them.

In the aftermath of the conflagration, the ILGWU organized a march on April 5 down New York's Fifth Avenue to protest the conditions that had led to the fire and among the 80,000 people who joined the procession were the women who had supported the factory girls in the previous year's strikes. In addition to joining the march, they collected funds for the survivors and vowed to pressure for safety laws in the factories. In October, yielding to civic pressure, the city government passed the Sullivan-Hoey Fire Prevention Law, which established safety guidelines for factories. Although passed, the laws were not rigidly enforced. Pointing to this fact and recalling the shirtwaist fire "where corpses of young girls were piled up like cordwood," Women's Trade Union League founder Rhetta Childe Dorr urged women to fight more passionately for the right to vote. "Only through voting," she declared, could "women push for political solutions to municipal problems."[12]

In the second decade of the twentieth century, appeals such as Dorr's had an ever increasing resonance among middle-class women. Reform-minded women came to realize that the methods of their Federations— rooted in antebellum strategies designed to raise consciousness and consciences among those in power—would not suffice, and they could not effect real reform until they wielded the power of the ballot. During the 1910s and the 1920s, women's public activity moved from the "municipal housekeeping" of the 1890s to the development of formidable state and national lobbies that secured legislation that could effectively address major social problems. Women's political pressure groups advocated numerous social reforms—such as the New York fire prevention law—including workman's compensation for victims of industrial accidents, better education, adequate nutrition, and inspections of factories and tenement houses. As historian Paula Baker has pointed out, "Progressive era women passed on to the state the work of social policy that they found increasingly unmanageable [and] social policy—formerly the province of women's voluntary work—became public policy."[13]

The Woman's Christian Temperance Union (WCTU) provides an excellent example of a women's organization that moved from antebellum strategies of consciousness raising and volunteerism to political activity. Transformation began in 1879 when Frances Willard resigned her presidency at Northwestern Women's College to lead the WCTU. Willard had always been an advocate of temperance. When she was 16, she asked her family to sign a pledge she had written in rhyming couplet that ended with the line: "So here we pledge perpetual hate/to all that can intoxicate." As an adult while pursuing an academic career that brought her to the presidency of Northwestern Woman's College in Evanston, she dedicated her voluntary time to the temperance crusade. But in 1874 while on a campaign that found her on her knees in a Pittsburgh bar singing "Rock of Ages" to a crowd of "unkempt, unwashed, hard drinking, men," she made the decision to leave her academic career and dedicate her life to the cause of temperance. At the same time, she determined that temperance was a women's issue that would never be resolved through legislation if it was left solely in the hands of men. She shocked her WCTU audience in 1876 when she declared that women should have the right to vote on matters relating to liquor.

Nevertheless, in 1879, they elected her president of the organization, replacing the antisuffragist president Annie Wittenmeyer. Immediately, she began to build alliances with the suffrage movement. Susan B. Anthony, for example, began to appear at WCTU conventions, and her niece became director of the WCTU lecture board. While Anthony was

Although originally organized to campaign for prohibition of alcoholic beverages, by 1896 the WCTU had expanded its agenda to include other women's issues including suffrage. (NY Daily News Archive via Getty Images)

"glad to see women awakened from their political apathy by the liquor wars," she chose to dedicate herself solely to the campaign for woman suffrage and refused to offer her opinion on any other public question. "My personal belief as to prohibition, pro or con, is nobody's business but my own."[14] Willard died in 1898; nevertheless, through her efforts for Prohibition—as Anthony pointed out—she awakened many women to political activism. She also raised the fear of the country's brewers, such as Adolphus Busch, who spearheaded a fundraising campaign that energized those who opposed giving the vote to women. "God pity our country," Busch proclaimed—and many agreed—"when the handshake of a politician is more gratifying to a woman's heart than the patter of children's feet. Is it not sufficient political achievement for women," he asked, "that future rulers nurse at their breasts, laugh in her arms, and kneel at her feet?"[15] The brewer's tactics proved self-defeating. The more they fought suffrage, the more they guaranteed women's antipathy once they got the vote. Indeed, many women who may have been neutral or even opposed to Prohibition voted for it in anger at the brewers who had unsympathetically and dishonestly dismissed them. In one three-year stretch in the 1910s, seven western states adopted Prohibition. All of them were states where women had been recently given the right to vote.[16]

As women moved into the political arena they maintained their own priorities, which tended to be more social and cultural in emphasis. Where the men might work for civil service, sound money, or tariff reform, the women labored for the promotion of art, education, civil beautification, closing "red light" districts, household economy, child labor laws, and pure food regulations. Moreover, divorce, birth control, and suffrage became identified as specifically "women's issues."[17]

In 1880, there was one divorce for every 21 marriages. By 1909, the number had soared to 1 in 10. This statistically verifiable social crisis worried Progressives, who sought legislative solutions to the problem. Despite the fact that it affected both genders, the issue quickly centered on the woman's role in marriage. The divorce law debate demonstrated that liberalism on social issues was not the glue that necessarily bonded Progressives; rather, it was the faith in legislation to solve social evils that did. Quickly, two camps emerged on the divorce issue. One side advocated the liberalization of divorce laws making them more accessible. Those who opposed this view wanted to use the power of the state to preserve marriage and make divorce laws more rigid. The opposing positions were not, as one might imagine, determined by gender, but rather by views held on marriage and family that transcended sex. On one side, Progressives—both men and women—affirmed that marriage was the bedrock of society and the state ought to wield its power to preserve it. The opponents of divorce, many of whom were driven by a utilitarian philosophy based on the principle of the greater good, railed against the selfish individualism—particularly on the part of women—that tore at the fabric of the community. *The North American Review* took women to task on the issue of increased divorce. In one of its forums entitled, "Are Women to Blame?" the *Review's* female panelists accused women of being "spoiled, romantic, impatient, and jealous of men and usurpers of the male's time honored functions." Margaret Deland, a well-known author and supporter of Progressive causes, declared that "civilization rested on the permanence of marriage." And women must forebear drunken, miscreant, and even adulterous husbands "for the sake of the greater good." She feared that if divorce became a facile solution to an unhappy marriage, it would mean "the end of everything," and "civilization must go upon the rocks."[18]

On the other side of the argument were those Progressives who believed that individual freedom was the cornerstone of a democratic society and ought to be preserved at all costs. Rather than protect irredeemable marriages, they believed the state ought to empower individuals—particularly women—to liberate themselves from the quasi-slavery of a failed marriage. Within a few years, the radical attack on marriage enlisted such big guns as H. G. Wells, who announced that monogamy was dissolving and sexual standards relaxing to the point where in a hundred years the present moral code "would remain nominally operative in sentiment and practice, while being practically disregarded ... " Although the majority of Americans did not embrace Wells's libertine views on sex and marriage, many did believe that traditional marriage was needlessly tyrannical and repressive and that it discriminated against women.

Those who viewed the marriage crisis through nineteenth-century domestic lenses were puzzled by the "new woman" of the twentieth century who questioned the institution. In the troubling convulsions of post-Civil War economic change, marriage seemed to be the key to female security and agency. Yet in the new century, women seemed to be turning their back or at least questioning this mythic paradigm. Although most people believed the family was woman's special interest and responsibility and its protection her primary concern, women seemed to be the driving force behind the increase in divorce. Statistically, the argument held weight since women had initiated two-thirds of the divorces in the Progressive age.[19] Some even accused modern women of wanting to destroy marriage. This remained far from the truth. Most women who supported lenient divorce laws still affirmed the importance of marriage, but they did not believe it should be preserved at all costs even to the point of tolerating an abusive husband, as many antidivorce advocates did. Feminists—both male and female—viewed divorce as an instrument for the emancipation of women, who if caught in an unhappy exploitative marriage were no more than sexual slaves. Benjamin O. Flower, who edited the populist *Arena*, argued that the common prostitute was "far freer than the wife who is nightly the victim of the unholy passion of her master." By 1914, even the respectable and cautious *Good Housekeeping* magazine questioned the propriety of a woman "allowing herself to be owned body and soul by a man she loathes . . . ."[20]

Since Progressives had lined up on both sides of the divorce issue, consensus was never reached in their era. In Pennsylvania, in 1906, Progressive governor Samuel Pennypacker hosted a National Divorce Congress attended by delegates from 42 states. Even after creating an effective alliance with Catholic bishops and other Christian leaders in a national campaign to enact a federal antidivorce law, it remained a state issue. In the Northeast where the influence of the Catholic hierarchy was strongest, Progressives succeeded in passing strong antidivorce laws. However, as the antidivorce argument moved westward in areas where there was less ecclesiastic strength and greater women's suffrage, it weakened. West of the Mississippi, Oklahoma, Nevada, and the Dakota territories had liberalized divorce and residency requirements to such a point that they became veritable divorce mills.

While most Progressive women affirmed the sanctity of marriage, they also wanted greater rights within the marriage contract. They proposed that marriage become "companionable," meaning that men and women would be treated as equal partners who shared in decisions related to family economics, living space, and recreation. Women also demanded sexual equality, and while marriages increased, birth rates declined as women sought and obtained greater accessibility to birth control information. The great heroine of this movement, Margaret Sanger, faced prison, revocation of her citizenship, and even threats on her life to ensure that women had access to information that enabled them to control their reproductive lives.

The growing belief that women should be entitled to enjoy the same pleasures as men brought women to golf courses, tennis courts, and to the new bicycle fad. Women's clothing that had previously restricted such activity also changed. They began wearing "Bloomers," blousy pants that appeared at first glance to be a skirt. This new clothing also became a political statement, as women who affirmed equal rights donned the quasi pants as a symbol of equality. These sartorial statements were not always accepted passively. For example, in Riverhead, a rural town in Eastern Long Island, when a woman cyclist peddled into the village in bloomers, word quickly spread, a crowd gathered, and she was soon run out of town on her bicycle. But the "new woman" of the twentieth century remained steadfast in their quest for equality in various areas where men had previously claimed exclusivity. In colleges and newly formed clubs, women also engaged in team sports for the first time, competing in basketball, volleyball, badminton, and softball.[21]

The myriad issues of the Progressive Era that affected women specifically began to orbit increasingly around the axis of the vote as more women began to realize that to effect real change they needed to have the power of the ballot. The issue of "granting suffrage" had been brewing ever since Elizabeth Cady Stanton issued the Declaration of Sentiments in Seneca Falls in 1848, but it had never garnered the strength of a significant mass of women.

A major impediment to women's suffrage until the twentieth century had been the Victorian middle-class myth that there existed two natural spheres in the public arena, and they were determined by gender. "Politics," read strictly as electoral and party politics, belonged to the aggressive, independent, and self-sufficient man. Management of the home, morals, ideals, culture, and education belonged to the virtuous, altruistic, fragile, and sensitive woman.

The idea of separate spheres even influenced women's political activity in the early years of the Progressive movement, as temperance, welfare, social reform, education, and consumerism dominated their political program. But as their political maturity grew so did their agenda.

Also, as historian Paula Baker argues, "The political realities of the late nineteenth century and Progressive legislation of the early nineteen hundreds had blurred the boundaries of the gender defined spheres of public life."[22] "Gone were not only the torchlight parades," she argues, "but also most of the manifestations of the male political culture that those parades symbolized." Men no longer claimed fierce allegiance to their political party, and actual political participation declined at the end of the nineteenth century. As political participation no longer was seen as a defining quality of masculinity, woman's demand for suffrage became less disturbing. On the other hand, by the early twentieth century because of Progressive legislative achievements—due in part to pressure exerted by women's reform groups—state and local government spent the largest portion of their budgets on schools, asylums, and prisons assuming some of the substantive functions of the home, previously seen as the woman's domain. And in an age that was replacing faith in religion and tradition with science and material progress, women no longer sought their mothers or grandmothers for advice on diet and childrearing but rather consulted books written by experts or government pamphlets produced by committee as result of scientific investigation.[23]

A clear sign that the myth of separate spheres defined by gender was breaking down came from that mainstay of Victorian masculinity and morality, Teddy Roosevelt, who while admitting that he had "somewhat changed his views," declared himself a zealous supporter of woman's suffrage. Many antisuffragists like social worker Lillian Wald feared that "when women had the vote they cut off their hair, they donned men's attire, and spoke in harsh voices." Roosevelt did not fear that suffrage would diminish women's feminine qualities or their influence in the domestic sphere if they used it not to masculinize themselves, but, he said, "to render better and more efficient service to the nation as mothers and wives, in accord with his understanding of the teachings of such social reformers as Jane Addams and Frances Kellor."[24]

Despite the breakdown of myths that had obstructed their path to the ballot box, women still faced considerable opposition in the beginning of the twentieth century. Opponents to women's suffrage were myriad and diverse. As mentioned earlier, the well-organized lobbying forces of the brewers and liquor industry opposed their vote because of the very visible role the WCTU was playing in the suffrage movement and because of the support given the women's movement by the increasingly powerful Anti-Saloon League lobby. German Americans, who wielded considerable political strength in the Midwest, also opposed women's suffrage simply because they found it offensive to their own traditions and culture. Big city politicians who often had connections to saloons opposed women's suffrage because of their perceived stand on temperance. Immigrants, especially from Italy and southern Europe whose entire universe rested on clearly defined gender roles, opposed women's suffrage, as did poor and uneducated urban workers whose votes were easily influenced by machine politicians. Finally manufacturers, especially in the textile industry, who benefitted from cheap female labor and feared the consequences of giving political clout to their exploited workforce, opposed women's suffrage.

On the other hand, women advocating for the vote had influential allies in their camp. Strong support came from the increasingly powerful Anti-Saloon League, which would claim their own political victory in 1920 with the passage of the Eighteenth Amendment and the Volstead

Act, which prohibited the sale, transportation, and production of alcohol in the United States. As a counterpoint to the opposition of the Catholic hierarchy, many native-born Protestants (outside the South) as well as Jews and Mormons rallied to the cause of women's suffrage. Most Progressives who advocated greater and wider political participation also favored women's suffrage. Middle-class and better educated Americans also supported the movement, as did the younger generation who had come of age in the Progressive Era. Such formidable adversaries promised for a long contentious political war over the issue of women's suffrage.

The early battles began when the older suffrage movements merged in 1890 to form the National American Woman Suffrage Association. They set out on a strategy to secure suffrage state by state. After early victories in 1890, which included the admission of Wyoming to statehood with a constitution that granted female suffrage, and the declaration of support by the American Federation of Labor, the movement suffered its first defeat when South Dakota rejected women's suffrage. However, in 1893, they rebounded with a victory in Colorado. But in 1894 after collecting 600,000 signatures to propose women's suffrage to the New York State Constitutional Convention being held that year, the motion was defeated by a coalition of downstate voters and urban political bosses. As the new century unfolded, momentum increased for the women's suffrage. But after a woman's suffrage victory in California in 1911, the opposition awoke and in the same year an eclectic and improbable coalition of clergymen, distillers, and brewers, urban political machines, and southern congressmen joined together to form "The National Association Opposed to Woman Suffrage (NAOWS)." Led by Mrs. Arthur Dodge, its members also included wealthy, influential women, and some Catholic corporate capitalists. Undaunted, the woman's movement continued on in the struggle. In 1912, Theodore Roosevelt's Progressive Party included a plank in its platform supporting woman's suffrage. And in the same year, Oregon, Kansas, and Arizona adopted woman suffrage. In 1914, Nevada and Montana granted woman the right to vote, and in 1916 Jeannette Rankin was elected to Congress from the state of Montana and the Democratic Party included women's suffrage as a plank in their platform. In 1917, the antisuffrage coalition began to disintegrate with the defeat of the New York City machine and the passage of a suffrage bill in that state. With opposition in the country's most populous state crumbling, the women's suffrage amendment moved quickly from House passage in 1918 to the senate where it was finally approved as the Nineteenth Amendment. Its passage became one of the last gasps of the waning Progressive Era.

Henry Adams, the grand commentator of nineteenth- and early twentieth-century American life, was confounded by the advances made by women in his lifetime. Presciently, he connected women's progress to the advances of science and technology in the nineteenth century. "There had never been a better or more capable, mother than the American woman," he observed "but at 40 her work was over. And she was left with no other stage." But since 1840, he observed, there were myriads of "new types—or type-writers—telephone and telegraph-girls, shop-clerks, factory-hands, running ... , without restraint or limit." He pointed out that women had made great progress in the latter half of the nineteenth century, even in the face of opposition of 9 out of 10 men who refused their request for equality. Although begun in 1840, he predicted that the consequences of the new paths women had established would not be realized for another century. Given the tumultuous path ahead, Adams writing in 1900 midway through the journey he foresaw, wistfully hoped that he could act the part of a horseshoe crab in Quincy Bay, and admit that all was uniform—that nothing ever changed—and that the woman would swim about the ocean of future time, as she had swum in the past, with the garfish and the shark, unable to change.[25]

But Adams could no more be a horseshoe crab than the world could be a changeless sea. Women continued through the twentieth century to increase their power and influence. The original demand to be companionable partners in the home expanded to the public arena and by the end of the century, standing on the shoulders of their Progressive Era sisters, women became the cocreators with their brothers—sometimes failing sometimes succeeding—in the quest for a more humane world.

NOTES

1. From the masthead of *The Revolution* (1868–1872), a weekly women's rights newspaper, the official publication of the National Woman Suffrage Association formed by feminists Elizabeth Cady Stanton and Susan B. Anthony to secure women's enfranchisement through a federal constitutional amendment.

2. Henry Adams, *The Education of Henry Adams* (Boston and New York: Houghton & Mifflin Company, 1918), 441–3.

3. Paula Baker, "The Domestication of Politics: Women and American Political Society, 1780–1920," *The American Historical Review* 89, no. 3 (June 1984): 620–47, 640–41.

4. Karen Abbot, *Sin in the Second City* (New York: Random House, 2009), 17–27, 31–46, 51–60, 64–67, 177–183, 231–238.

5. Joanne Reitano, "Working Girls Unite," *American Quarterly* 36, no. 1 (Spring 1984): 112–34, 118.

6. Ibid., pp. 124–6.

7. Ibid., p. 114.

8. Ibid., p. 116.

9. *New York Times* (December 19, 1909): SM5.

10. *New York Times*, "Facing Starvation to Keep Up Strike" (December 25, 1909), 2.

11. *The New York Tribune* (March 26, 1911), 1.

12. *New York Times*, "Fire Story for Suffrage" (December 27, 1914), 7.

13. Baker, p. 644.

14. Daniel Okrent, *Last Call: The Rise and Fall of Prohibition* (New York: Scribner, 2010), 17–20.

15. Ibid., pp. 55–56.

16. Ibid., pp. 65–66.

17. Maureen A. Flanagan, "Gender and Urban Political Reform: The City Club and the Women's City Club of Chicago in the Progressive Era," *The American Historical Review* 95, no. 4 (October 1990), 1032–50.

18. Ibid., pp. 208–10.

19. William L. O'Neill, "Divorce in the Progressive Era," *American Quarterly* 17, no. 2, Part 1 (Summer 1965): 203–17, 203–4.

20. Ibid., p. 211.

21. Elliott Gorn and Warren Goldstein, *A Brief History of American Sports* (Urbana: University of Illinois Press, 2004), 198–9.

22. Baker, pp. 620–47.

23. Ibid., pp. 637–9.

24. Arnaldo Testi, "The Gender of Reform Politics: Theodore Roosevelt and the Culture of Masculinity," *The Journal of American History* 81, no. 4 (March 1995): 1529–33.

25. Adams, p. 447.

CHAPTER 6

African Americans in the Progressive Age

We refuse to allow the impression to remain that the Negro-American assents to inferiority, is submissive under oppression and apologetic before insults ... the voice of protest of ten million Americans must never cease to assail the ears of their fellows, so long as America is unjust.

—W. E. B. Du Bois and William Monroe Trotter[1]

"The white folk of Altamaha [Georgia] voted John a good boy,—fine plough-hand, good in the rice-fields, handy everywhere, and always good-natured and respectful. But they shook their heads when his mother wanted to send him off to school." All the white folk believed that "Education would ruin him." In *Souls of Black Folk* (1903) W. E. B Du Bois tells the story of "John" whom some white southerners deemed unfit for southern life because of his northern education. He returned home to teach in the ramshackle schoolhouse built for the black tenant farmers' children. The local judge sized him up and warned him,

John, I want to speak to you plainly. You know I'm a friend to your people. I've helped you and your family, ... Now I like the colored people, and sympathize with all their reasonable aspirations; but you and I both know, John, that in this country the Negro must remain subordinate, and can never expect to be the equal of white men. In their place, your people can be honest and respectful; and God knows, I'll do what I can to help them. But when they want to reverse nature, and rule white men, and marry white women, and sit in my parlor, then, by God! We'll hold them under if we have to lynch every N ... in the land. Now, John, the question is, are you, with your education and Northern notions, going to accept the situation and teach the darkies to be faithful servants and laborers as your fathers were,—or are you going to try to put fool ideas of rising and equality into these folks' heads, and make them discontented and unhappy?[2]

Du Bois's story depicted the realty of race relations in the South in the post-Reconstruction era. An understanding of blacks in the Progressive Era necessitates an understanding of the conditions in which 90 percent of black America lived at the turn of the century. This world, which had been crafted by the children of the defeated white southerners, left blacks in a condition that made many observers wonder what had been gained by the war.

When the Civil War ended, blacks in the South had reason to celebrate their new freedom and nurture hope that their lives and those of their families would be quite different from what it had been under slavery. Legislation followed to solidify what the war had accomplished. In 1865, Congress passed the Thirteenth Amendment ending slavery as a legal institution everywhere in the United States; the amendment was ratified in December. In 1866 the Civil Rights Act made the former slaves citizens by establishing birthright citizenship. In 1868, the Fourteenth Amendment embedded that principle in the Constitution. It also prohibited the states from taking away basic civil rights or freedom without due process. Southern states fought against the amendment but reluctantly accepted it as a condition for reentry into the union. Finally, the Fifteenth Amendment, ratified in 1870, guaranteed the former male slaves the right to vote, which theoretically gave them a voice in the formation of the new post-slavery South. To enforce the three amendments, which collectively were designed to bring about a social revolution in the South, Congress passed the Civil Rights Bill of 1875, to which the South gave the derogatory name of the "Force Act." The bill guaranteed African Americans equal treatment in public accommodations, public transportation, and prohibited exclusion from jury service. With the former leaders of the slavocracy seemingly vanquished, and the newly freed slaves empowered by the federal Constitution and protected by an occupation army, small though it was, a new South where former slaves and former slave owners would move forward together seemed to appear on the horizon; or so hoped most optimistic observers of the postwar era.

But four years of the bloodiest war the country had ever fought resulting in the destruction of the South, and a virtual rewriting of the Constitution as it pertained to individual rights, was not enough to deconstruct an economic and social structure 200 years in the making. Within a generation of the war, the white power structure of the South—with the acquiescence or at least indifference of the northern victors—had reasserted their dominance over the blacks.

White subjugation of blacks in the South was a gradual and systematic process that coalesced legal, economic, and—when necessary—violent forces into a campaign to reestablish white supremacy. It began with a reassertion of white economic dominance of the land, the true source of power in the South. Radical Republicans proposed legislation designed to overturn white economic power by confiscating the land of plantation owners and giving it to the former slaves who had worked it. But the bill, which in popular parlance promised newly freed blacks "forty acres and a mule," never passed and whites were able to maintain control of the land. Faced with the challenge presented by a landless labor force and a cash poor landowner class, former slaves and former slave owners worked out new economic relationships through various forms of farm tenancy. The freed people offered their labor to get access to the land, and landholders recruited workers with the promise of a share in, or control over harvest or other arrangements.

The most common and widespread new labor system was "share cropping," whereby former slaves could continue to live on the plantation, and work the fields in exchange for a share in the profits after harvesting the crop. However, deductions from the share for rent and food provided by the landowner often left the sharecropper with very little profit or even further in debt. Consequently, at harvest time, a sharecropper might discover that after months of hard labor in the field he owed more than he had gathered and thus found himself and his family tied to another year of field work. The fact that many poor whites also found themselves in this position did not discourage southern power brokers from adopting sharecropping as a viable alternative to slave labor.

Some fortunate sharecroppers were able to put away a little money, and pay for their use of the land in cash rather than produce. This elevated them to tenant farmer status, and in some cases they even became land owners. But success did not assure security. A successful black tenant or land-owning farmer lived in an insecure and precarious world. He might wake one morning to find livestock poisoned or a barn burned by a jealous or controlling group of usually poor whites who felt the need to put an uppity black man with dreams to rise above his appointed station in life back in his place.

For those who refused to become tied to the land, strict vagrancy laws were passed that resulted in the arrest by the local sheriff, who rented jailed inmates out to local plantation or factory owners. With their economic domination secured, whites reasserted their hegemony over the political landscape of the South. After the war, roughly 12,000 federal troops remained in the South to ensure that legal rights for the newly Freedmen for whom they had fought, and to maintain order. But the U.S. Army's relatively small contingent could not be everywhere and the Redeemers—the name that white southern politicians and insurrectionists gave themselves—launched a war of terrorism and intimidation that kept blacks from voting or in any way directly challenging the white authority. Terrorist groups riding on horseback under banners such as "Knights of the White Camelia" or "Ku Klux Klan" intimidated blacks through night visits, burning crosses, and random shots into their homes to convince them that it would be prudent to remain at home on Election Day. Northern Republicans railed in frustration as they witnessed the unraveling of the Fifteenth Amendment in the South. Speaker of the U.S. House of Representatives, Thomas Reed, published an article outlining the egregious actions of so-called Redeemers of the South. "When the collections of gentlemen in a Southern District," he wrote, "go forth to fire guns all night in order to—as a member from that district phrased it in open House—'let the niggers know there is going to be a fair election that next day' they are guilty of intimidation."[3]

Weaving around and sometimes crashing through the voting rights established by the Fifteenth Amendment, southern states contrived outrageous maneuverings of the law. South Carolina, for example, passed the "eight box ballot," a long box with eight separate slots each designated for a specific candidate or party. The voter had to match his choice to the correct slot or the vote was invalid. The system made it impossible for an illiterate person to cast a valid ballot. Illiterate whites were assisted by poll workers, but for blacks no help was available. John Richardson, the governor of South Carolina, bragged that with the eight-slot voting "we now have the rule of the minority of 400,000 [whites] over a majority of 600,000 [blacks]."[4] Within a dozen years of their surrender at

Appomattox Courthouse, in the face of challenges posed by constitutional amendments and military occupation, white southern leaders—through violence and chicanery—had regained power. As J. J. Chrisman, a Mississippi judge, observed, " it is no secret that there has not been a full vote and a fair count in Mississippi since 1875 we have been stuffing ballot boxes, committing perjury, and here and there in the state carrying elections by fraud and violence." Systematically and relentlessly, whites dismantled the Republican Party in the South, and in the 1874 election led by resurgent Southerners, Democrats took control of the U.S. House of Representatives for the first time since before the Civil War.

In 1875, in the waning days of their political dominance, a lame duck Republican Congress passed the strongest civil rights bill the country had ever seen. The bill mandated open access to all public facilities—including public conveyances, inns, and places of amusement except schools and cemeteries. Its passage represented the last triumph of a dying campaign for racial justice. But it did not endure. Energized by their new political power, Southerners immediately began an all-out legal assault on the hated Civil Rights Bill. The Supreme Court abetted this assault by deciding in various cases that the Fourteenth Amendment pertained only to actions by states. Individuals, therefore, had the constitutional right to exclude whomever they wished from their private establishments or services. Three-quarters of a century passed before that opinion changed.

Southern white reassertion of power in the postbellum South was ratified by the rest of the country in 1877 in a proverbial smoke-filled room in Washington, D.C. The presidential election of 1876 had been very close, perhaps the closest in the history of the Republic. The Democratic candidate, Samuel Tilden, governor of New York, garnered more popular votes than his Republican opponent Rutherford B. Hayes, but he did not win the election. He had fallen one vote short in the Electoral College as the votes from Florida, Louisiana, South Carolina, and one from Oregon remained contested after Election Day. At this point—according to accepted interpretation—a group of reasonable men gathered at Wormley's Hotel in Washington, D.C., and worked out a compromise. Southern Democrats would trade off the presidency if federal troops were withdrawn from the South. The deal was struck, and as one of his first orders of business after his inauguration, Hayes ordered Federal troops in the South to stand down and Reconstruction officially came to an end. A small irony is that the hotel where this sellout took place was owned by James Wormley, a man of color. In the absence of the U.S. Army, southern whites became more emboldened in their efforts to return the social structure of their homeland as close as possible to what it had been before the war had destroyed it.

By 1877 Americans had grown weary of the campaign to reconstruct the South. Furthermore, new distractions occupied and fascinated the collective consciousness of Americans in the rest of the country. A second industrial revolution was well underway, and newspapers fascinated readers with continual revelations of mechanical wonders wrought by the new age of applied science. Engineers and inventors crowded generals and war heroes off the stage of the American pantheon, as people marveled at the dizzying pace at which the new high priests of applied science created one miracle after another. Just prior to the Civil War, the transatlantic cable had reduced communication with Europe from 10 days to about 15 minutes. And shortly after the war ended, travel from New York to California was reduced from about six months to five days. The barriers of time had been broken. In 1883 after centuries of wishing, Brooklyn was finally connected to Manhattan Island by John and Washington Roebling's suspension bridge, and other mechanical wonders followed. The telephone, electric motors and lights, adding machines, typewriters, sewing machines, and gramophones all convinced Americans that they were on a dawn of a new age that promised new opportunities and they were willing to leave the South in its old world and to let them deal with their old problems in their own way. The future was too exciting to agonize over failures of the past. Freed from the scrutiny of their northern conquerors, southern whites drew up new state constitutions and passed new laws that eliminated blacks from the economic, political, and social power structure of the South.

In the last decade of the nineteenth century, having successfully reasserted political power and emasculated civil rights legislation, southern whites completed their subjugation of the black community by dismantling provisions in their state constitutions, which had been forced on them by Republicans during Reconstruction. As Mississippi Governor—and later senator—James Vardaman admitted, "There is no use to equivocate or lie about the matter, Mississippi's constitutional convention of 1890 was held for no other purpose than to eliminate the nigger from politics . . ."[5] When Mississippi's actions remained unchallenged by federal authority, other southern states followed suit. In 1895, South Carolina adopted a constitution that required a literacy test and a poll tax, and disqualified anyone from voting who had committed a crime no matter how small. That same constitution also mandated segregated schools and prohibited marriage between a white person and any person of one-eighth or more African blood. In 1898, Louisiana convened a constitutional convention "for the express purpose of disenfranchising the Negro in order to establish the supremacy of the white race." In 1901, Alabama followed suit with a constitutional provision that stipulated that voters must be able to read and write or own property assessed at $300 or more. In order to keep poor illiterate whites on the voting books, the new state constitutions included "Grandfather Clauses," which allowed a person to register if their grandfather had voted in the 1860 election.

Emboldened by their new power, the all-white Louisiana legislature passed the "Separate Car Law" in 1890. The law, which demanded the separation of the races on public railways, was not without opponents. Soon after its passage a political committee was formed in New Orleans composed of doctors, lawyers, newspaper publishers, and prominent businessmen. Its leader was Louis Martinet, doctor and lawyer, and part of a proud tradition of Louisiana blacks who had family roots that preceded the Louisiana Purchase. Given the less racist policies of Spain and France, free blacks who proudly referred to themselves as *Gens de couleur libre*, successfully negotiated a respected place in white society, even to the point of marriage. They established businesses, sent their children to the best schools and colleges, and enjoyed many of the same privileges as any person of means in any city.[6] They also considered themselves superior to their less fortunate brothers and sisters still working in the fields, who traced their roots to slave plantations. But in the last decades of the nineteenth century they had seen their privileges erode and—in the minds of whites—their proud heritage of 200 years no longer distinguishable from that of ex-slaves. The street car law affirmed their final decline, and they decided that a battle against this law would be where they would launch their final—albeit hopeless—battle to maintain their dignity and rights.

Martinet believed he did have one trump card. He assumed that the train officials would object to a law that demanded duplicate, and therefore costly, services. He hoped to ally his cause with the railroad corporations, one of the most powerful economic forces of the latter nineteenth century. He argued that the segregation law, which mandated government interference into railroad company policy represented a clear violation of the sacred—in the minds of corporate leaders—principle of *laissez faire*. He knew that the owners of the Louisville and Nashville road balked at the unnecessary requirement of providing extra cars and enlisted the railroad bosses as allies in his planned assault on the law.

For the test case Martinet chose Homer Adolph Plessy. Although a man of color, he could pass for white if he chose. Plessy bought a first-class ticket and after taking his seat, he announced to the conductor that he was a man of color. The prearranged arrest was carried out and attorney James Walker for the defendant asked for dismissal. Also as part of the plan, Judge John Ferguson, who was sympathetic to the attempt to overturn the law, refused dismissal, which allowed Walker take the case to a higher court. Walker went directly to the U.S. Supreme Court where he argued that the law violated the Fourteenth Amendment's equal access provision. The state attorney countered by invoking the Tenth Amendment's guarantee of state rights to pass laws for the common good of its citizens. Five weeks after arguments were presented the Supreme Court made its ruling in the case known as *Plessy vs. Ferguson*. Writing for the majority in a 7–1 decision, Justice Henry Billings Brown wrote that a law "which implies merely a distinction between white and colored races ... has no tendency to destroy the legal equality of the two races ... [and] the state is at liberty to act with reference to the established usages customs and traditions of the people and with a view to the promotion of their comfort and the preservation of the public peace and good order ..."[7]

Brown assumed that because of "established usages customs and traditions," both whites and blacks would be more comfortable apart from each other in separate cars. And as long as segregation laws provided for equal facilities for both races, it was in accordance with the Fourteenth Amendment. Thus was established the misconceived concept of "separate but equal," which remained in place for the next 60 years. Standing alone in his dissent, Justice John Marshall Harlan ridiculed Brown's conclusion that everyone would be happier in their own segregated facilities. He pointed out that even the premise was ludicrous since everyone knew the law was not passed to keep whites away from blacks but rather to keep blacks out of superior white facilities. "Since no one, would assert the contrary. Such a law," he declared, "implies class differences based on race," and "in view of the constitution," he argued, "there is in this country no superior, dominant, ruling class, of citizens." He asserted that the "constitution is color blind and neither knows nor tolerates classes among citizens ... when [their] civil rights as guaranteed by the supreme law of the land are involved."[8]

Two years after ratifying southern segregation laws the Supreme Court affirmed the legality of southern voting laws, which denied blacks suffrage. In the case *Williams vs. Mississippi* the court declared that since the word *Negro* was not specifically mentioned in the voting law, Negroes could not prove that the laws were written specifically against them. As with the *Plessy* case, the country accepted the suffrage decisions without protest. For those southern blacks who dared to object to the new order, there was violence and intimidation.

In 1899 Sam Hose, a sharecropper, got into a dispute with his boss, Alfred Cranford, over wages owed him. Angered by the audacity of his black worker, Cranford pointed a shotgun at him and told him he was going to shoot him on the spot. In self-defense Hose threw an ax at Cranford, which split his head open and killed him. Crawford ran, but the sheriff soon caught him. Within a week an angry mob dragged Sam Hose from jail to a lynching field, which the *Atlanta Constitution* described as "an ideal one for such an affair ..." The lynching drew a crowd of 4,000 spectators including ladies in their finest Sunday dresses. Men tied Hose to a tree and after smearing his body with oil they stacked kerosene soaked wood at his feet. Before lighting the fire, men in the mob mutilated his body. They sliced off his ears, his fingers, and then his genitals. Finally, they ignited the bloody mutilated body of Sam Hose. As the heat rose, his eyes popped out and his veins burst. "The stake bent under the strains of the Negro's agony and his sufferings cannot be described," the *Atlanta Constitution* reported.[9]

From 1889 to 1918 more than 2,400 African Americans were hanged or burned at the stake. Many lynching victims were accused of little more than making "boastful remarks," "insulting a white man" or seeking employment "out of place."[10] Through segregation, disenfranchisement and brutal intimidation to the point of murder, within a generation of the Civil War, white southerners could bequeath to their children a social economic system based on race they thought that their parents had lost forever. And by the same means by which they had obtained it they would maintain that system for another 70 years.

Southern whites legitimized their actions by rewriting the narrative of the post-Civil War era. From the southern point of view, Reconstruction was a failure because undeserved faith had been put in the ability of newly freed slaves to govern and function in democratic society. White southerners believed that by regaining political power and relegating blacks to a position of second-class citizenship not only restored order to the South but put blacks back into a position where they were more comfortable and productive. The rest of the country accepted the southern white argument, and except for black intellectuals and some Republicans their ascendancy went unchallenged. The country even celebrated the mythic collective memory of the well-ordered tranquility and general contentment of the old plantation South. For example, the 1897 Tennessee centennial exposition featured a plantation scene with 12 log cabins that provided comfortable shelter to 30 to 50 "native darkies" who sang and danced as they processed cotton. The exhibition demonstrated the happy productive plantation of the time "befo the wah."[11] In 1915 D. W. Griffith produced *Birth of a Nation*, the first feature-length film—an event that enthralled thousands including President Woodrow Wilson who had a private screening in the White House. The movie celebrated the white insurrectionist activities of the South as necessary to throw off the tyranny of Radical Republicans and to protect oppressed whites from rape, robbery, battery, and worse, and to bring order to the chaos created by corrupt northern carpetbaggers and incompetent ex-slaves. The film also reinforced stereotypes of intellectually dull and sexually promiscuous blacks.

Not just the general public but American scholars affirmed this interpretation of a benevolent southern plantation system that was destroyed by the Civil War and Reconstruction. The eminent Columbia University historian William Archibald Dunning wrote that black suffrage had been a political blunder and that the Republican state governments in the South that rested upon black votes had been corrupt, extravagant, unrepresentative, and oppressive. His point of view, first expressed in the 1890s, remained dominant among American historians through the first half of the twentieth century. "Dunningite" historians condemned the use of troops during Reconstruction as an undemocratic usurpation of power by a radical Congress and sympathized with the white Southerners who ousted the Republicans from state power through legal opposition and even extralegal violence. From the ivory towers of academia to the popular culture of movie theaters and fairs, white America gave their collective approval to southern white paternalism and opposition to a free labor market, and allowed the South to impose this view on the black community often through violent and extra-legal means. The period certainly was, as one historian has described it, the nadir of black history on the United States.

Even the high idealism of Progressives, which brought about workman's compensation mandatory education, and protection of women in the workplace, failed to arrive at a collective response or legislation designed to reaffirm the social justice promised by the Republicans at the close of the war. Although Progressives abhorred the abuses of slavery and applauded its demise, many, especially southern Progressives, held that slavery "had brought blacks from the condition of the savage to a status where [they were] fitted for the privileges of American citizenship."[12] Progressive white southerners welcomed the legislation and court decisions that had brought about the stabilization of race relations after the 1890s. They were convinced that segregation would guarantee social order, economic progress, and white supremacy in the polling place that would place the vote "on the highest plane possible in a republic." According to one historian, "The comparatively sanitary policies of disfranchisement and educational segregation appealed to the Progressives, who were enamored with the idea of regional advancement through discrete adjustments to the social order." Armed with such "rational" techniques for maintaining white supremacy, Progressives "shielded themselves from the contradictions inherent in their program for black uplift."[13]

Most Progressives accepted the liberal southern attitude toward blacks was influenced by the intellectually fashionable racism of the era. For them racial conciliation was in perfect harmony with the spirit of service underlying the Progressive ethos. Progressives rejected the image of blacks as beasts of burden and replaced it with a paternalistic counter-image of blacks as dependent children. For example, in discussing the alleged problem of black intemperance, one southern progressive educator suggested that "under the fairest conditions, this child-race, so clogged by appetite and passion, finds it difficult to get on well in the world." Progressives agreed that blacks had been morally and intellectually stunted by slavery and were thus capable of improvement only under the guidance of liberal-minded southerners.[14]

Abandoned by whites, African Americans at the turn of the twentieth century built on or created their own associations and institutions to improve the condition and status of thousands of former slaves and their children. Black churches provided one pillar of support for the African American community. In addition to establishing an organizational platform and spiritual support in trying times, they became the training ground for black leadership, which would continue up through the high water mark of the civil rights movement in the 1960s. In addition to the church, blacks also pursued more secular means of self-improvement.

As in the white Progressive movement, black women played an important role in social reform in their community. On July 21, 1896, in the 19th Street Baptist Church in Washington, D.C., black women, primarily from the North and overwhelmingly middle-class in background formed the National Association of Colored Women (NACW), whose goal was to attack racism and in particular to fight discrimination against black females, who suffered under a stereotypical image of being wanton, immoral, lazy, and promiscuous. In her first address as leader and organizer of the movement, Mary Church Terrell declared

> We have become National, because from the Atlantic to the Pacific, from Maine to the Gulf, we wish to set in motion influences that shall stop the ravages made by practices that sap our strength, and preclude the possibility of advancement.... We call ourselves an Association to signify that we have joined hands one with the other, to work together in a common cause. We proclaim to the world that the women of our race have become partners in the great firm of progress and reform.... We refer to the fact that this is an association of colored women, because our peculiar status in this country ... seems to demand that we stand by ourselves.... Our association is composed of women ... because the work which we hope to accomplish can be done better ... by the mothers, wives, daughters, and sisters of the race.[15]

Although not overwhelming in numbers—comprised primarily of well-educated business women, doctors, and lawyers—the NACW did achieve significant goals. Among their most important accomplishments was the creation and institutionalization of kindergartens, day nurseries, and mothers' clubs. Within a year of its founding, the NACW had established kindergartens and day nurseries in 14 cities large and small, North and South.[16] They also established training schools and boarding houses for young women in urban areas both North and South and help centers in the South that instructed young girls in basic principles of home management and taught boys job oriented skills such as blacksmithing, carpentry, and practical farming.[17]

The NACW also attacked the convict lease system and the lynch law, which Frederick Douglass described as the "two great outgrowths and results of class legislation which our people suffer today." They waged a petition campaign against convict labor in every southern state, and over the first two decades of the twentieth century they saw these laws eventually repealed across the South. The NACW also attacked lynching, particularly through the efforts of founding member Ida Wells. Born as a slave in 1862, in Mississippi, she left that state as a young woman and supported herself by teaching while getting a degree from Fisk University. She later moved to Memphis where she became a journalist and a leading member of Memphis black society, an aristocracy based on complexion, education, and talent.[18]

In 1887, the National Afro-American Press Convention named her the most prominent correspondent for the American black press. In the same year she purchased a third interest in the (Memphis) *Free Speech and Headlight* and used it as a forum to attack the horrors of lynching. She challenged the myth that lynching was necessary to curtail the irrepressible lust of black men for white women. In an article, which responded to the lynching of eight black men in one week, Miss Wells declared, "Nobody in this section of the country believes the old thread-bare lies that Negro men rape white women. If southern white men are not careful they will over-reach themselves and public sentiment will have a reaction, or a conclusion will be reached which will be very damaging to the moral reputation of their women."[19] Wells so outraged the white community with her remarks suggesting white female promiscuity that she had to leave town. The Memphis sheriff closed and sold her newspaper.

She moved to Chicago where she wrote and financed an antilynching pamphlet for distribution at the 1893 World's Columbian Exposition in Chicago. Soon after she carried her antilynching crusade to England. After two successful visits to England and the publication of *The Red*

Record, a 100-page pamphlet describing lynching in the United States, Wells became the leading advocate of antilynching in the country.

In a pamphlet published in 1892, Wells wrote that the lesson learned from lynching was that every African American should understand that a Winchester rifle should have a place of honor in every black home, and it should be used for that protection, which the law refused to give. "When the white man who is always the aggressor knows he runs as great a risk of biting the dust every time his Afro-American victim does," she continued, "he will have greater respect for Afro-American life. The more the Afro-American yields and cringes and begs, the more he has to do so, the more he is insulted, outraged and lynched."[20]

Over 80 percent of the lynchings in the United States occurred in the South, and at the end of the nineteenth century many of those victims were members of the Colored Farmers Association, an organization dedicated to elevating the economic and social status of black farmers to equality with their white counterparts. At its height in 1891 the Association boasted a membership of over 1,200,000 and was probably the largest black organization in the history of the country. The Colored Alliance urged its members to learn new farming techniques, acquire ownership of their homes, and improve their level of education. It sponsored co-operative stores and established exchanges through which members bought goods at reduced prices and obtained loans to pay off mortgages. It published newspapers and in some areas raised money to provide longer public school terms.[21]

Whites perceived the Colored Farmers Alliance as a threat to their hegemony and acted accordingly. Several times white violence obstructed Colored Alliance attempts to improve the economic position of blacks. For example, Oliver Cromwell of the Colored Farmers Alliance success-fully organized a boycott of white store owners and a strike for better wages for cotton pickers in Leflore County, Mississippi. In reaction, 200 armed whites descended on the county shooting or hanging 20 black members of the Colored Alliance. Similar acts of violence occurred throughout the South wherever the Colored Farmers Alliance successfully organized black farmers. Given the violent resistance of whites, the Alliance could not survive. Black farmers intimidated with beatings and death threats abandoned the Colored Farmers Alliance, and the movement did not sur-vive into the twentieth century. Some offshoots of the Colored Farmers

Alliance such as the Farmers Improvement Society of Texas, a black farm club founded in 1890 that restricted its activities to improving farm productivity, did continue well into the twentieth century. But the Colored Farmers Alliance, which had the broader goal of raising up the black community, threatened white hegemony and members suffered violent deaths for their efforts.[22]

Not all blacks were cowed by the threat of white brutality. Jack Johnson, born in Galveston, Texas, in 1878, not only remained undaunted by white intimidation but he also challenged through word and action their assertions of superiority. In 1908, he knocked out Tommy Burns and became the first African American heavyweight champion of the world. He then horrified an already astonished white America by disdaining claims of white racial superiority and flaunting established rules of decorum. He drove fast cars, boasted about his wealth, and openly dated white women. He even visited the famous Everleigh Club in Chicago, the most exclusive house of prostitution in the country and demanded services usually reserved for barons of corporations and European princes.[23]

All that disgruntled white America could do was complain and hope for a white champion who would humble the man they considered to be a braggadocios pretender. In 1910 the dream of "A Great White Hope" collapsed as Johnson pummeled former undefeated champion James J. Jeffries in what was billed at the time as the "fight of the century." After the fight Jeffries confessed, "I couldn't have hit him. No, I couldn't have reached him in 1,000 years." As word of Johnson's victory spread across the country, numerous riots broke out when angry whites reacted to badgering by young black men who taunted them about their inferiority in the manliest of sports.

A movement to ban the showing of a film of the fight even received support from Theodore Roosevelt. Congress agreed and passed a law forbidding the showing of all boxing films. Congress explained the law was needed in order to prevent gambling. But everyone knew the real purpose was to eliminate the spectacle of a white man suffering a severe beating at the hands of a black man. White America eventually extracted their revenge on their bombastic nemesis. In 1912 Johnson was convicted on charges of violating the Mann Act when he transported his white girlfriend across state lines. He fled to Europe to avoid imprisonment, but at the end of the First World War he returned and served his sentence. He died in a car accident in 1946. The spontaneous celebrations that broke out after Johnson's victory over Jeffries were the result of sheer joy of the black community who finally had a champion who stood up to white oppression. But the average black person could not pummel a white man. In many places they could not even organize a protest without violent recrimination.

The only effective mass protest in the first decades of the twentieth century remained migration out of the South. In response to black flight from the South, southern states instituted laws, which echoed the sentiments of the antebellum Fugitive Slave Act. Often blacks who attempted to leave were arrested after being accused of trying to abandon legal debts or of vagrancy. Some leaders of the migration movements even suffered attacks by the Klan and lynching for organizing movements out of the South, and business agents representing northern companies willing to hire blacks often found themselves in jail on trumped-up charges. Nevertheless, after 1910 a slow but steady migration north began. Sometimes it was the action of an individual or a single family, but often an exodus was organized by a pastor who would take his whole congregation or by a store clerk or barbershop owner who would persuade and then lead his clients north. Migrants were urged on by black northern newspapers like the *Chicago Defender* and *Pittsburgh Courier* that celebrated in biblical terms the "paradise" of the North compared to the "hell" of the South. Also songs like those of Bluesman Robert Johnson urged southern blacks to come to "Sweet Home Chicago." Often upon arrival they discovered that the North was no paradise. They lived in segregated neighborhoods in overcrowded and often unsanitary apartments with inappropriately high rents. There were also scammers ready to take their few hard-earned dollars, and there was job competition. On the other hand, there was no debt slavery, convict labor, or fear of lynching. There were no "separate but equal" facilities, nor did bathrooms, water fountain buses or waiting rooms bear the marker "Colored." And they could vote. Over the next decades the trickle of black movement from the South became a deluge. In 1910, 89 percent of all African Americans lived in the South. By 1920 the number of blacks living outside the South had increased to 15 percent, as over half a million blacks moved North.[24] The movement not only radically changed the lives of many black families, it also transformed the cultural landscape of urban America. For black migrants brought with them their own music, stories, art, and perceptions of America, which would be realized in the musical phenomenon in the 1920s known as jazz and the explosion of literary and artistic talent centered in the Harlem Renaissance, which wove black talent and sensibilities into the fabric of American cultural life.

Poor whites also migrated North in these years bringing their racial prejudice with them. In the North, tensions between poor whites and blacks were not tempered by social conventions established by white intimidation as they were in the South. White intimidation or offenses against blacks in the North was often met with resistance not meek submission. Consequently, tensions between poor whites and blacks frequently erupted into violent urban warfare, especially in the post-World War I years when poor whites and blacks competed over living space and jobs. During the summer of 1919, 25 riots broke out across the nation. One of the bloodiest occurred in Chicago when a black boy accidently drifted on a wooden raft into the commonly accepted white zone of Lake Michigan. The boy was killed by a barrage of rocks thrown at him by an angry white mob. Angry blacks reacted and a riot broke out that lasted for 3 days and left 23 blacks and 15 whites dead, 537 people injured, and over a million dollars of property damage.

The violence of 1919 was but one expression of the dismal position blacks found themselves in the first decades of the twentieth century. It was hardly a time that black leaders could call "Progressive," and they debated over what proper course to take to transport the black community out of the social and economic quagmire created by white racism. Two strategies emerged. There were those who believed that their energy should be centered on technical education and self-help programs. They avoided direct action against racial injustice and advocated a position of accommodation to the white community. On the other hand, there were those who believed that self-help programs would be fruitless without addressing the causes of the marginalization of black society. Therefore, they advocated a policy of attacking segregation, disenfranchisement, and lynching with legal and public challenges.

Booker T. Washington, who advocated accommodation, and W. E. B. Du Bois, who called for confrontation, became the leading spokesmen for these contrasting responses to racism. Washington was born a slave in 1856 in Virginia. In the post-Civil War years with money from white donors he established Tuskegee Institute as a center of learning designed to teach industrial trades, agricultural skills, and domestic training to black students. For whites, this meant a curriculum that would keep the graduates "down on the farm." For Washington, it represented a non-threatening means for improving blacks economically by giving them useful trades. At the same time he hoped that a skilled black population indispensable to whites would help erode the laws and prejudices, which had made blacks second-class citizens in the South. In 1895 in a speech that became known as the "Atlanta Compromise," Washington defined his position. "In all things purely social we can be as separate as the five fingers," he declared, "and yet one as the hand in all things essential to mutual progress." Such a position, which implied a subservient place for blacks in the emerging hierarchy of industrial capitalism, was met with agreement by whites, and Washington became the recipient of white acclamation and financial support and was designated by whites as the spokesman for black America.

W. E. B Du Bois who possessed the most articulate voice on the other side of the discussion recoiled at Washington's advocacy of accommodation to a social and economic world built on a foundation of racism and injustice. Born in Massachusetts and educated in the North, he was a grown man before he had experienced that environment of bigotry, hatred, and intimidation in which Washington had lived his entire life. He therefore had quite a different vision of where black aspirations could lead. In the South, black demands for equality and justice most probably terminated at the end of a hangman's noose. But in Du Bois's world such aspirations put him at the forefront of academia. His study of blacks in Philadelphia defined him as one of the leading sociologists in the country and a recognized leader in higher education.

In February, 1905, partly in response to Washington's declaration of accommodation, Du Bois along with William Monroe Trotter called for the formation of an all-black board to create a more radical strategy for fighting social and racial injustice. They met in Niagara Falls, Canada, that same summer and established the Niagara movement. Initially comprising a group of 29 black intellectuals and activists, they demanded abolition of "all caste distinctions based simply on race and color [and] a recognition of the principal of human brotherhood." They called for access to the "stuff of liberty and opportunity," which included "education, decent travel, civil rights and the ballot."[25] To put an exclamation mark on their demands, the Niagara group called for their second meeting to be held at Harpers Ferry, Virginia, where in 1859 John Brown launched a fateful attack on the U.S. arsenal designed to begin a slave insurrection. By 1909 the Niagara movement evolved into the National Association for the Advancement of Colored People (NAACP), a biracial organization that initiated a legal assault on the laws of segregation and disenfranchisement. The NAACP also launched the important journal *Crisis*, which Du Bois edited. It exposed the horrors of violence against blacks in the South and at the same time demonstrated the intellectual ability of black authors. Du Bois admitted that whites and many blacks recognized Booker T. Washington as "the spokesman of his ten million fellows, and one of the most notable figures in a nation of seventy millions." But, he concluded, "so far as Mr. Washington apologizes for injustice, North or South, does not rightly value the privilege and duty of voting, belittles the emasculating effects of caste distinctions, and opposes the higher training and ambition of our brighter minds," he must oppose him. Du Bois promised that he would continue by every peaceful means possible to strive for "the rights which the world accords men." Rather than reach a compromise with the South, Du Bois declared that the leaders of that region ought to be criticized and urged to do their "full duty to the race [they have] cruelly wronged and [are] still wronging."[26]

Washington held great dreams of white goodwill when Theodore Roosevelt and the Progressives took the reins of national leadership in 1901, but that hope was quickly dashed by the reality of racism which rushed over him in a flood when the new president invited him to the White House for dinner. It was an innocent invitation innocently accepted without much thought given to effect. In the past Roosevelt had invited conservationists, industrialists, and authors to the White House to learn through conversation something he had little knowledge of. In this spirit he invited Washington to discuss how best to improve conditions for blacks in the South. Roosevelt planned the dinner as an informational event not a manifestation of his views on race. But the public did not see it that way. Response—especially in the South—was immediate and vitriolic. In a large headline the *Atlanta Constitution* condemned the "Action of the President [which] was Roundly Censored." and in a later edition lamented that Roosevelt had ruined the "best Negro in Alabama." One southern senator declared, "We people of the South have been born and raised so that we cannot accept the Negro as our social equal and we cannot accept any man who does." White southern

EQUALITY

DINNER GIVEN AT THE WHITE HOUSE BY PRESIDENT ROOSEVELT TO BOOKER T. WASHINGTON, OCTOBER 17TH, 1901

President Theodore Roosevelt outraged southerners when they learned that he had invited Booker T. Washington, a man of color, to dine at the White House. (David J. & Janice L. Frent Collection/Corbis)

sensibilities were further outraged when they learned that Mrs. Roosevelt had joined the dinner. A white man and black man sitting to dine as equals was reprehensible, but a white woman at the table marked a total degradation of all laws of southern white propriety. The desk of Washington's secretary overflowed with death threats and a group in Louisiana actually took up a collection and hired an assassin. Fortunately, the attempt failed when the would-be killer was injured jumping from the train outside of Tuskegee. Not only Washington but also blacks throughout the South suffered from the event as white violence increased dramatically over the next few months. Senator Ben Tillman of South Carolina railed that "the action of President Roosevelt will necessitate our killing of thousands of niggers in the South before they will learn their place again"[27] By the beginning of the twentieth century, southern whites had declared a new mantra for their part of the country which asserted that "all white men are created equal." And they used trickery, manipulation of the law, and even violence to maintain it for over half a century.

The story of John which began this chapter was the story of many young blacks who chose to dream of a better life in the South. The story ends with John walking in the woods after being dismissed from his job for the things he taught the children. "I'll go away," he said slowly; "I'll go away, and find work, and send for [my family]. I cannot live here longer." Suddenly, the screams of a young girl rattled him from his thoughts. Running toward the commotion, he found a young white man—the Judge's son—raping his sister. He hit the man with a tree branch and killed him. In the white South of the early twentieth century, there was but one resolution to his action—John was lynched.

> Amid the trees in the dim morning twilight he watched their shadows dancing and heard their horses thundering toward him, until at last they came sweeping like a storm, and he saw in front that haggard white-haired man, whose eyes flashed red with fury, and wondered if he had the coiling twisted rope. Then, as the storm burst round him, he rose slowly to his feet and turned his closed eyes toward the Sea. And the world whistled in his ears.[28]

In an instant John became one of the strange fruits lamented by singer Billy Holiday.[29]

NOTES

1. "Niagara's Declaration of Principles." 1905. The Gilder Lehrman Center for the Study of Slavery, Resistance and Abolition, Yale University. Accessed September 16, 2014. http:/www.yale.edu/glc/archive/1152.htm.

2. W. E. B. Du Bois, *The Souls of Black Folk* (New York: Pocket Books, 2005), 233.

3. Lawrence Goldstone, *Inherently Unequal: The Betrayal of Equal Rights in the Supreme Court 1865–1903* (New York: Walker and Company, 2011), 132–33.

4. Ibid., pp. 132–33.

5. Ibid., p. 135.

6. Ibid., pp. 152–53.

7. Ibid., p. 165.

8. Ibid., pp. 166–67.

9. Ibid., p. 5.

10. Accessed February 23, 2014. http://www.digitalhistory.uh.edu/learning_history/lynching/lynching_menu.cfm.

11. David J. Peavler, "African Americans in Omaha and the 1898 Trans Mississippi and International Exposition," *The Journal of African American History* 93, no. 3 (Summer 2008): 339.

12. Michael Dennis "Schooling Along the Color Line: Progressives and the Education of Blacks in the New South," *The Journal of Negro Education* 67, no. 2 (Spring 1998): 148.

13. Ibid., p. 142.

14. Ibid., p. 143.

15. Beverly W. Jones, "Mary Church Terrell and the National Association of Colored Women, 1896 to 1901," *The Journal of Negro History* 67, no. 1 (Spring 1982): 234.

16. Ibid., p. 26.

17. Ibid., p. 30.

18. David M. Tucker, "Miss Ida B. Wells and Memphis Lynching," *Phylon: The Atlanta University Review of Race and Culture* 32, no. 2 (Summer 1971): 112–22.

19. Ibid., p. 113.

20. Ida B. Wells, *Southern Horrors: Lynch Law in All Its Phases.* 1892. *Digital History* ID 3614. Accessed January 16, 2014. http://www.digitalhistory.uh.edu/disp_textbook.cfm?smtid=3&psid=3614.

21. William F. Holmes, "The Demise of the Colored Farmers' Alliance," *The Journal of Southern History* 41, no. 2 (May 1975): 187–200, 187.

22. Ibid., p. 200.

23. Karen Abbot, *Sin in the Second City: Madams, Ministers, Playboys, and the Battle for America's Soul* (New York: Random House, 2007), 179–81.

24. Taeuber, Karl E., and Taeuber, Alma F., "The Black Population in the United States," *The Black American Reference Book,* Smythe, Mable M., editor, (New York: Prentice-Hall, Inc., 1976), 165.

25. "Niagara's Declaration of Principles." 1905. The Gilder Lehrman Center for the Study of Slavery, Resistance and Abolition, Yale University. http://www.yale.edu/glc/archive/1152.htm.

26. W. E. B. Du Bois, *The Souls of Black Folk* (New York: Simon and Schuster, 2005. Original 1903), 46, 53, 60, 61.

27. Deborah Davis, *Guest of Honor: Booker T. Washington, Theodore Roosevelt, and the White House Dinner That Shocked a Nation* (New York: Simon and Schuster, 2012), 227.

28. W. E. B. Du Bois, *The Souls of Black Folk* (Boston: E Purdy, 1914), 177–79.

29. "Strange Fruit" Lewis Allan, Dwayne P. Wiggins Copyright: Edward B. Marks Music Co., Music Sales Corporation, Marks Edward B. Music Corp., Dwayne Wiggins Pub Designee, WB Music Corp.

CHAPTER 7

LITERATURE IN THE PROGRESSIVE AGE

A person who won't read has no advantage over one who can't.

—Mark Twain[1]

B y the end of the nineteenth century 95 percent of Americans could read. Even 45 percent of the most illiterate group—poor black farmers in the South—possessed this skill, and the printed word was the most accessible source of entertainment and information in the United States. From the novels and urbane magazines that lay on tables in middle- and upper-class homes, to the almanacs and agricultural journals that arrived in farm houses, by rural free delivery, to the pulp magazines scattered on tables in working-class bars and barbershops, reading materials in the United States were ubiquitous. Social activist Jane Addams commented that because of the universality of reading, "we find in ourselves a new affinity for all men, which probably never existed in the world before."[2]

Probably every literate person took some time to read the newspapers, which played an instrumental role in affecting the course of the public's debate on the major issues of the time. Some papers challenged, others maintained the status quo. On the one hand, there were investigative reporters like Elizabeth Cochrane, who worked as a servant to expose white slavery in Pittsburgh and faked insanity in order to study a mental institution from within and on the other hand, there were newspapers like the *Miami Evening Record* that celebrated the despoiling of South Florida's natural environment in the name of progress. For example, the paper headlined the draining of the Everglades to create 6,000,000 acres of reclaimable farmland as "Governor Napoleon Broward's GREAT PROJECT."[3] Whatever their editorial views, which they often did not hesitate to include in their so-called objective reporting of events, the newspapers held great sway over public opinion. Undoubtedly, the greatest example of this tremendous influence occurred in 1898 when William Randolph Hearst convinced the American people through his newspapers that it was imperative for the United States to go to war against Spain in order to liberate the island of Cuba.

Aside from newspapers, the most common form of literature was the magazine. Selling for anywhere from 10 cents for the *Police Gazette* to 35 cents for the more sophisticated *Century*, magazines informed and entertained with a variety of material. Content included biography, poetry, fiction, sports, and news. The great—and not-so-great novelists—of the era usually introduced their work in serial form in the magazines.

In this era, class usually determined preferences. For the working class the material of choice was a collection of magazines collectively known as the "pulps." The name referred to the quality of the paper used to publish these low priced journals. The appearance of these magazines stood in stark contrast to the glossier and attractive magazines known as "slicks." And like the paper they were printed on, "pulps" documented the less glossy side of late Victorian life. Tom Wolfe described them as the only contemporary chronicles of "a style of living that was not so much the opposite of high Victorian gentility as its underside"[4] Their pages revealed the world of sport, crime, and lost innocence. They celebrated the "Sporting Man," the macho dandy who betted on anything and enjoyed "all the minor vices (gambling, lechery, gluttony, profanity and blood sports) that were kept leashed in the social sphere above him."[5]

The *National Police Gazette* remained the most popular of the pulps. It had its origins in the antebellum urban North, but its most successful years date from the late nineteenth to early twentieth century when it came under the editorship of Richard Kyle Fox, an Irish journalist who took over the faltering magazine in 1878 for back wages. He printed the magazine on eye-catching pink paper with a front page that always featured the picture of a scantily clad woman over a headline that suggested she had been the victim of a sexually charged transgression. Tough but good-hearted detectives, who protected women of similar characters provided subject matter for the short stories in the *Gazette*. In addition to providing lurid details of crime—both real and imagined—the inside matter of the magazine contained a regular fare of scandals involving powerful people, disasters such as fires or train wrecks, and sports with up-to-date information on baseball and boxing. The format attracted myriad enthusiastic followers, particularly among the working class. Impressed with the success of the *Gazette* newspaper, publishers William Randolph Hearst and Joseph Pulitzer began to employ similar tactics to sell their newspapers. Indeed, Fox's pink-papered *Gazette* gave rise to the so-called yellow journalism of Hearst and Pulitzer.

In order to increase sales, Fox became a great promoter of boxing matches. One of the *Gazette*'s most important contributions to boxing was the promotion of a fight between their appointed champion Paddy Ryan and the upstart from Boston James J. Sullivan. The promotion of this fight not only sold thousands of *Gazette* special editions but launched Sullivan's illustrious career.[6] According to historian Elliot Gorn, Fox's magazine also contributed to the eroticization of the culture especially of sports. He points out that not only did the magazine contain numerous ads for contraceptives and aphrodisiacs, it also covered subjects like the famous late nineteenth-century strongman Eugene Sandow, whose particular skill lay on the frontier between sport and eroticism. The *Gazette* reported that after a scantily clad Sandow posed before a New York audience, he wanted the people to know that his body was pure hard muscle so he took the gloved hand of a young woman and ran it over his chest. " 'It's unbelievable,' she gasped just before fainting."[7] Although many respected authors wrote for pulps, the magazines are best remembered for their sexually charged stories and sensational cover art. But these magazines were more than lurid entertainment for the lower class. The hero detectives in the pages of these magazines provided important lessons for young working-class men. They taught them how to dress, how to talk, and even in some ways how to attract a woman. They also provided lessons in more abstract virtues such as self-respect and manly dignity.[8]

Printed on finer material and selling at a higher price, the "glossies" (usually selling for around 35 cents) provided reading material for the middle and upper classes. *The Century*, which began in 1881, was typical of this type of magazine that contained serialized novels, short histories or biographical sketches, and poems. Often politicians contributed articles to explain their views to the electorate. For example, in the January 1904 edition of *Century* along with the initial chapter of Jack London's novel the *Sea Wolf*, an article by Senator Henry Cabot Lodge on immigration appeared. In this article, he defended legislation proposed to restrict immigration. He warned Americans that a "new wave of Italians and Eastern Europeans people, with whom we have never amalgamated or had relations of any kind, are entering the country and if not soon restrained, will before long affect fundamentally the quality of our citizenship."[9]

Magazines also contained many poems. This was an age when Woodrow Wilson carried Rudyard Kipling's poem "If" in his breast pocket and often read it aloud when concluding a speech. In his poem Kipling observed:

> If you can keep your head when all about you/ Are losing theirs and
>   blaming it on you. . . .
> If you can talk with crowds and keep your virtue . . .,
> If neither foes nor loving friends can hurt you,
> If all men count with you, but none too much:
> . . . Yours is the Earth and everything that's in it,
> And—which is more—you'll be a Man, my son!

In the post-World War I era, poetry became increasingly the medium of the intellectual elite, but in the Progressive Era—and before—poems were read for comfort and enjoyment by the general public. Therefore, magazines of this era that did not contain a good number of poems were deemed incomplete. Robert W. Service—whose work by later critics was considered "doggerel"—was a favorite poet at this time and at least a few verses of his poem, "The Cremation of Sam McGee," which began *There are strange things done in the midnight sun/ By the men who moil for gold*; were known by almost every American of school age and older.

Magazines were the means by which the era's most popular novelists were introduced to the reading public. Jack London's *The Call of the Wild* (1903) and *Sea Wolf* (1904) were first published, in serialized form, as was Henry James's novel *The Ambassadors* (1903). And before starting his own magazine, Samuel S. McClure created a syndicate that sold over 50,000 words a week to various publications. His efforts introduced Americans to Robert Louis Stevenson, Rudyard Kipling, Emile Zola, Thomas Hardy, and Arthur Conan Doyle.

Middle-class women also had their own magazines. The most important in terms of readership was *Ladies' Home Journal*, which at the beginning of the twentieth century had a circulation of well over a million copies. The magazine was directed to middle-class married women and maintained a relatively inexpensive subscription price of a dollar a year. It included short stories of particular interest to women and also gave advice on cooking, child rearing, health, and home entertainment. While it frequently contained cute pictures of children, and the popular "Ruth Ashmore Advice Column" for young girls, written by Isabel Mallon, it also assumed a certain level of education among its readers and articles included subjects such as "Letters from Europe," or comments from a senator or cabinet member's wife presenting a woman's view on contemporary political issues. At the turn of the twentieth century, the magazine also published the work of social reformers, such as Jane Addams and home designs by famed architect Frank Lloyd Wright.

Magazines also introduced children to heroes who—thanks to the film industry—continued to fascinate young people through the century. In William Rice Burroughs's *Tarzan* (1912) first published in *All Story*, a pulp magazine designed for a younger audience, a small boy is left marooned on an island. Although written for children, the story reflects popular behaviorist and racial perceptions of Anglo-Saxon Americans of the era. In the story young Tarzan masters his environment, and is worshipped as a god by the African tribe who discovers him in the jungle. Rudyard Kipling's *Jungle Book* (1894) also finds a boy alone in the jungle. The boy is raised by a wolf, a bear, and a jaguar, and as many behaviorists in the period predicted, he becomes a product of his environment. But his Anglo-Saxon roots prevail in the end. He eventually has to fight a tiger. Merging jungle skills with genetically inherited ingenuity, he prevails.

Another turn of the last century children's book that has endured is the *Wonderful Wizard of Oz* (1900) by Frank Baum. Although free of Anglo-Saxon predispositions to superiority inherent in other children's literature, the book has not escaped analysis for deeper meaning by some who have concluded that the book is a political allegory. This novel made famous for another generation in 1939 by a film version tells the story of a Kansas girl just trying to get home after being blown away by a tornado. Dorothy dances along the yellow brick road (i.e., gold standard) to the emerald city (prosperity) in silver shoes, which are seen as a nod to Silverites who took control of the Democratic Party in 1896. The tin man representing industry lacks a heart and is dependent on oil to keep moving, and the straw man representing the Populist farmers has no brain. The cowardly lion has been seen as a comment on our less than heroic war against the Spanish in 1898. Mercifully most children's stories remain just that, and therefore free from political analysis. Such is the case with *Peter Pan* (staged 1904) or *Peter and Wendy* (1911), published as a play and later as a book in 1911 by J. M. Barrie. Both versions tell the story of a mischievous little boy who can fly and refuses to grow up.

The political agenda of the authors of children's books can be debated. However, a group of novelists collectively referred to as "naturalists" clearly reflected and in turn influenced Progressive perceptions of the world. They affirmed a Progressive axiom that humans are inescapable products and often victims of their environment. A corollary to this assumption was that through proper scientific study, social conditions and in turn human behavior, can be modified. At the same time they raised the social consciousness of their middle-class readers by introducing them to a world isolated from their own. As Jane Addams pointed out, thanks in part to these novelists, people of the middle—and upper classes have learned the experiences of—and their affinity to—the poor with whom otherwise they had little or no contact. She concluded that from a raised social consciousness proceeds an elevated ethical and political consciousness because "much of the insensibility and hardness of the world is due to the lack of imagination which prevents a realization of how others live." And if after becoming aware of our common humanity "we grow contemptuous of our fellow," she warned, "we not only tremendously circumscribe our range of life, but limit the scope of our ethics."[10]

Exemplary of the generation of Naturalist writers were Stephen Crane and Theodore Dreiser both of whom turned their attention to the human condition of their time. In *Maggie, Girl of the Streets* (1893) Stephen Crane tells the story of a blameless young girl who follows her heart and is destroyed by her environment. Crane describes the urban slum as a monster, which swallows the innocent and excretes them on the filthy streets that front the tenements and saloons of the slums. Even a good-hearted, loving, and innocent young girl like Maggie cannot avoid the inevitable consequences of life in such a place and in the end she dies, a young, poor, sickly, and pregnant prostitute.

In *Sister Carrie* (1900), Dreiser also begins his novel by painting the picture of an innocent girl. In this story Carrie, a country girl, is driven from the farm by life's monotony and lured by the promise of material well-being and happiness of the big city. Unlike Maggie, Carrie is able to harden her heart to the harsh urban world she has entered and achieves the material wealth she sought. In the end, however, she learns that material well-being without spiritual comfort is an empty reward and the things she thought would bring her happiness do not. Throughout the novel she avoids those matters of the heart that might uplift her human spirit but may in the process cause pain. At the end of the novel that has taken her through a number of generous lovers, a successful career in the theater, and a life of complete material comfort, she finally realizes that things alone do not make a person happy. For, as Dreiser tells his readers, "Amid the tinsel and shine of her state" Carrie, walked unhappy.

> As when Drouet took her, she had thought: "Now am I lifted into that which is best"; as when Hurstwood seemingly offered her the better way: "Now am I happy." But since the world goes its way past all who will not partake of its folly, she now found herself alone. ... In her walks on Broadway, she no longer thought of the elegance of the creatures who passed her. Had they more of that peace and beauty which glimmered afar off, then were they to be envied.[11]

Novelists like Crane, Dreiser, and others presented a world little known by the middle class and in the end contributed to the growing awareness of the conditions of the poor living in the bowels of their cities. In addition to informing the general public, these novels also provided ammunition for Progressive politicians arguing for social legislation.

Bridging the terrain between Naturalist writers' experiments with social realism and actual conditions of the poor at the time was the Socialist novelist Upton Sinclair. Since the late nineteenth century radical writers had been publishing their dreams of a better world. But aside from Edward Bellamy's *Looking Backward* (1888), which described the utopia that the United States would become at the end of the twentieth century by following socialist formulas, they rarely reached mainstream readership. Sinclair was the exception. Sinclair, a socialist, wrote a novel on the conditions of the packinghouse workers in Chicago. In order to gather material for his work, he moved to the Packinghouse district of Chicago, put on tattered clothes, and carried a lunch pail into the meat processing plants, where he wandered and observed unnoticed. What he saw horrified him. The packinghouses utilized an assembly line or rather disassembly line for their industry. Dead animals moved along a belt as workers stood on each side with sharp knives cutting sections of the cadaver as it passed by them. Workers were paid by the piece so they worked rapidly with sharp blades in hand. Since choice cuts were a priority, they were often fought over, resulting in wounded workers. Sinclair described the scene:

> The pig hung by its legs on a chain ... squealing (until he was killed). Now he passed by two lines of men who were standing on a platform each one hacking at a piece of the animal as he passed by.[12]

At the end of the day what had fallen on the floor including sawdust, human blood, spit, and flesh, dead rats, and moldy meat was doused with borax and ended up as sausage or ground canned meat. Hams of unbearable smell were injected with chemicals to mask the odor and sent to market. After collecting the data Sinclair was not sure how to present it. One night at a wedding celebration of a young Lithuanian couple in the Packing House District known as "Back of the Yards," the idea came to him to create a novel of a young immigrant and his struggle for survival as a slaughterhouse worker. The novel became the *Jungle* (1906), and the public outcry from its readers was a major force in the passage of the Pure Food and Drug Act of 1906. This landmark bill that authorized the federal government to examine the contents of processed food and medicine would not have had "the slightest chance of passing the House," Senator Albert Beveridge observed, if it had not been for the "agitation produced by the meat inspection amendment."[13] Later the socialist Sinclair lamented, "I aimed for the public's heart and hit its stomach." Other novels such as Frank Norris's *Octopus* (1901), which told the story of the struggle between wheat growers of California and the railroad conglomerates, also informed the public of the social upheavals created by the new industrial age, but none equaled the *Jungle* in terms of political and public influence.

While a number of good novels that provided glimpses of a world unknown to the middle-class played an important part in moving the Progressive agenda, nonfiction—especially works that looked at society scientifically—maintained preeminence in the hierarchy of Progressive literature. The popularity of nonfiction in this era was based on the premise that if a problem could be analyzed, then it could be solved. The study of humanity became a science, and the preeminent social scientist of the era was W. E. B. Du Bois, whose University of Pennsylvania sponsored book *The Philadelphia Negro* (1899) redefined sociology as a statistically based scientific discipline. Four years later he produced his seminal work *Souls of Black Folk* (1903), which like most literature of the time first appeared as a series of articles in a magazine, the *Atlantic*. In this work, which examines the struggle of blacks in the South, he defined the color line that existed not only in that region but throughout the United States and—in anticipation of his later views on Pan Africanism—throughout the world. But this sociological, "scientific" study also contained a metaphysical theme, which is suggested throughout the book but then clearly stated in the last chapter. While playing on the word *soul* to define black society, he created a contrast to the overt materialism, which had become the driving force of white society in the early twentieth century and he suggests that white people need black people in order to recover their soul that they had lost in the rush for material gain. He concludes the book by explaining the gifts that the African people have given America, the most important one being the gift of Spirit. For over 300 years of American history, he wrote:

> We [blacks] have called all that was best to throttle and subdue all that was worst; fire and blood, prayer and a sacrifice, have billowed over this people, and they have found peace only in the altars of the God of Right. Nor has our gift of Spirit been merely passive. Actively we have woven ourselves with the very warp and woof of this nation,—we fought their battles, shared their sorrow, mingled our blood with theirs, and generation after generation have pleaded with a headstrong careless people to despise not Justice, Mercy and Truth, lest the nation be smitten with a curse. Our song, our toil, our cheer, and warning have been given to this nation in blood brotherhood. ... Would America have been America without her Negro people?

In his final paragraph he concludes, "If somewhere in this whirl and chaos of things there dwells eternal good" then white America "shall rend the veil and the prisoned shall go free ... swelling with song ... with life. ..."[14] In 1909, Du Bois became a founding member of the National Association for the Advancement of Colored People, which formally began the campaign to liberate white America from its prejudices and the campaign continues to the present.

Another writer of nonfiction whose work flowed into the current of Progressive thought was William James. His publication of *Pragmatism: A New Name for Some Old Ways of Thinking* (1907) gave Americans a philosophy they could embrace as their own. In its most simple form

Pragmatism defined the value of an idea by its practicality; and if Americans were anything they were practical. Pragmatism also became the philosophical foundation for Progressive politicians who abandoned established theoretic models and implemented or abandoned legislation based on one simple criterion: "Does it work?"

Two additional nonfiction writers who made significant contribution to the Progressive view of things were Jacob Riis and Jane Addams. Novelists like London and Dreiser had painted fictional images of the conditions in the bowels of the industrial city. Riis and Addams went into those areas, lived among the people there, and through their eyewitness accounts transformed the novelists' images into objective fact. Jacob Riis was born in Denmark in 1849 and migrated to America in 1871, where he found a career when he became the police reporter for the *New York Tribune*. In this position, Riis worked at the most crime-ridden and impoverished slums of the city. Through his own experiences living in poorhouses as a recent immigrant and witnessing the conditions of the poor in the city slums, he decided to make a difference for them. While continuing his day job as a reporter, he spent his evenings speaking to civic groups about the conditions of the poorest inhabitants of their city. He began experimenting with a camera, which allowed him to dramatize his talks with photos of the slums of the Lower East Side. In doing so he joined a new but expanding army of photo journalists such as Lewis Hine and Elizabeth Cochrane who with slide shows and statistics convinced groups of socially minded citizens of the need for public and government participation in reform.

Riis's photos along with his essays became an 18 page article in the December 1889 issue of *Scribner's*. And a year later, it was expanded and published as a book entitled, *How the Other Half Lives: Studies among the Tenements of New York by Jacob A. Riis with Illustrations Chiefly from Photographs Taken by the Author* (1890). Through words and photos Riis detailed the terrible living conditions of people who are forced to live in what he described as the "most densely populated neighborhood in the world."[15] In the process, he also created an image of the multicultural polychromatic quilt that the Lower East Side became in the late nineteenth century. Riis noted that a visitor to that part of Manhattan, "may find for the asking an Italian, a German, a French, African, Spanish, Bohemian, Russian, Scandinavian, Jewish, and Chinese colony. Even the Arab, who peddles 'holy earth' from the Battery as a direct importation from Jerusalem," can be found in the neighborhood.[16] With a suggestion of racial prejudice common to the era he described the distinct ethnic groups of the Lower East Side and their typical characteristics as seen through his eyes. In the Italian neighborhood he reported, "The Italian learns slowly, if at all."[17] And of the Chinese on Mott Street he wrote, "all attempts to make an effective Christian of John Chinaman will remain abortive. ...."

> Ages of senseless idolatry, a mere grub-worship, have left him without the essential qualities for appreciating the gentle teachings of a faith whose motive and unselfish spirit are alike beyond his grasp. He lacks the handle of a strong faith in something, anything however wrong, to catch him by. There is nothing strong about him, except his passions when aroused.[18]

"Thrift" he notes was "the watchword of Jewtown, as of its people the world over."

> It is at once its strength and its fatal weakness, its cardinal virtue and its foul disgrace. Become an over-mastering passion with these people who come here in droves from Eastern Europe to escape persecution, from which freedom could be bought only with gold, it has enslaved them in bondage worse than that from which they fled. Money is their God. Life itself is of little value compared with even the leanest bank account. In no other spot does life wear so intensely bald and materialistic an aspect as in Ludlow Street.

The newly appointed New York Civil Service Commissioner Teddy Roosevelt read Riis's book and declared it to be an "enlightenment and inspiration." He commented that it would "go a long way toward removing the ignorance" of comfortable New Yorkers about the hardships confronting their less fortunate neighbors. As was his custom after reading an impressive author, Roosevelt sought out Riis for conversation and out of the meeting grew a friendship that Roosevelt described as "one of my truest and closest."[19]

The written work of Jane Addams also brought the reality of the poor right into the reading rooms of the middle class. Known prominently for her work as a social reformer, pacifist, and feminist during the late nineteenth and early twentieth centuries, Addams was born on September 6, 1860, in Cedarville, Illinois, one of nine sisters and brothers. Her father was a state senator and businessman and the most important men of commerce and politics, including Abraham Lincoln, passed through the portals of their home. At 17, she graduated as valedictorian from the Rockford Female Seminary in Illinois in 1881. She spent the next six years studying medicine,—a career curtailed by sickness—travelling, and studying in Europe. In 1887 with a friend, Ellen Gates Starr, she returned to England. They visited Toynbee Hall a famous settlement house for the poor of London. She and her friend Starr were so moved by the experience that they decided they were going to create a similar enterprise in Chicago. They called their center, Hull House, which was named after the building's original owner. The house, a two-story brick mansion built in neo-classic style in 1856, provided food, housing, employment information, and day-care services for the immigrant and poor population living in the Chicago area. They also provided technical and language classes designed to empower the new arrivals to the United States. It became a model for similar houses throughout the country, and Jane Addams became internationally famous and the preeminent name in social work in the United States. Realizing that her efforts alone would not ameliorate the conditions of the urban poor, she also worked tirelessly for social legislation, the right of women to vote, and for peace. In 1931 she was awarded the Nobel Peace Prize for her life's work. In 1912 she published *Twenty Years at Hull House*, which put a palpable face on poverty and encouraged others to take up similar work in their own cities.

She wrote of people like Mrs. Moran, who was returning one rainy day from the office of the county agent with her arms full of paper bags containing beans and flour, which alone lay between her children and starvation.

Although she had no money she boarded a street car in order to save her booty from complete destruction by the rain, and as the burst bags dropped "flour on the ladies' dresses" and "beans all over the place," she was sharply reprimanded by the conductor, who was the further exasperated when he discovered she had no fare. He put her off, as she had hoped he would, almost in front of Hull-House. She related to us against the rain nor the conductor, nor yet against the worthless husband who had been set up to the city prison, but, true to the Chicago spirit of the moment, went to the root of the matter and roundly "cursed poverty" her state of mind as she stepped off the car and saw the last of her wares disappearing; she admitted she forgot the proprieties and "cursed a little," but, curiously enough, she pronounced her malediction, not.[20]

It was also during this winter, Addams recalled, that I became perma-nently impressed with the kindness of the poor to each other;

> the woman who lives upstairs will willingly share her breakfast with the family below because she knows they "are hard up"; the man who boarded with them last winter will give a month's rent because he knows the father of the family is out of work; the baker across the street who is fast being pushed to the wall by his downtown competitors, will send across three loaves of stale bread because he has seen the children looking longingly into his window and suspects they are hungry.

There were also the families, she pointed out "who, during times of business depression, are obliged to seek help from the county or some benevolent society, but who are themselves most anxious not to be con-founded with the pauper class, with whom indeed they do not in the least belong."[21]

Through her writing Addams opened the doors of the hovels of the poor to the hearts and minds of the better off. The leitmotif of her work was that most of the poor were not in their condition by choice, they had moral values, dreams, and love for their family, equal to those of any of her middle-class readers. But her writing also espoused the Progressive credo that despite the fact that the poor may share basic values with the middle class, they would never achieve that status without education and an improved environment. The work of Addams at Hull House first appeared in magazines like *Scribner's* and *McClure's* and along with Jacob Riis's essays and photos added ammunition to the Progressive's arsenal in their struggle for political and social reform.

The written word became a powerful force for change at the turn of the last century. Indeed, it could be said that the most powerful catalysts for reform were the investigative journalists of the early twentieth century who gave a voice—in powerful and factual language—to the collective but undefined outrage that many felt against the new economic forces including monopolies, unions, and political machines, that seemed to be intruding into their lives with increasing frequency. The leader in this journalistic campaign was Samuel S. McClure. Born in Northern Ireland in 1857, at the age of seven he came to the United States along with his three brothers and recently widowed mother, who made the journey in steerage in an attempt to keep the family together. His mother remarried a poor farmer, but at 14 with $1 in his pocket McClure abandoned farm life and travelled alone to Valparaiso to seek a college education.

After graduation he convinced one of his college newspaper's sponsors Alexander Pope, whose company produced the famed Columbia Roadster bicycle, to finance a magazine dedicated to cycling, which would he hoped, "weave the bicycle into the best literature and art." Along with his friend John Philips, McClure published the *Wheelman*, which the *Nation* rated among 10 "most attractive of the monthly magazines," and McClure's publishing career was launched.[22] Soon after the successful launching of *Wheelman*, which evolved into the still very popular *Outdoor* magazine, McClure accepted the position of editorial assistant of the prestigious *Century* Magazine.[23]

Soon the demons that continually drove his frenetic life engulfed him, and in 1884 newly married to his college sweetheart Harriet Hard and with the first of his four children on the way he began to grow restless at the *Century*. With a month paid vacation and little else he set out to create a Literary Associated Press to buy short stories wholesale and then resell them to various magazines. This unexplored frontier of journalistic capitalism proved quite fruitful and by 1887 McClure was dispersing 50,000 words a week to well over a 100 journals. Despite his financial and literary success, McClure was soon restless again, and in 1892 along with his friend and partner, John Phillips began planning a new magazine. In a megalomaniac moment he declared "my blood is like champagne" and in a short time, he promised to down all the competition and "dominate the world" of journalism. At that moment the famous muckraking journal *McClure's* was born.

The first step in burying the competition came with underpricing them. To present a magazine that was pleasing to the eye a minimum of 35 cents per copy had to be charged, which limited readership to the "moneyed" middle- and upper-middle class. McClure proposed to sell his magazine for 15 cents to put it into the hands of everyone with literary taste regardless of their economic status. This was the price of the "Pulps," skeptical critics observed, and the idea of putting quality content into a cheap format seemed unrealistic if not revolutionary. But McClure had technology on his side. The high price of the "Glossies," McClure realized, was due to the costliness of the process of photo engraving pictures, but a new method that allowed photographs to be directly transformed to the printed

The cover of an issue of *McClure's Magazine*. With its January 1903 edition *McClure's* launched an era of investigative journalism, which President Roosevelt described as "muckraking." (Library of Congress)

page eliminated the need for costly wood engravings and cut the production price dramatically.[24]

McClure envisioned a magazine that contained four sections: "The Edge of the Future," featuring articles by entrepreneurs like Thomas A. Edison and Alexander Graham Bell; "Human Documents," which showcased portraits of famous people; "Conversations," which contained interviews between two famous people, and finally a short story section that drew from the best fiction available. The magazine also contained an ample number of poems. Instead of paying writers for work randomly submitted or solicited, he kept a permanent staff, the core of which became the standard bearers of journalism in the first decade of the twentieth century. Built around a nucleus of Ida Tarbell, Ray Stannard Baker, Lincoln

Steffens, and William Allen White, the plan was an expensive one, which his competitors eschewed, but McClure was not in the game for the money. He believed that journalism was the vehicle that moved the conscience of the nation and called the country to action. And he wanted to put himself at the wheel of that vehicle. He wanted his magazine "to become above all else a power in the land, a power for good." And he confessed that if given the choice, he would rather "edit a magazine than be President of the United States a hundred thousand times over."[25]

Readers of the first issue, which appeared on the stands in June, 1893, gave it an enthusiastic reception. The *Review of Reviews'* editor commented, "It is not often that a new periodical begins with prestige enough to make its success a certainty with the first number."[26] Over the next seven years the magazine met with enormous literary and financial success. McClure was even able to expand his personal mission of "becoming a power for good" by financing the publication of promising books that exposed the abuses of corporate power such as Frank Norris's *The Octopus: A Story of California* (1901), which told the story of how predatory railroads with their highly inflated shipping rates and arbitrary routing and shipping policies broke hard-working farm families leaving behind them a path of domestic destruction and driving men to crime and women and girls to (Victorian) ruin.[27]

In 1900 when things were going very well, McClure's hyperactive mind began to whirl out of control again. This time he overreached by trying to buy the very successful publishing house of Harper and Brothers. This deal, which promised to bring five more magazines under McClure's control, collapsed and drove the psychologically challenged McClure to the point of a nervous breakdown.[28] At the suggestion of his colleagues and to satisfy his own frenetic nature, McClure decided to go to Europe "to take the cure," a panacea of recuperation reserved for the well to do. The European "cure" included leisurely tours and visits to the natural springs that had been utilized as curatives at least since the time of the Romans. After six months in the famous spa towns of Aix-les-Bains and Divonne-les-Bains and a steady milk diet, McClure was energized, enervated, and prepared to bring himself, along with his manic—but creative—mind, back to New York.

He arrived in the offices and announced a new plan to his writing team. *McClure's* was going to change format. They were going to dedicate the magazine to expose the corruption that had been eating away at American life. The idea was not without precedent. Henry Demarest Lloyd's diatribe against monopolies, *Wealth against Commonwealth* (1894), had been on bookshelves for almost a decade. Newspapers had been uncovering public and private corruption for decades. But McClure's approach was novel. The exposure would not be based on abstract facts and statistics but rather, he hoped to put a human face on corruption. He proposed, for example, to expose unethical business practices by presenting the biography of a corporate baron. The chosen subject was John D. Rockefeller, and the biographer would be Ida Tarbell. No one was fit for such an assignment than Tarbell, who came from western Pennsylvania, where her father, an oil pioneer, had been run out of business by the newly formed Standard Oil Trust. Her knowledge of the topic, although it could be suspect of bias, could not be questioned. And her skill as a biographer was unmatched. McClure had met her in Paris in 1893 while she was working on a biography of Mademoiselle Marie-Jeanne Roland, and McClure convinced her to write a biography of Napoleon whose reputation at the time was experiencing a favorable reconsideration and he wanted a piece on him for his new magazine. On the strength of her biography of Napoleon, McClure's circulation doubled. In the wake of the enthusiastic reception of the Napoleon article, McClure assigned her to write a biographical sketch of Abraham Lincoln. Tarbell uncovered scores of people who had known him in his early days and shared hitherto unknown stories. The result was a magnificent piece filled with new information and detail of the life of the increasingly beloved Lincoln, and when it first appeared *McClure's* circulation increased by 40,000 copies to 190,000. After this initial success her permanent position at *McClure's* was secured.[29]

Given her demonstrated skill as a biographer and her personal history, which connected her to the oil industry, McClure could not have made a better choice than Tarbell to take on the subject of oil industry giant Rockefeller. Travelling from Washington to New York by way of Pennsylvania, Ohio, and Kansas on an unlimited expense account provided by McClure, she researched old depositions, newspapers and even pamphlets published during various stages of the corporation's takeover of smaller companies. Finally she arrived at corporate headquarters in New York. Although she could not get an interview with the reclusive Rockefeller, she did develop a warm relationship with Henry Rogers, a Standard Oil partner who believed that she would present the story of Standard Oil fairly.[30] Tarbell's painstaking research concluded with a series of articles that uncovered a system of espionage and bribery that Standard Oil used to crush independent oil producers in America. Her own father's experience could not have been far from her mind as she wrote about, "The man who had begun with one still and had seen it grow through his own energy and intelligence to ten and then a five hundred barrels of oil a day." For this man, she wrote, "his refinery was the dearest spot on earth, save his home." Therefore, Tarbell explained, "he resisted Standard Oil's takeover attempts with all his strength." But, where persuasion and intimidation failed, Rockefeller had other weapons, Tarbell explained. He crafted a system of espionage by which Standard Oil bribed railroad agents to access secret shipping records which detailed quantity, quality, and price of independent shipments. With this information, Standard Oil knew exactly how much to undercut a competitor to drive him out of business.

Tarbell quoted a producer who had a client in New Orleans who purchased from 500 to 1,000 barrels a month, but the client was lost when Rockefeller came in and promised the client $10,000 a year in rebates for a five-year contract to buy exclusively from Standard. Tarbell ended her series of articles with the question "What are we going to do about it?" Urging the American people to action, she told them that "it is our business, we the people of the United States and nobody else must cure whatever is wrong in the industrial situation, [as] typified by the narrative of the growth of the Standard Oil Company."[31]

Ray Stannard Baker also contributed to the first issue of the refocused McClure's. Born in 1870 and raised in LaCroix, Wisconsin, he went to Michigan State University and then on to the University of Michigan Law School. But he was soon drawn to writing and to the English department, and after graduating he went to work for the Chicago Record and shortly thereafter the plight of the industrial workers captured his attention. In March 1894 he went to Massillon, Ohio, to cover the "Coxey's Army" march. He appeared objective and indifferent to the quixotic campaign but as he got to know the men and walked with them his attitude changed. Soon they were talking about "their homes in Iowa, and Colorado, and Illinois, and Chicago, and Pittsburg, and the real problems they had to meet."[32]

After his return to Chicago he was sent to cover the Pullman strike. While most newspapers blamed the strikers and created the impression that federal troops saved Chicago from anarchy, Baker carefully recounted what he had observed and reported that no strikers had appeared to participate in the violence; that it was mainly outside provocateurs. When the Pullman strike ended, so did editorial interest in labor issues at the *Record*, and Baker's bosses relegated him to stories of murder, arson, and robberies, for which he held little interest and began submitting articles on labor issues to *McClure's*, where he was finally invited to join the staff of the newly formatted investigative magazine. Baker went to the anthracite coal mines of Pennsylvania where a bitter strike had been broken. He went into the homes of those who had gone back to work, both union and nonunion men. He discovered in the process the horrible conditions of the mines, the corruption of some mine owners and union leaders both, and the dangers that men faced when they returned to work not only in the mines but on their way to the mines at the hands of those trying to continue the strike.[33]

Lincoln Steffens wrote the third article for *McClure's* inaugural investigative edition. By the time McClure made his acquaintance, Steffens was a well-known and powerful newspaper man in New York. He had built a reputation as the best journalist New York had ever had. Steffens by his own admission led a privileged and for the most part a happy life. Born in California in 1866 in a palatial Sacramento mansion, which would eventually become the governor's residence, he was the oldest child and an only boy with three affectionate younger sisters. After graduating from the University of California at Berkeley, with his father's continued financial support he traveled and studied in the major centers of learning in London, Germany, and Paris.

Eventually, Steffens returned to the United States to find gainful employment. Armed with a letter of introduction from the friend of a father, Steffens was given a job at the *New York Evening Post*. Because of his background and connections to the moneyed class, Steffens was put on the Wall Street beat where he covered the crash of 1893 first hand and also wrote a number of successful investigative pieces on fraud and embezzlement at the country's most prestigious financial institutions. He then began a column dedicated to local crime, which brought him to a detailed study of the inner workings of the police department. Consequently by the time Teddy Roosevelt was made Police Commissioner of the city in 1894, Steffens was a recognized expert on police operations and was one of the men Roosevelt called on to give him the inside story of New York City police procedures. These credentials and connection inside the city administration brought him an invitation to join McClure's team.

With the new direction for his magazine in mind, McClure sent Steffens on an odyssey. "Get out of here," he told Steffens, "travel, go somewhere, buy a railroad ticket get on a train." With this mandate— and McClure covering travel expenses—he began an investigative journey through the nation's largest cities. He spoke to political bosses, ward heelers, tavern owners, newspaper editors, bartenders, public work employees, police, prostitutes, and anyone else who had contact at any level with city functionaries. The result of Steffens's journey was the famed book, *Shame of the Cities* (1904), which uncovered political corruption in six major American cities. The book began, as Steffens writes in his introduction, as a series of articles for *McClure's* magazine. The first article began by explaining the techniques that bosses used to take political control of cities, and in the process "supplanting democracy with autocracy." One example was Minneapolis where Boss Albert Alonso Ames, better known as "Doc Ames," ran the city. Under his jurisdiction, gambling parlors, unlicensed taverns, and houses of prostitution functioned under the protection of local law enforcement. But the protection came at a price. For example, the mayor's agents supervised the slot machines and collected $15,000 annually for the mayor as his share of the earnings. Unlicensed tavern owners and prostitutes also paid stiff protection fees. In order to cover their trail of corruption, city functionaries created imaginative means of collecting money. The police department, for example, organized a baseball team and their clients were forced to buy blocks of tickets to their games. Women were forced to turn over jewelry to the police.[34]

Steffens's initial article on political corruption in the cities, along with Tarbell's article on Rockefeller, and Baker's on unions, all appeared in the groundbreaking January 1903 edition of *McClure's*, which launched the muckraking era of American journalism. In a postscript to this edition McClure called on the public to right the wrongs exposed by his journalists. In this issue he wrote, "should make every reader stop and think. ... 'The Shame of Minneapolis,' could have been called 'The American Contempt of Law,'" and that title, he pointed out, could also have served well for Tarbell's article on oil or Baker's article on unions. With "Capitalists, workingmen, politicians—all breaking law, or letting it be broken," he asked, "Who is left to uphold it?"

> The lawyers? Some of the best lawyers in this country are hired to go into court not to defend cases, but to advise corporations and businesses firms how they can get around the law without too great a risk of punishment. The judges? Too many of them so respect the law that for some "error" or quibble they restore to office and liberty men convicted on evidence over-whelmingly convincing to common sense. The churches? We know of one Trinity Church in Manhattan an ancient and wealthy establishment which had to be compelled by a Tammany holdover health officer to put its tenements in sanitary condition. The colleges? They do not understand. There is none left; none but us.

And if the people don't act he warned, "the sum cost will be our liberty."[35] The January 1903 issue of *McClure's* sold out within days, faster than any previous issue, and the articles became talking points in cities across the country. As a result of the widespread circulation at 15 cents a copy for the first time, as one historian points out, a considerable number of small businessmen and white-collar workers were joining factory hands and farmers in a restless questioning. McClure called the issue the "greatest success we have ever had."[36] He told Ida Tarbell, "You are today the most famous woman in America!"[37] And the politics of corruption uncovered by Steffens played a major role in the unseating of a number of corrupt mayors across the country in the 1904 elections. "The day of the Boss is passed," declared the *Baltimore Herald,* and they pointed out that "few men in the country have done more to bring the ... defeat of municipal bosses than SS McClure and Lincoln Steffens."[38] The success of McClure's January 1903 edition persuaded editors at a dozen leading magazines to pursue a similar course, and the age of investigative journalism soon to be called "muckraking" had begun, and the literary legacy of an era was established. Investigative journalism, one historian observed, "assumed the proportions of a movement hardly less important than that of Theodore Roosevelt himself."[39]

By 1906 McClure was considered one of the most important men in America, but that same year his empire built on reform unraveled. It began with another of McClure's creative but disquieting inspirations. One day he announced to the staff the launching of a new magazine he would call *McClure's Universal Journal*. He also planned to invest the company's funds in a new weekly magazine. This most recent disrupting and narcissistic enterprise exasperated his longtime friend and partner, John Phillips, who had not been consulted. He told Tarbell that if he could not convince McClure to abandon his vainglorious scheme, he would resign. Of course, McClure could not be persuaded and Philips left taking the brilliant writing team of Tarbell, Baker, and Steffens, as well as William White, the popular Midwest political commentator, and others with him. They put their resources together and purchased a magazine *The American*, which they described as a "writers collective."

The breakup of the prestigious writing team at *McClure's* coincided with Teddy Roosevelt's angry tirade against the investigative journalists who had been his allies in his successful 1904 election and in early campaigns against the monopolies. Irritated by attacks launched against the senate by William Randolph Hearst, his political rival, Roosevelt lashed out at all investigative journalists at a speech at the Gridiron club on March 17, 1906. He compared them to the muckraker in John Bunyan's *Pilgrim's Progress* who spent his day raking in the mud and could look nowhere but downward. Bunyan's muckraker, Roosevelt suggested, "Typifies the man who in this life consistently refuses to see that which is lofty and fixes his eyes with solemn intentness only on that which is vile and debasing." The next day, an angry Lincoln Steffens called the president and told him he had just "put an end to all these journalistic investigators that made you." In retort, Roosevelt complained that Steffens and his friends with their relentless push for reform failed to understand, "the requisites of practical leadership—a sense of when to move forward when to hold back, when to mobilize the public when to negotiate behind closed doors."[40]

The metaphor created by Roosevelt stuck, and soon Americans were collectively defining investigative journalists as "muckrakers." Numerous journals continued to publish the work of investigative reporters, but with the downfall of its pioneer McClure, and the condemnation of the popular president, their power as a dominant political force had subsided. Roosevelt's muckrakers speech was more than an angry outburst provoked by his feud with Hearst. As he had done throughout his presidency, he had captured and elicited the public mood. As literary critic Edwin Slosson noted at the time, "The public cannot stand at attention with its eyes on one spot indefinitely. It is bound to get restive and seek diversion." And a Wisconsin judge expressed the resentment of many when he said, "It is getting so nowadays that the man or corporation that accumulates property to any extent is made the subject of attacks." Finally, the folk philosopher of the era, the Irish bartender Mr. Dooley, who appeared in Peter Finley Dunne's popular cartoon of the time, caught the public mood, as he so often did, when he commented that there once was a time when reading the popular magazines calmed the mind, leaving the reader with a "glad sweet song." Now, he lamented, after turning the pages of any magazine, a reader discovers that "everything is wrong. Corruption and double dealing today were so common that the world is little better than a convicts' camp."[41]

After the breakup of his staff, McClure put together a new team of writers that included Willa Cather, whose first piece, which ran for 18 months, was an exposé of Mary Baker Eddy, the founder of the Christian Scientists. But Cather's true talent lay in literature and historic narrative not exposés. And her talent marked the new direction of *McClure's*, which from 1907 onward became more noted for its quality fiction and poetry than its investigative reporting. Indeed, Cather's most important early work, *Alexander's Bridge* (1912) and *O Pioneers* (1913), the first of her Prairie Trilogy, began as installments in *McClure's*. The magazine's continued success after its departure from investigative journalism can be attributed to the changing public mood as across the country the literature of distraction was replacing the literature of inquiry.[42]

In the first decades of the twentieth century, Americans enjoyed a reading list that was eclectic, international, abundant, and of high quality. It included children's literature by writers such as L. Frank Baum, Edgar Rice Burroughs, and James Matthew Barrie that continues to entertain; poetry by writers such as Robert Service, Wallace Stevens, and Rudyard Kipling that was loved and recited by many; fiction that ranged from fantasy adventures to social realism to psychological introspection by writers such as Arthur Conan Doyle, H. G. Wells, Zane Grey, James Joyce, Joseph Conrad, D. H. Lawrence, C. K Chesterton, Somerset Maugham, and playwrights such as Anton Chekov and George Bernard Shaw that became classics; and nonfiction by historians such as Henry Adams, sociologists such as W. E. B. Du Bois, and philosophers such as William James that continues to inform.

Despite the quantity, variety, and excellence of the work produced, the literary legacy of this era will always be linked to investigative journalism. Such a phenomenon persuades historians to seek reasons. Perhaps part of the answer is that in an age that remained greatly divided by class, gender, and race—even as this chapter points out—in literary taste, the so called muckrakers transcended these barriers for a brief moment and brought the country together in a common cause; one that called for honest government, just dealings with shopkeepers and clients, cooperation between workers and owners, and an honest government that would strive for and ensure these goals. In bringing these ideals to print they created a common ground where most could walk comfortably and defined the goals and aspirations of a period of history called "Progressive." Most historians would concur with the judgment made at the time by a reporter for the *Independent* who predicted, "When the historian of American literature writes the opening years of the century he will give one of his most interesting chapters to the literature of exposure, and he will pronounce it a true intellectual force."[43]

NOTES

1. Although attributed to Mark Twain, this author could not find the quote in print before December 31, 1914, in the *Aberdeen Daily American*, "How to Keep Well" by Dr. W. A. Evans, Quote Page 2, Column 5 and 6, Aberdeen, South Dakota. Accessed September 19, 2014. http://quoteinvestigator.com/2012/12/11/cannot-read/.

2. Jane Addams, *Social Ethics and Democracy* (New York: The Macmillan Company, 1902), 7.

3. *Miami Evening Record* (May 23, 1905): 1.

4. "About the Police Gazette," *Police Gazette*. Accessed May 10, 2014. http://policegazette.us/About.html.

5. Erin A. Smith. *Hard-Boiled: Working-Class Readers and Pulp Magazines* (Philadelphia: Temple University Press, 2000), 32–6.

6. Elliot Gorn and Warren Goldstein, *A Brief History of American Sports* (Urbana, IL: University of Illinois Press, 2004), 122.

7. Gorn, p. 118.

8. Smith, pp. 23–36.

9. Henry Cabot Lodge, "A Million Immigrants a Year: Efforts to Restrict Undesirable Immigrants," *Century Magazine* (January 1904): 466–69.

10. Addams, p. 7.

11. Theodore Dreiser, *Sister Carrie* (New York: Pocket Books, 2005), 501–2.

12. Upton Sinclair, *The Jungle* (Gutenberg Project Release Date: March 11, 2006 [EBook #140] Last Updated: January 9, 2013. Accessed November 14, 2013. http://www.gutenberg.org/files/140/140-h/140-h.htm#link2HCH0007

13. Goodwiin, pp. 460–65.

14. W. E. B. Du Bois, *The Souls of Black Folk* (New York: Simon and Schuster Pocket Book Edition, 2005), 252–53.

15. Jacob Riis, *How the Other Half Lives: Studies among the Tenements of New York by Jacob A. Riis with Illustrations Chiefly from Photographs Taken by the Author* (New York: Charles Scribner's Sons 1890), 10.

16. Ibid., p. 21.

17. Ibid., p. 49.

18. Ibid., p. 92.

19. Ibid., p. 205.

20. Jane Addams, *Twenty Years at Hull House with Autobiographical Notes* (New York: The Macmillan Company, 1912), 160.

21. Ibid., p. 163.

22. Doris Kearns Goodwin, *The Bully Pulpit: Theodore Roosevelt, William Howard Taft, and the Golden Age of Journalism* (New York: Simon and Schuster, 2013), 162–67.

23. Goodwin, p. 196.

24. Ibid., pp. 166–68.

25. Ibid., pp. 168–70.

26. Ibid., p. 169.

27. Ibid., pp. 327–28.

28. Ibid., p. 328.

29. Ibid., pp. 177–78.

30. Ibid., p. 334.

31. Ibid., p. 339.

32. Ibid., p. 185.

33. Ray Stannard Baker, "The Right to Work: The Story of the Non-Striking Miners," *McClure's Magazine* 20, no. 3 (January 1903): 334.

34. Lincoln Steffens, "The Shame of Minneapolis: The Rescue and Redemption of a City That Was Sold Out," *McClure's Magazine* 20, no. 3 (January 1903): 227–30.

35. S. S. McClure, "Editorial," *McClure's Magazine* 20, no. 3 (January 1903): 336–38.

36. Goodwin, p. 325.

37. Ibid., p. 339.

38. Ibid., pp. 381–83.

39. Frank Luther Mott, *A History of American Magazines* (Cambridge, MA: Belknap Press, 1957), Vol. 4, pp. 207, 607.

40. Goodwin, pp. 480–84.

41. Ibid., p. 483.

42. Ibid., p. 489.

43. Ibid., p. 384.

CHAPTER 8

RELIGION IN THE PROGRESSIVE AGE

A Christian cannot believe any of those who promise that if only some reform in our economic, political, or hygienic system were made, a heaven on earth would follow.

— C. S. Lewis[1]

As in other ages, Americans in the Progressive Era celebrated their belief in God and their vision of eternity in a variety of ways. While most people clung to their religious traditions, the idea of "progress" touched religion as it had literature, politics, family, and every other aspect of American life at the turn of the century. The material progress experienced in the United States in the decades following the Civil War dazzled the minds of those who experienced it. Observing the world from the vantage point of 1900, one could celebrate the achievements of the recent past and assert the inevitability of its continuation. "Progress" became the mantra of the age.

Progress had always been a theme of Western civilization, but at least since the time of the Middle Ages up to the Enlightenment, progress had usually been measured in spiritual terms, as defined by John Bunyan's Pilgrim. However, with the scientific and technological miracles of the late nineteenth century, including turning night into day with Thomas Edison's lightbulb, the promise of material progress had trumped the spiritual. The results had been awe inspiring. Railroads had crossed the nation, industrial production made goods available to unprecedented numbers, public health had improved, material comforts and economic well-being unfathomed in previous ages had been realized. But while many people, including many religious leaders, hailed the material progress of the age, many troubled over the cost to the human spirit. They feared that in the course of pursuing material wealth, Americans risked destroying the social relations that cemented the community. John Winthrop's vision of a "City on a Hill," where Americans "delight in eache other, make others Condicions our owne, rejoyce together, mourne together, labour, and suffer together [*sic*]" had given way to a world of greed, competition, and oppression of those not able to keep pace with the velocity of the modern world. Consequently, theologians could correctly observe—and lament—that

> the present generation was wandering confused and bewildered, without guidance from any standard of ethics. A moral anarchy had been created in which men treated other men as commodities rather than as human beings. Moreover the anarchy was destroying democracy because it was dissolving the homogeneity, the ability of the people to act together on important issues.

But these same theologians who condemned the age also embraced the myth of "Progress," as defined by their times, and therefore, believed that solutions to societies' problems did not lie in the past but in the future. They did not beckon souls back to traditional values but rather they formulated a practical Christianity that addressed the problems of the day. Many theologians of the era not only studied the Bible, they also developed economic theories, studied sociology, and in the process formulated a practical theology that they hoped would transform the social cacophony created by the industrial revolution into new harmonious human society. As one theologian of the era proclaimed, "The progress of humanity ... is proceeding according to an intelligent plan, that line of march is irresistible, and the reformer's work is to remove one by one the obstructions in its way, strip off from growing man the outworn, out-grown forms at the instant of transition from one period to another. ... Mankind's progress is towards absolute truth."[2]

A new theology for this new age developed, which became known as the "Social Gospel." Advocates believed that although the industrial age in its early phases seemed to create class hatred, it also created the means —through trains, telephones, telegraphs, and cities—to bring humanity closer together, and therefore, closer to their basic God-given instincts of charity. Theologians admitted that certain inequities had occurred in the early stages of industrial development, but they believed that these anomalies caused by human frailty could not divert humanity away from God's plan. Once those diversions had been corrected by a raised social and spiritual consciousness, the benefits of the recent material progress would be shared by all and the Kingdom of God would be at hand. In this spirit, Social Gospel advocates went beyond the pulpit into the world of politics, economics, sociology, and activism.

An early and important influence in the Social Gospel movement was Henry George. Born in Philadelphia in 1839, this mostly self-educated man identified the land monopoly of the newly formed corporations as the primary reason for the massive poverty among the working class. He also believed that this imbalance went beyond economics; it was a violation of the law of God. He believed that land, like the air, was a gift from God to all humanity to share and use equally to create their own economic security. To correct the imbalance created by the massive land grab of the monopolies, especially the railroads, he proposed a tax on all profits made from land. The proceeds of this tax should be distributed to landless workers. As one historian has pointed out, "George conceived of land monopoly as a violation of God's law." Rooting his single-tax plan firmly in divine law, he was certain his plan would usher in a new Christian society and he proselytized with the fervor of missionary. As with Leo Tolstoy—who influenced George's ideas as well as that of many social gospelers—George believed in the practical application of the principles of the gospels. To follow Christ's teaching, he wrote, would lead to "the culmination of Christianity—the City of God on earth." George's reintroduction of the forgotten phrase, "Kingdom of God on Earth," became a central theme of the entire Social Gospel movement.[3]

George ran twice unsuccessfully for mayor of America's financial center, New York, where he hoped to implement his plan for economic and spiritual salvation. Although he never won election, his "Single Tax" idea captured the imagination of reformers and "Henry George Tax Clubs" sprang up in every major city in the nation. His frequent references to God and God's justice attracted a large number of theologians and clergy who were looking for a religious response to the social injustice they saw around them.[4]

George had a great influence on the thinking of Walter Rauschenbusch, who is often referred to as the principal theologian of the Social

Gospel movement. Born in Rochester in 1861, Rauschenbusch embodied an important characteristic of the Social Gospel movement: the marriage between social science and religion. He studied economics and theology at the University of Berlin and industrial relations in England. In his seminal work *Christianity and Social Crisis*, Rauschenbusch presented an outline of history that explained the economic crisis that most workers faced as a result of the industrial revolution. In the agricultural age he asserted the chief means of enrichment was to gain control of large landed wealth. The chief danger to the people lay in losing control of the great agricultural means of production, the land. Although in the preindustrial age there were wealthy classes who controlled more land than their poorer neighbors, possession of even a small amount of land meant some degree of economic independence. However, in the new industrial age, he wrote, access to "factories, the machines, the means of transportation, the money to finance great undertakings, are controlled by monopolies, and inaccessible to the average person." The people, Rauschenbusch concluded, "lost control of the tools of industry more completely than they ever lost control of the land." Additionally, the simple craft worker had been eliminated because he too lost control of his simple tools and had no ownership of the machines that now dominated the workplace. In the industrial capitalist system, he concluded, "human relationships have been reduced to competitive tension between a small group which owns all the material factors of land and machinery and a large group which owns nothing but the personal factor of human labor power." In this process, he wrote, "the propertyless group is at a fearful disadvantage. Furthermore, the new industrial wage system has destroyed the concept of a fair or just wage that existed in a previous era when craftsmen dominated the production process." Under the new industrial capital system Rauschenbusch observed that "no attempt is made to allot to each workman his share in the profits of the joint work. Instead he is paid a fixed wage." He further noted that "if a worker is poor or if he has a large family, he can be induced to take less wages." If his family is sick, or hungry, or for other reasons desperate for money, he may take even less. Therefore, Rauschenbusch concluded that the less the worker needs, the more he can get; the more he needs, the less he will get. This system, he argued, was contrary to natural law and the law of the family, "where the child that needs most care gets most."[5] The human community in times past could be compared to the family but in recent times, Rauschenbusch lamented, the family values of community and charity had been replaced by an amoral pursuit of profit and destructive competition.

To those who condemned the poor as being immoral, lazy, and in other ways solely responsible for their condition, Rauschenbusch responded that the industrial system was the root cause of immorality among the poor. "This constant insecurity and fear pervading the entire condition of the working people," he argued "is like a corrosive chemical that disintegrates their self-respect." He cited the example of an old man, who in the preindustrial age was able to look about him on the farm or business he had built up by the toil of his life, "with a profound satisfaction, that served as an antidote to the sense of declining strength and gradual failure." But in the industrial age an old man after a lifetime of honest work has nothing and is turned out of his work as useless, and is forced to eat the bread of dependence, in pitiable humiliation. Or, Rauschenbusch continued, "think of a man that is out of work for weeks, after offering his work and his body and soul at one place after the other, and to be told again and again that nobody has any use for such a man as he. It is no wonder that men take to drink when they are out of work." He concluded. To solve this growing social crisis Rauschenbusch called on industrial leaders to become "statesmen, prophets, and apostles who set truth and justice above selfish advancement [and] a new tide of religious faith and moral enthusiasm [with] new standards of duty and a new capacity for self-sacrifice." And, he concluded

> if the strong learn to direct their love of power to the uplifting of the people and see the highest self-assertion in self-sacrifice-then the entrenchments of vested wrong will melt away; the stifled energy of the people will leap forward; the atrophied members of the social body will be filled with a fresh flow of blood; and a regenerate nation will look with the eyes of youth across the fields of the future.[6]

Rauschenbusch's many allies in his call for a new age of Christianity included Washington Gladden a journalist turned preacher, who became the first well-known religious leader to support the unionization of workers. Also a founding member of the American Economic Association, Gladden, as many other social gospelers used "scientifically proven" social and economic facts to support his theology that called for an applied

Christianity that would Christianize the industrial age and thus ensure continued human progress toward the Kingdom of God. Other important leaders on the movement included Charles Sheldon, whose book entitled *In His Steps*, asked the practical question, "What would Jesus do?" if he lived in the contemporary world of industrialist exploitation and abject poverty of the working class. Another advocate of the Social Gospel, Richard Ely, also a cofounder of the American Economic Association, authored a book called *The Social Aspects of Christianity and Socialism*, in which he called for the practical application of Christian principles to social problems. The intersection of economic thought and theology at the turn of the century underscores the moral dilemma many economists suffered when they realized that the new industrial conglomerates had undermined the immutable—and what they believed to be—moral laws of Adam Smith.

Many Protestants picked up the banner of the Social Gospel. Although they came from various denominations, they struck a common theme that could be best summarized by excerpts from a sermon delivered by George Herron entitled "The Message of Jesus to Men of Wealth," which he delivered before the Minnesota Congregationalist Club in Minneapolis in 1890. He told his congregation that the existing social and religious order was wrong "because it placed a premium on competition, self-interest, and material power. Such a civilization failed to secure morality and justice," he warned, "since it put the weak at the mercy of the strong and at the same time minimized the paramount Christian principles of stewardship and sacrifice." Advocates of the Social Gospel determined that only a radical moral revival would stop the trend toward the amoral—profit motivated—world created by the industrialists. In this struggle they were eager to enlist government on their side, and clerics, whose religion, for centuries had eschewed the ways of the world suddenly embraced it, creating an alliance between economists, sociologists, theologians, and politicians.

Probably the most important example of the marriage between Social Gospel message and politics was the political career of William Jennings Bryan. Despite his strong identification with the Christian Fundamentalists who represented a counterpoint to the theology of the Social Gospel movement, Bryan stood firmly in the camp of those who called for the application of Christian principles to the social and economic inequalities of the day. When asked how he could be a Fundamentalist and at the same time support the applied Christianity of the Social Gospelers, Bryan replied. "People often ask me why I can be a progressive in politics and a fundamentalist in religion. The answer is easy. Government is man-made and therefore imperfect" and as such "it was made to be improved." On the other hand, "If Christ is the final word, how may anyone be progressive in religion?" Although not satisfied with government as it was, he was quite "satisfied with the God we have, with the Bible and with Christ." Bryan carried his religious precepts into his everyday world of politics. He understood that "a good democratic speech is so much like a sermon that you can hardly tell the difference between them." A good sermon, he believed was "built upon the ten commandments, the sermon on the mount, and the eleventh commandment, 'Thou shalt love thy neighbor as thyself.' And a good democratic speech is built upon the doctrine of human brotherhood, equal rights, and self-government, charity and justice." Although he preferred the term *Applied Christianity* to *Social Gospel*, in thought and action he was one with those who carried the banner of the latter.[7] That Bryan believed religion to be the source of his political ideas can be seen by many of his statements. "Whether I speak on politics, on social questions, or on religion," he declared, "I find the foundation of my speech in the philosophy of Him who spake as never man spake; who gave us a philosophy that fits into every human need and furnishes the solution for every problem that can vex a human heart or perplex the world."[8]

In the light of these principles, Bryan urged government ownership of those aspects of the economy, which should be enjoyed equally by all. That list included railroads, utilities, telegraph lines, pension plans, and the telephone. When accused of being a socialist, Bryan replied, "every cooperative effort of the government is open to that objection including the post office." The way to stop the spread of socialism and to protect property rights, he asserted, was to support reform and social justice.[9] Eventually Bryan's faithful reliance on his reading of the gospel to formulate political positions would bring him in conflict with Progressives. Just as Progressives were gearing the country up for entry into the great world war, Bryan's reading of the gospel convinced him the correctness and virtue of pacifism. Guided by the biblical admonition, "thou shalt not kill," and Christ's Sermon on the Mount, which blessed the peacemakers, he had to resign his position as secretary of state under President Woodrow Wilson when he thought his leader's actions after the sinking of the *Lusitania* would draw the country into war.

Although the Social Gospel movement was rooted in Protestantism, the Catholic Church at the time also had leaders who saw the need for a practical application of the gospels in order to rebalance the inequalities wrought by the industrialization of the late nineteenth century. Some Catholics were even drawn to the same thinkers that had attracted the Protestant reformers. For example, Father Edward McGlynn, for 30 years pastor of St. Stephen's, New York City's largest Roman Catholic Church, became Henry George's most devoted personal follower. He believed he did not mock sacred scriptures when he said, "There was a man sent of God whose name was Henry George."[10] Indeed, Father McGlynn considered *Progress and Poverty* "not merely political philosophy," but "a poem, a prophecy [and] a prayer." While most Catholic journals and authors dismissed George's ideas as dangerously socialistic, Father McGlynn remained the outstanding exception. Following George, he told his parishioners, to prepare their heart and mind "to receive and act out the old evangel of Him, who taught the universal Fatherhood of God and the equal Brotherhood of man."[11] Unfortunately for McGlynn, the Catholic hierarchy did not share his enthusiasm and Archbishop Michael Corrigan of New York —who considered George a dangerous radical—defrocked McGlynn when he refused to abandon his support for George.

McGlynn was eventually reinstated thanks to the efforts and influence of John Cardinal Gibbons of Baltimore, himself a great advocate for social justice. Warning the Pope that the Church could not afford to lose the working class in America as they had in Europe, he convinced the Pope of the workers' right to organize and thwarted an effort in Rome to excommunicate anyone who joined the Knights of Labor. Gibbons was also instrumental in the writing of the great Encyclical on the rights of workers, *Rerum Novarum*, in which Pope Leo XIII condemned abuses committed against laborers and told employers they had a moral obligation to pay workers a living wage, which he described as an amount sufficient for a worker to support his family, own a small piece of property, and to save enough for hard times when they came.

Despite theological differences among the various denominations, the Social Gospel movement drew them together on many common themes. They shared a common optimism that the new discoveries in technology and the social sciences created possibilities for a better world for everyone and that practical application of the gospels to the new challenges created by industrialization would help usher in a new age of grace. For the first time in many centuries Christians began to speak again of bringing the "Kingdom of God" to Earth, as opposed to living for the "hereafter." Another common theme of the Social Gospel was its masculinity. Despite the fact that a number of women such as Jane Addams and organizations such as the Woman's Christian Temperance Movement were closely linked to the Social Gospel, the movement remained an expression of masculinity. Social Gospelers believed that in order to address the moral challenges presented by the new industrial age, a new more muscular Christianity had to replace the sentimental and feminized religious expression of the nineteenth century. In 1911 and 1912, an interdenominational religious revival called Men and Religion Forward Movement (M&RFM) inspired male religious feelings across the country. Over a million men attended M&RFM events; organizers spent hundreds of thousands of dollars promoting events in seventy-six major cities and over a thousand small towns. The most unusual aspect of the revival was not its scope but its sex. The movement's purpose was to masculinize the Protestant churches by getting as many men as possible active in religion. According to *Collier's* magazine, the common sentiment was un-mistakable, "The women have had charge of the church work long enough." Addressing primarily a white, native-born, middle-class audience, the movement was sponsored by nearly every national Protestant men's organization and attracted the active support of a wide spectrum of prominent Protestant churchmen.[12] Although not its original intention, by creating a definite program of manly church work, the Men and Religion Forward Movement became what some historians have labeled a Social Gospel campaign. Social Gospel ministers, anxious for wider acceptance of their controversial call for a religiously mandated social activism, were able to use the Men and Religion Forward Movement as a vehicle for propagating the Social Gospel. They accomplished this by showing that the Social Gospel and social service activity could provide the churches with that elusive but all important element of masculine church work fit for manly men. They believed—correctly, as it turned out—that men looking for manly church work would respond to their vision of establishing the Kingdom on Earth by vigorously reforming the urban environment. Social Gospel theologian

Walter Rauschenbusch could write of the M&RFM, "The movement has probably done more than any other single agency to lodge the Social Gospel in the common mind of the Church. It has made social Christianity orthodox." One reason for this great success was that the Social Service Committees of the M&RFM addressed many of the same concerns which had originally led to middle-class men's fears of social effeminacy: cultural upheaval, a consumer economy, and threats to class dominance. Working on Social Service Committee projects allowed laymen to resist those threats both as Protestants and as men.[13] Armed with this new "scientific" knowledge, local "Men and Religion Forward," activists could move, as men, to take control over their communities by acting on a virile moralism—which had nothing to do with the old feminized religion—by closing brothels, working to improve housing regulations, or addressing labor unrest.[14]

Defined by its title, the Social Gospel movement was exclusively a Christian movement, but the desire to reform or to create moral values on an amoral economic system transcended religious differences. Often finding themselves excluded from Christian-driven charities, Jews in this era also began to form organizations to encourage the more fortunate of their co-religionists to be more charitable to the less fortunate of their own. By the middle of the second decade of the twentieth century, there were over 3,500 individual Jewish agencies in New York dedicated to helping indigent, sick, orphaned, and elderly Jews. In 1917 these diverse groups organized into the United Jewish Appeal. In that same year the new organization collected over $2 million that funded orphanages, hospitals, agencies for the sick and needy, and a home for the aged.

If the Social Gospelers could be seen as a positive reaction to the challenges presented by the new age of progress, Fundamentalists, who rejected all efforts to compromise their religion with the new sciences, represented the opposite. Social Gospelers advocated a practical application of theology designed to create a new morality for the industrial age. On the other hand, Fundamentalists rejected the new age of science and placed their entire trust in the Bible as the source of all wisdom. While Social Gospelers envisioned a collective salvation that would lead to a more just world guided by charity, Fundamentalists advocated individual redemption that would eventually usher in a renewed Christian—and therefore just—society.

Fundamentalists followed the wisdom of Dwight Moody, who could be considered the inspirational founder of the movement. His choice of books followed a simple rule. "I do not read any book," he said, "unless it helps me understand *the* Book." Fundamentalists eschewed theological nuance for the theatrical and emotional side of Christianity. They created a spirit of optimism, fellowship, and good feeling with the hope for a better future, which would arrive through an upheaval of love fueled by the energy of a Christian revival. Although often defined as a reaction to turn of the century progressive Christianity, the movement has earlier roots in an evangelical crusade launched by Dwight Moody in the 1870s. After attracting thousands of followers in England with his exuberant preaching, Moody returned home to the United States in 1876 and began the largest evangelical crusade the country had ever seen. Preaching an ardent message of their Savior's love, Moody in concert with the robust hymn singing Ira Sankey traveled throughout the Northeast and Midwest attracting thousands of followers. On January 19, 1876, President Ulysses S. Grant along with 12,000 others filled the old Pennsylvania freight depot in Philadelphia to listen to a Moody revival. That same year, in New York, about 60,000 people a day filled the halls at the Great Roman Hippodrome on Madison Avenue for the daily rallies held from February 7 to April 19. Over the next two decades, Moody's conversion caravan moved on to places such as the West Coast and middle-sized cities across America. His last crusade started in November, 1899, in Kansas City, where shortly after delivering a sermon on excuses, he died.

Upon Moody's death William B. Riley, a young Baptist preacher who had adopted much of Moody's style and was often described in the press as a "second Dwight L. Moody," immediately became recognized as his spiritual successor. From the late 1890s through the first decade of the twentieth century in revival meetings around the Midwest and Northwest, Riley told crowds to follow the Bible. "God is the one and only author," he declared, and "every book, chapter, sentence, and even word," which came straight from God was absolute authority. The Bible's integrity, he declared, "extends to history as well as to morals and religion, and involves expression as well as thought." His simple and forceful message resonated especially with persons on the bottom rungs of the middle class who filled his rallies. Expressing the fundamentalist belief that reform would come through an upheaval of Christian love and not political action, Riley asserted that only when the electorate becomes a unified body of "God-fearing, righteous-living men," will politics become a powerful influence. Until then he urged individually saved Christians to serve the urban poor. In the end he hoped that politics would become a tool of a strongly Christian nation. He disagreed with Social Gospelers who compromised their religion thus allowing Christianity to become tool of politicians when in a truly Christian world the opposite should be true. He condemned Social Gospelers' willingness to allow scripture to be manipulated for political purpose. Protestant denominations were coming increasingly under the sway of modernism and what Riley called its "awful harvest of skepticism." The only true path to salvation, he insisted, was to follow his hyper literal approach to the Bible and accept that supernatural forces have shaped history. Riley urged delegates to stand by their traditional faith in the face of the modernist threat: "God forbid that we should fail him in the hour when the battle is heavy."[15]

Much of the attraction to fundamentalism was energized by the emotional ecstasy experienced by believers captivated by the stirring orations delivered by charismatic preachers who with great skill produced verbal portraits of the fires of hell, the evil of the Devil, the goodness of God, and the wonders of heaven. More often than not these preachers had very little education. They had no diploma from schools of divinity or theology, but rather they had received a "personal call" from God to preach his Word. One such example was Billy Sunday, born in 1862 in Iowa and raised in an orphanage. He used his baseball skills to lift himself out of poverty, and after a respectable career as a professional ball player, Sunday experienced a conversion and a "call" to serve the Lord. He left baseball and began preaching in the Midwest. Soon he attracted large crowds who listened as he told his story of personal redemption from drunken, rowdy ball player to a humble God-fearing Christian. They watched him wrestle with the devil on stage, call out to sinners in the audience to renounce their life of perdition, and generally left his listeners convinced they had witnessed the Holy Spirit in action. As his fame grew, he attracted more followers than any other evangelist in the preelectronic age. Over 300,000 followers of Billy Sunday committed themselves to follow the preacher's "sawdust trail" to salvation. His successful career brought him a financial fortune and invitations into the homes of the

One of scores of Christian fundamentalist preachers who urged listeners to embrace "old time religion" as an answer to the complexities of modern life, Billy Sunday enthralled crowds by wrestling with the devil as he preached on stage. (Library of Congress)

country's most powerful and influential people. Sunday accepted the dominant myth of the age, the inevitability of human progress. Along with the material progress already realized, he anticipated a spiritual upheaval that would bring a better future for all including those suffering from social injustice. But like most fundamentalists he believed that social reform would come as a result of personal salvation. In his famous "Booze Sermon" he declared that,

> Jesus Christ was God's revenue officer ... I challenge you to show me where the saloon has ever helped business, education, church, morals or anything we hold dear. ... I go to a family and it is broken up, and I say, "What caused this?" Drink! I step up to a young man on the scaffold and say, "What brought you here?" Drink! Whence all the misery and sorrow and corruption? Invariably it is drink.[16]

"I am a temperance Republican down to my toes," Sunday told listeners, and his tirades against alcohol played an important part in the passage of the Eighteenth Amendment, but most of his fellow Fundamentalists eschewed politics. They opposed Social Gospelers who were clearly interpreting the Bible for their own purpose and who made alliances with skeptics and nonbelievers in their pursuit of social reform. They opposed, for example, Rauschenbusch for comparing Jesus to a modern sociologist. Fundamentalists believed that social injustice was the result of people abandoning God for mammon. And reform would not come from political action or alliances but rather as a result of collective and individual actions of those who had been personally redeemed. This policy changed in the 1920s when they became actively involved in legislation outlawing the teaching of Darwinism.

Despite theological differences, both the Social Gospelers and the Fundamentalists agreed that much of the social injustice that existed at the turn of the century was the result of greedy individuals who pursued their own wealth selfishly and without regard to the suffering they caused for thousands of less fortunate workers, whom they exploited for their own gain. In response, those who saw virtue in the pursuit of material gain proclaimed the "Gospel of Wealth" as outlined by Andrew Carnegie in an article he wrote in 1889.

"The problem of our age is the proper administration of wealth, so that the ties of brotherhood may still bind together the rich and poor in harmonious relationship," wrote Carnegie. He noted that in the recent past "the conditions of human life have not only been changed, but revolutionized," and it is the duty of those who have accumulated wealth in this new age "to set an example of modest, unostentatious living, shunning display or extravagance; to provide moderately for the legitimate wants of those dependent upon him." But he warned, charity should not be given indiscriminately. "For one of the serious obstacles to the improvement of our race is indiscriminate charity. . . . It were better for mankind that the millions of the rich were thrown in to the sea than so spent as to encourage the slothful, the drunken, the unworthy." There are deserving and undeserving poor, he pointed out, and it is the moral obligation of the prudent rich to determine carefully who should receive charity. "In bestowing charity," he pointed out, the main consideration should be to help those who will help themselves; to provide part of the means by which those who desire to improve may do so. "Those worthy of assistance, except in rare cases, seldom require assistance," he believed, and "The really valuable men of the race never do, except in cases of accident or sudden change." The only person that can call himself a true reformer, therefore, is the one who "is as careful and as anxious not to aid the unworthy as he is to aid the worthy, and, perhaps, even more so, for in alms-giving more injury is probably done by rewarding vice than by relieving virtue." But like Fundamentalists and Social Gospel advocates, Carnegie believed in the inevitability of human progress, he may have disagreed with his co-religionists who advocated Christian charity as the vehicle to human betterment but he did agree, that the world would soon reach its destiny which is "to solve the problem of the Rich and the Poor, and to bring 'Peace on earth, among men Good-Will.' "[17]

The material advance that came at a dizzying pace in the last decades of the nineteenth century captured the imagination of everyone to-the point that a new mantra, "Progress" entered the conversation of every aspect of American life, including religion. Although most Protestants continued to worship in the centuries old manner prescribed by Martin Luther, John Calvin, and John Wesley, and Catholics continued to celebrate Mass in the format established by the Council of Trent in 1563, no one could deny the forces that affected their own time. And no matter how people of faith in America viewed God they all could agree that they were living in a blessed time and place and that forces both material and physical were converging toward the point where they could realize the "Kingdom of God" on Earth.

NOTES

1. C. S. Lewis, "The Problem of Pain," *The Complete C.S. Lewis* (New York: Signet Classics, 2002), 618.

2. David W. Noble, "The Paradox of Progressive Thought," *American Quarterly* 5, no. 3 (Autumn 1953): 207.

3. Fred Nicklason, "Henry George: Social Gospeller," *American Quarterly* 22, no. 3 (Autumn 1970): 649–50.

4. Ibid.

5. Walter Rauschenbusch, *Christianity and the Social Crisis* (New York: Macmillan, 1907), 232–43.

6. Ibid.

7. Willard H. Smith, "William Jennings Bryan and the Social Gospel," *The Journal of American History* 53, no. 1 (June 1966): 41–2.

8. Ibid.

9. Ibid., pp. 45–6.

10. Fred Nicklason, "Henry George: Social Gospeller," *American Quarterly* 22, no. 3 (Autumn 1970): 650–51.

11. Ibid., p. 657.

12. Gail Bederman "The Women Have Had Charge of the Church Work Long Enough: The Men and Religion Forward Movement of 1911–1912 and the Masculinization of Middle-Class Protestantism" *American Quarterly* 41, no. 3 (September 1989): 432.

13. Ibid., pp. 448–49.

14. Ibid.

15. Douglas O. Linder, "Putting Evolution on the Defensive: William B. Riley and the Rise of Fundamentalism in America," 2005. Accessed July 2, 2014. http:/law2.umkc.edu/faculty/projects/ftrials/conlaw/Fundamentalism.html.

16. Billy Sunday, *Billy Sunday Speaks*, David Gullen ed. (Philadelphia: Chelsea House Publishers, 1980), 53.

17. Andrew Carnegie, "Wealth," *North American Review* 148, no. 391 (June 1889): 653–65.

CHAPTER 9

PRESIDENT THEODORE ROOSEVELT TAKES ON BIG BUSINESS, BIG LABOR, AND CONSERVATION

This country will not be a permanently good place for any of us to live
in unless we make it a reasonably good place for all of us to live in.
—Theodore Roosevelt[1]

In 1901 Progressives mourned the assassination of President William McKinley. But their grief was tempered by the consolation of knowing that after fighting the battle for reform in the trenches of local and state government for over a decade they now had one of their own in the White House. Roosevelt, of course, was shaken by the assassination (the third within the lifetime of many), and it was a terrible way to enter the presidency, but it did not hinder him from embracing it with the energy and enthusiasm that defined his entire life. Years later, when the American businessman and diplomat William vanden Heuvel commented to Roosevelt's daughter Alice that the president must have suffered a "terrible moment of sorrow," she responded "Are you kidding?" On the Sunday morning after the assassination, Roosevelt awoke and after fueling his already explosive nature with a generous supply of caffeine exclaimed, "I feel Bully!"[2] More than likely most reform-minded Progressives felt the same.

With one of their own in the White House, Progressives could now take on challenges that required national leadership. Specifically, Progressives sought to stem the seemingly uncontrollable abuses of power of big business, the devastation of the environment for purposes of economic gain, and the increasingly violent nature of labor-capital relations, which threatened to undermine the political principles on which the country stood. In Roosevelt, many Progressives believed they had found their champion, though some doubted his ability to work with the still divided Progressive movement. Immediately after McKinley's burial in Ohio, Roosevelt rushed back to Washington and the next morning sprang up the steps of the White House, entered his new office in the West Wing, sat behind the desk that a week before had been McKinley's, and began dictating letters to William Loeb. "He looked as if he had been there for years" an observer remarked, "quite the strangest introduction of a Chief Magistrate . . . in our national history."[3]

Using his "Bully Pulpit" President Roosevelt introduced Progressives' concerns into the national political agenda. (Library of Congress)

But the enthusiasm soon dissipated. After five months in office Roosevelt had done nothing more notable than enrage Southerners by inviting Booker T. Washington to dine at the White House and confound the senate's attempt to formulate a proposal to build a canal through Nicaragua. Jokes began to circulate that "Terrible Teddy" was good for nothing but dining with black men and exercising the diplomatic corps. Roosevelt knew he had to do something to assert his own power and control over the office, and although Republican political boss Mark Hanna warned him to go slowly, his own nature as a man of action would not allow him to passively allow events to dictate his course. "The time has come," he told a friend, "when my course has to be definitely shaped." An editorial cartoon that appeared in *Life* magazine suggested what that action should be. Edward Kimble had drawn a giant ogre with knife in hand gorging and grinning on plates of helpless trussed human beings. Scratched across his belly was the word *Trusts*. Below the giant, the president climbed up a beanstalk with clenched teeth and an ax in his belt. Under the cartoon a caption read "Will Jack reach the Ogre?"[4]

The cartoon was not a whimsical dart at the president. The people wanted Roosevelt to grapple with the "ogre" corporations. At that moment, the bull's-eye on the target of American's antitrust sentiment was the great Northern Securities Company, which J. P. Morgan had recently formed to control virtually all rail lines that connected the burgeoning Northwest to eastern markets. In the previous months, the superior financial and legal power of Northern Securities crushed the attempt of the governor of Minnesota, Samuel Van Sent, to break up the company by court order. Most Progressives agreed that nothing less than the power of the federal government was needed to address these powerful new economic forces. Novels such as the *Octopus* (1901) and nonfiction works such as *Wealth Against Commonwealth* (1894), and the enthusiastic response to the investigative reporting of *McClure's* magazine, reflected the disquieting effect that the rapid rise of corporations had on many Americans, especially those in the middle class and the working class. Small independent family-owned businesses, whose proprietors believed that they paid workers a fair wage and charged a fair price, based on ethical and practical economic theory, feared that large corporations disrupted the eternal laws of supply and demand as enumerated by Adam Smith, whose principles had been ingrained in them since their schooldays. Corporate violation of these eternal laws had already disrupted the established order of things. Myriad failures of small businesses, riots in Homestead, Pennsylvania, and Pullman, Illinois, the Populist uprising in the farm country, and the unionization of workers in the cities all served to underscore the consequences of the distorted economic order that the trusts had created and over which they ruled.

For the sake of making sense out of their shifting economic world, Americans attached names to the phenomena of capital growth. None stood out more boldly than J. Pierpont Morgan. Born in 1837 in Hartford, Connecticut, to Juliette Pierpoint and her wealthy banker husband Junius Spencer Morgan, the young Morgan received the most sophisticated education the times could offer. After attending the English High School of Boston, he went to universities in Switzerland, Germany, and London. In addition to mastering European banking and finance practices, his education abroad enabled him to gain fluency in both French and German. After completing his studies, he began his career in the London branch of the banking house of Peabody, Morgan, and Company, which his father had cofounded. In 1858 he moved to New York where he continued to work for his father's banking house. During the Civil War he purchased 5,000 defective rifles from an army arsenal at $3.50 each and resold them to the army for $22 apiece. With these profits he partnered with the Drexel family of Philadelphia to form in 1871 what would eventually become the J.P. Morgan banking house. He continued to amass his fortune by buying troubled businesses, reorganizing them, and selling them at huge profits— a process that became known as *Morganization*. By 1900, the J.P. Morgan banking house was the largest in the United States and one of the most powerful in the world. The company controlled an annual income and expenditure nearly equal to that of Imperial Germany, paid taxes on a debt greater than that of the smaller nations of Europe, and employed 250,000 men, who supported a population of over a million. In the latter years of the nineteenth century, the House of Morgan had rescued the country from financial collapse on three different occasions.[5]

In 1901 his business acumen thwarted another near economic catastrophe. Averill Harriman, president of the Union Pacific Railroad, and J.P. Hill of the Great Northern Railroad, two of the largest railroads in the United States, sought to gain control of the Burlington Railroad in order to connect their western lines to the vital railroad hub of

Chicago, Illinois. The internecine bidding war that ensued threatened to break both railroads and to bring down the entire stock market as well. J.P. Morgan stepped into the fray and his negotiations brought corporate peace. The treaty called for joint ownership by Harriman, Hill, Rockefeller, and Morgan of a new holding company named Northern Securities, which in effect would monopolize railroad transportation between the Northwest and Chicago. To a collective public mind raised on the principles of fair competition, this latest amalgamation of economic giants, if not criminal, certainly represented an impediment to fair competition, which—common knowledge agreed—stimulated economic progress.

With his sensitive hand on the public pulse, Roosevelt knew he had to take action on this issue that his predecessor had been reluctant to undertake. Attorney General Philander C. Knox assured Roosevelt that, if properly argued, the Sherman Anti-trust Act could be used to break up the Northern Securities Trust, and "If you instruct me to bring such a suit," he assured Roosevelt, "I can promise we will win." Moved by public anxiety and his attorney general's confidence, Roosevelt instructed Knox to proceed with the suit. Shortly after the announcement that "within a very short time a bill will be filed by the United States to test the [combination of] Northern Pacific and Great Northerner Systems through the instrumentality of the Northern Securities Company," the tickers that rattled out financial information in all the major banking houses of the country reported a rapid collapse in the market. After spending the day buying up stock in order to bolster prices, a flabbergasted J.P. Morgan and a coterie of his officers descended on Washington, D.C. Morgan announced that he was in town to dine with his good friend Senator Chauncey Depew. But the meal was anything but convivial; Henry Adams later wrote that "Pierpont sulked like a child throughout the meal." After dinner they received an invitation from Roosevelt for an evening cordial, which they accepted. They certainly did not want to be convivial with this young upstart who wanted to upset years of cultivated and purchased government compliance, but a presidential invitation, of course, could not be declined. The meeting was coldly cordial and without substance. Each side remained formally polite, and neither party mentioned the Northern Securities case.[6]

But the next morning Morgan arrived alone to find the president in his office with his attorney general at his side. There they stood—the de facto financial leader of the country against the democratically elected leader of the people. An observer in the room would have heard the following:

MORGAN: Why had the administration not asked us to correct irregularities in the new trusts charter?

ROOSEVELT: That is exactly what we did not want to do.

MORGAN: If we have done anything wrong, send your man to my man and they can fix it up.

Roosevelt: That can't be done

KNOX: We don't want to fix it up we want to stop it.

MORGAN: Are you going to go attack my other interests, the Steel trust and others?

ROOSEVELT: Certainly not—unless we find out that in any case they have done something we regard as wrong.

Alone with Knox, Roosevelt later mused, "That is a most illuminating illustration of the Wall Street point of view." Morgan could think of the president of the United States only as "a big rival operator" with whom he had to cut a deal.

In the weeks that followed, the great financial leader Morgan could do nothing more than plead not to be included in the lawsuit by name and forced to testify. Morgan's attorneys had argued that the indignity of a courtroom appearance would undermine the credit of the United States. But Knox was adamant, and James Hill and J. Pierpont Morgan were both named as defendants. Hill was the angriest and most determined to take the case to the Supreme Court. Hill declared that he was damned if he was going to dismantle the world's greatest transportation combine because of "political adventurers who have never done anything but pose and draw a salary."[7] But in the end he did.

On Monday, March 14, 1902, word spread that the anticipated Supreme Court decision would be announced that day. Chief Justice Melville Fuller seated himself and waited until the chamber had settled. After dealing with some less substantial issues, he finally nodded to Justice John Marshall Harlan and asked for his opinion on case number 197, the Northern Securities case. Noisy movement of chairs and doors followed as clerks ran off to alert congressmen that the Northern Securities decision was about to be rendered.

Justice Harlan summarized the facts, which showed that in 1901 defendant Hill and defendant Morgan had combined the Great Northern and Pacific railroads into a holding company headquartered in New Jersey making the interests of all stockholders of the various companies identical. "No scheme or device," he decided, "could more certainly come within the words of the [Sherman] Act or could more effectively and certainly suppress free competition. The judgment of the Court is that the decree below be and hereby is affirmed." Each justice in turn voted, and in the end the decision was a five to four. It represented a victory for Roosevelt but not the decisive one he had hoped for. The surprise vote in favor of the trust came from Oliver Wendell Holmes, whom Roosevelt had counted as a political and intellectual collaborator. Dissenting from Harlan's majority opinion, Holmes lectured that "Great cases . . . make bad law. For great cases are called great not by reason of their real importance in shaping law of the future but because of some accident of immediate overwhelming interest which appeals to the feelings and distort the judgment." He implied that "an accident of immediate overwhelming interests"—namely Theodore Roosevelt—had made "an emotional issue out of the Northern Securities case which exaggerated its legal significance."[8]

Roosevelt felt betrayed. He doubted Holmes's intellectual integrity and surmised that his presumed ally had collapsed under the political pressure of the business wing of his Republican Party. "I could carve out of a banana a judge with more backbone than [Holmes]" he decried.

When he heard the president's comment, Holmes, ever the gentleman, retorted, "I have such confidence in his great heartedness that I don't expect for a moment that after he has had time to cool down it will affect our relations."[9]

Roosevelt's decision to take on Northern Securities evolved from the mind of a thoughtful man, who understood the fears that many in the middle class had for unbridled power of the newly formed corporations. But he understood the complexity of the role of corporations in a rapidly transforming economy. In his first address to Congress he shared his thoughts on trusts:

> The mechanism of modern business is so delicate that extreme care must be taken not to interfere with it in a spirit of rashness or ignorance. Many of those who have made it their vocation to denounce the great industrial

combinations which are popularly, although with technical inaccuracy, known as "trusts," appeal especially to hatred and fear. These are precisely the two emotions, particularly when combined with ignorance, which unfit men for the exercise of cool and steady judgment[10]

On one hand, trusts brought order to the very disorderly economic expansion of the post-Civil War years. On the other hand they had the potential to suppress competition, control prices, and exploit workers. He also worried that a constitution, conceived in a preindustrial world, could be fashioned to address challenges created by modern corporations. Roosevelt's thought process brought him to the conclusion that there were good trusts that should survive and bad trusts that should be broken up, and that the only force up to the task was a well-informed federal government empowered by popular will. Or as he told Congress, it was his "sincere conviction that combination and concentration should be, not prohibited, but supervised and within reasonable limits controlled; and in my judgment this conviction is right." The corollary to this conclusion was that since the president was the only person elected by all the people, he alone should in the name of the people be the final arbitrator who distinguished good trusts from bad.

In order to wield this power, Roosevelt forged a new weapon, the Bureau of Corporations, which would have the power to investigate the activities of trusts and corporations and make recommendations to the president based on those investigations. Fearing political opposition, Roosevelt began the creation of this bureau by supporting a bill to establish a Department of Commerce and Labor, the Elkins Anti-Rebate bill, and a bill to expedite the handling of cases originating under the antitrust and interstate commerce laws. To this bill he urged an additional rather innocuous appearing amendment that created a Bureau of Corporations within the newly proposed department.[11] The responsibility of the bureau, as set forth in the bill, was simply to gather information and data on companies doing interstate business in order to enable the president "to make recommendations to Congress." The bill also allowed the president to publish—at his discretion—any information obtained by the bureau. Roosevelt believed he could use the threat of negative publicity to cow corporations he considered "bad." The point was not lost on congressmen who opposed giving the president such unrestricted power. "We all know," one congressman complained, "that the President has repeatedly said that there are 'good and bad trusts.' Who should be the judge on such a question? It should not be one man. It should be the law, under the rules and regulations prescribed for eliciting the truth."[12] Despite opposition from some members of Congress and major corporations, such as Standard Oil, Roosevelt got his Bureau of Corporations. It soon became his principal weapon for exercising substantial executive control in the regulation of big business. Like any new weapon, Roosevelt had to learn how to use it.

His first attempt to wield his new power ended disastrously. In order to strengthen the prosecutor's case against the Beef Trusts, he released the results of a bureau investigation of the industry. Lawyers for the defendants claimed that since the testimony given to the bureau by their clients was compelled, it violated their Fifth Amendment rights. The judge concurred, and the case was thrown out. However, in 1906 when senators friendly to the meatpackers refused to support the passage of a bill providing for a rigid federal meat inspection program, Roosevelt threatened to reveal his inspectors' report, which described meat packing facilities in a condition far worse than described in Upton Sinclair's *Jungle*. They reported, "Pillars caked with offal, dried blood, and flesh [and] unspeakable uncleanliness." Faced with this threat, the senate resistance collapsed.[13] Later cases such as the one against Standard Oil successfully used testimony obtained from the Bureaus of Corporations. According to one historian, "In publicizing corporate abuses and in helping to prosecute offenders, the Bureau proved very useful to the President in his role as 'trustbuster'." It also helped him to meet the needs of a transition period in the development of public policy toward big business and to fulfill his promise to Progressives that he would bring big business under control.[14] Finally, Roosevelt's bureau helped reduce to some extent the anxiety of many Americans, who trusted that their president had the ability to distinguish good trusts from bad trusts and the power to act accordingly.

While public attention remained focused on the trusts, Roosevelt held an equal concern for the forces emerging in the industrial working class, which remained the neglected child of the newly emerging corporations. He believed that the rising tide of unionism, socialism, and anarchism, which threatened American life—as he viewed it—were the consequences of corporation owners' indifference to the welfare of wage workers. *Homestead, Pullman, Haymarket, Mother Jones, Debs, Goldman,* and *Czolgosz*—all were flash words that warned middle-class Americans that their ordered universe was threatening to spin out of control. Roosevelt determined that unless the federal government addressed the terrible imbalance of power between labor and capital, the accelerating forces of labor unrest could explode into all-out class war. His immediate barrier to addressing the problem was his own political party. Republicans had controlled the national political agenda since the election of Lincoln and had not only endorsed the growth of corporations but also had supported it with land grants to railroads, protective tariffs, and benign indifference to monopolization. When workers finally started to organize and protest their wretched conditions, the government continued support of corporations by using court injunctions and federal troops to crush strikes.

Unless the government began to take a more evenhanded approach to labor relations, Roosevelt believed less rational voices could drive collective anger of the workers to class war. His first opportunity to alter the historic role of the federal government in labor relations came early in his administration when the miners of Pennsylvania took on the largest coal conglomerate in the nation. In 1900, coal fueled 90 percent of the American industrial economy. Coal provided the fuel that heated homes and powered the engines that drove the factories, which had made the United States the greatest producer of manufactured goods in the world by the end of the nineteenth century.

A prolonged halt in the production of coal threatened to have a devastating effect on the economy, and on May 12, 1902, that possibility became more probable when 140,000 coal miners in Pennsylvania went on strike. They demanded a 20 percent increase in pay, an eight-hour work day, and recognition of the United Mine Workers (UMW) as their sole bargaining agent. John Mitchell, the charismatic president of the UMW, said if the American people could see "the sorrows and heartaches of those who spend their lives in the coal mines, they would sympathize with the mineworkers." He lamented that "the lives of those who delve into the bowels of the earth . . . remained darkly hidden . . . from the sight of their fellow beings."[15] The coal miners had a hard battle to fight. Like beef, oil, and the railroads, the coal industry had also created a tremendous holding company comprising of a few owners who held oligarchic power over the industry. Before being taken over by the trusts, local mine owners had lived close to the miner, so that not only did they understand their workers interests and problems, they knew a strike could devastate their business. Based on that relationship, operators and workers could negotiate livable although not always satisfactory agreements. In the new order of things, financiers with vast mine field holdings had little concern over a job action in one mine. Working from big city corporate offices far removed from the minefield, with little knowledge of the industry or its challenges, they made labor contract decisions—as they made any other contract decisions —based on nothing more than the bottom line. For example, in the months preceding the strike, the miners had agreed to ask for a 5 percent increase in pay, which would have represented an increase in expenses of $3,000,000 for an industry realizing $75,000,000 in profit. But George Baer, president of the Philadelphia Reading Railroad and director of the coal industry trust, flatly refused. With an arrogance nourished by his unchallenged power, he pre-dicted that with the mere threat of a coal shortage he could bring public opinion to his side and pressure the workers back to the mines. He told a concerned citizen's group, "I beg of you not to be discouraged. The rights and interests of the laboring man will be protected and cared for—not by labor agitators, but by the Christian men to whom God in his infinite wisdom has given control of the property interests of the country."[16]

But Baer misjudged the public animus. By midsummer public opinion was moving in favor of the workers and union president John Mitchell was becoming a folk hero to many. In a time when unions received very little favorable publicity, one reporter wrote, "No better strike leader than John Mitchell has ever emerged in anytime of industrial strife." He con-ducted himself without "bitterness or retort." When the public learned that Baer had refused Mitchell's promise to comply with the decision of an impartial arbitration committee, support for the union leader increased. When asked by a reporter why he did not agree to work out a compromise based on the findings of a mutually agreed on arbitration committee, Baer responded, "Anthracite mining is a business, and not a religious, sentimen-tal, or academic proposition. . . . I could not delegate this business manage-ment to even so highly a respectable body as the Civic Federation, nor can I call to my aid . . . the eminent prelates you have named."[17] Aided by the arrogance of Baer, the UMWs were clearly winning the battle for public support as the strike dragged on through the summer.

As the strike continued into the fall and the winter approached, Roosevelt became increasingly concerned, "A coal famine in the winter is an ugly thing," he told Mark Hanna, "and I fear we shall see terrible suffering and grave disaster."[18] As was his nature, he decided to use his own powers of persuasion to break the impasse. Before summoning the conflicting parties, he sent his secretary of labor and commerce to the coal field to investigate and with the same self-confidence that told him he could determine good corporations from bad ones, he decided with proper information he could determine if a strike was justified. With report in hand he determined that the strikers had legitimate grievances that had remained unaddressed by the owners and decided to break precedent by using his presidential power to urge the owners to negotiate with the union. On October 1, 1902, he sent identical telegrams to the coal operator's board of directors and to the directors of the UMW. For the first time in the country's history the president had beckoned leaders of capital and labor to the White House to negotiate on equal terms. The newspapers already leaning to the side of union president Mitchell in this dispute faithfully reported that representatives of the owners each arrived in their own elaborate carriage in plume-covered livery, while the union representatives trudged down Pennsylvania Avenue from Union Station with their grips still in hand and boarded streetcars to the White House.[19]

Roosevelt began the meeting by stating that, "three parties [were] affected by the situation in the anthracite trade—the operators, the miners, and the general public." He assured the representatives that he spoke for neither side present but rather for the general public, and he appealed to their shared patriotism—that he mistakenly believed all felt to the same degree he did—to set personal considerations aside and "make individual sacrifices for the general good." Moved by the president's appeal, Mitchell jumped up and enthusiastically restated his promise to negotiate any time, any place, with anyone and affirmed his willingness to abide by conclusions reached by any mutually agreed upon arbitration board even if the decisions went against his own views. Roosevelt was pleasantly taken aback by Mitchell's eagerness to settle the dispute on the spot, but he admitted that he was not prepared to respond to such a statement. He then asked the mine owners what they thought of Mitchell's proposal. Unsurprisingly, George Baer stood up and—much to Roosevelt's chagrin—declared, "We cannot agree to any proposal put forth by Mr. Mitchell." Roosevelt later confided that he was stunned by "the stupidity and bad behavior of the mine operators," who belittled Attorney General Knox for not invoking the Sherman Antitrust Act to put an injunction on the strike and even criticized the president for not sending in federal troops to preserve order. "Mr. Mitchell towered above them all," Roosevelt noted. At one point in the discussion, he confessed that he wanted to take one of the mine owners "by the seat of the breeches and nape of the neck and chuck him out the window."[20]

A frustrated Mitchell returned to the coal fields and an arrogant Baer to New York, and the strike raged on. When outbreaks of violence left several dead and hundreds injured and a general strike threatened, Roosevelt ordered Secretary of War Elihu Root to put 10,000 troops on immediate alert. At the same time he sent Root to New York to meet with J.P. Morgan, who had agreed to do what he could to end the impasse. Although still smarting from the Northern Trust suit—which he considered a personal affront—filed only eight months earlier, he recognized the looming catastrophe of a coal shortage and agreed to help the president. Roosevelt planned for more drastic action. Placing General John Schofield in charge of the reserves, he told him, "I bid you pay no heed to any authority ... [not even] a writ from a judge ... [you will follow] only my commands." He told Schofield he "must be ready at a half hours' notice to invade Pennsylvania, dispossess the operators, end the strike, and run the mines as a receiver for the government." When Republican House Whip James Watson railed against the president's actions asking "What about the Constitution?" An exasperated Roosevelt grabbed the congressman by the shoulder and shouted, "The Constitution was made for the people not the people for the Constitution!" After a day and a half of negotiating on Morgan's yacht the *Corsair*, Root and Morgan worked out an arbitration compromise that included an impartial commission appointed by the president. In essence it comprised the same conditions as proposed by Mitchell during the Washington meeting, but Baer, a railroad president, with deep roots in America's moneyed class, would never have negotiated directly with Mitchell whom he considered nothing more than a "common coal miner." Morgan met with Baer and other mine owners at the Union Club in New York City. After some modifications the owners accepted the arbitration compromise. After agreeing to name the Bishop of Baltimore John Lancaster Spalding and Edgar E. Clark chief of the Railroad Conductors Union to the commission, Mitchell also agreed and immediately called off the strike. The miners returned to work, the violence and the threat of a general strike subsided and a disastrous energy crisis was averted. The arbitration commission continued its work for three months. They heard testimony from over 500 witnesses representing each side of the dispute. In his final presentation, Baer tried to convince the committee that coal workers were not suffering. How could they? He exclaimed, "Half of them don't even speak English!"[21]

In the end the committee concluded that although conditions in the mines were bad, they were not as drastic as the coal miners depicted. They recommended a nine-hour work day (not the eight-hour day proposed by the union) and also an increase in pay of 10 percent (less than the 20 percent demand of the strikers). Much to the chagrin of Mitchell, the arbitration committee did not recommend recognition of the union as the sole arbitrator for the workers. But as promised, Mitchell abided by all the recommendations of the committee and urged his workers to do the same. Despite the defeat of union recognition and the limited gains won, the arbitration marked a great turning point in the labor history of the United States. With Roosevelt's decision to promote arbitration and his willingness to use armed forces to seize the mines, he reversed the U.S. government role in labor relations from strike breaker to evenhanded negotiator. Once again he stretched the president's constitutional powers from their preindustrial roots into the industrial age. He also gained popular acclaim for working out what he called "A Square Deal" that benefited all interests.

Corporation arrogance not only led them to abuse of human resources but the country's natural resources as well, and many Progressive reformers took up the call to protect the country's rapidly depleting natural heritage. Actually, the conservation movement predated Progressivism as a political movement. In the early 1890s groups such as the American Forestry Association along with lobbyists such as John Muir, George Grinnell, and Theodore Roosevelt and the future senator of Nevada Francis Newlands were beginning to be heard, and in 1891 Congress passed the Forest Reserve Act of 1891, which allowed the president of the United States to set aside forest reserves from the land in the public domain. The movement gained momentum in the decade of the nineties. It was spurred not in small part by the growing sentiment that the frontier was an essential part of the national character and—as documented by the 1890 census—was rapidly disappearing. In 1893 at a presentation given at the World's

Fair in Chicago, Frederick Jackson Turner, influenced greatly by Theodore Roosevelt's *Winning of the West* (1889), told the American people that their frontier had created a new and unique type of citizen, but that the frontier phase of American history was passing and a new urban United States, which would redefine the country, was emerging. Then in 1901 fate had placed the person who had inspired Turner's reimaging of the frontier in the White House.[22] Following his cautionary swipes at corporations and his precedent-setting resolution of the coal strike, President Roosevelt launched into his conservation campaign full steam.[23] To Roosevelt, forest management and national greatness were one and the same.[24] Upon entering office in 1901 he discovered that bureaucratic confusion reigned supreme in the area of resource management. From 1886 to 1918, for example, Yellowstone, Grand Sequoia, and several other national parks remained protected by the U.S. Army. But the land adjacent to the park was under the supervision of the Department of Interior.[25] Immediately Roosevelt deviated from McKinley's policies of benign neglect, which used positions charged with protection of the country's natural heritage as political rewards. Roosevelt told Interior Secretary Ethan Allen Hitchcock that nobody should be employed in the Interior simply for political reasons. Instead Roosevelt wanted "good plainsmen and mountain men able to walk and ride and lie out at night as any first class men must be able to do"[26] With this mandate, the professionalization of forestry and wildlife protection in both the Departments of Interior and Agriculture began.[27] He also appointed Gifford Pinchot the head of the Division of Forestry within the Department of Interior. Born in 1865, Pinchot's father made a fortune in lumbering and land speculation, for which he later had a deep regret for the harm he had done to the natural environment. In his later years the elder Pinchot made land restoration his central ambition and urged his son to go into forestry. After studying at Yale and later at the French National School of Forestry, Gifford Pinchot returned to the United States to become a leading force in the burgeoning forestry movement that promoted the establishment of a national forestry policy. It was Pinchot who appropriated the word *conservation* to describe the movement to preserve the nation's natural resources.

Roosevelt promised Pinchot that his decisions on conservation would become de facto policy of the Interior Department. Later, Pinchot would become the first chief of the new Forestry Service created by Roosevelt in 1905.[28] Roosevelt was determined to protect the wilderness of the country. His first address to Congress included 10 paragraphs that dealt directly with conservation. "The preservation of our forests is an imperative business necessity," he told Congress, and he promised to save as much of the United States' pristine land as possible while it still existed. "We have come to see clearly," he continued "that whatever destroys the forests, except to make way for agriculture, threatens our own wellbeing." In the future, he declared, the federal government, not big business, would make decisions about leasing land for logging or mining. Again demonstrating that he was willing to stretch the powers of the presidency to meet contemporary challenges, he asserted that since the president already had the power of transferring lands needed by the Departments of War and the Navy, he would use those powers to enforce his new land use policy throughout the west, not just near national parks. He would not allow the Pacific Northwest Ranges, he promised, to be turned into "heaping mounds of slag" as had occurred in Appalachia. Once again, as he had done in his relationship with the trusts, Roosevelt had mobilized the implied power of the presidency and wielded it in a manner never before attempted by his predecessors. As historian Douglass Brinkley has pointed out, as a best-selling author, a wilderness trooper, birdwatcher, hunter, cow herder, and moral advocate for nature, Roosevelt knew he spoke with authoritative expertise on the issue. Roosevelt firmly believed that his position on conservation was the only correct one. He remained uncompromising and used any tool available to enforce his will.[29] In 1902, when Roosevelt turned his attention to the nation's forests, the United States had approximately 43 million acres of forests reserves at its disposal. Roosevelt mandated the Department of Interior to double or triple that amount immediately.

A plan for land reclamation accompanied his concern for forest preservation. In his first address to the Congress he stated that along with the forests, water problems were "the most vital internal questions of the United States."[30] The early pioneers of the West, he observed, settled near rivers and streams, which they could channel for their own use. But vast land areas of the West that were not near water could be made arable through judicious policies of damming and rechanneling for irrigation. Since water flow did not respect state boundaries and since the project was far greater than the resources of any single state, he believed that the federal government should take on the responsibility of land reclamation. Partly as a result of Roosevelt's persuasive power and partly the collective will of those who saw the great possibilities of making the vast arid lands of the West economically profitable, the 1902 Congress passed the Newlands Act, which created the Bureau of Reclamation. It rankled Roosevelt a bit that the bill, which he had championed bore the name of a Democratic senator and he noted upon its passage, "I regard the irrigation business as one of the great features of my administration and take a keen personal pride in having been instrumental in bringing it about."[31]

Unaware of the potential ecological disasters imminent in such radical change to the environments, eager engineers dug through lands previously untouched by the new machinery of the industrial age. Water appeared where it never was, railroads arrived at previously unreachable destinations, and bridges crossed distances that had been considered prohibitive. All these accomplishments made engineers the new miracle workers of the twentieth century. In describing his plans for a canal, one young engineer told a reporter, "God did not finish his work here so we are doing it." Roosevelt celebrated the wonders of practical science and encouraged similar engineering projects wherever they seemed possible. For example, he applauded efforts in Florida where his friend, Governor Napoleon Bonaparte Broward, was pushing forward with a program to drain the vast wetlands of the Everglades to populate the millions of acres with an equal number of people on an area thought to be nothing more than useless swampland. How this new population on this reclaimed "swampland" would obtain water after they pulled the plug on the massive Everglades aquifer never entered the governor's mind, and his drainage program left Florida with an ecological challenge that continues to beg resolution.[32] As in the case of Florida, the Newlands Reclamation Act had mixed results in the West. It destroyed many natural wonders, but it drew millions of new settlers and soon small hamlets such as Los Angeles, Santa Barbara, San Bernardino, and San Diego were booming with people and economic activity. Eventually Roosevelt's prediction that the population west of the Mississippi would soon equal that east of the Mississippi was realized.[33]

The Florida Everglades proved to be one of the most disastrous calamities of the Progressive urge to transform nature for the benefit of humanity, but Florida was also the place where one of Roosevelt's most noteworthy conservation practices began. In March 1903, ornithologists from Florida, Frank M. Chapman of the American Museum of Natural History and William Dutcher, Roosevelt's only rival as an expert on Long Island birds, visited the White House and explained to Roosevelt the plight of the brown pelican in Florida. This once prolific fishing bird was rapidly becoming extinct, he said, because their friendly nature had made them easy prey for poachers who were profiting from the new consumer rage for feathers. After listening to their description of failed efforts to try and purchase a small island near Palm Beach just north of Sebastian Inlet called Pelican Harbor, with a "little more than a wave of the hand," Roosevelt declared Pelican Island to be a bird preserve protected by federal regulations. It was the first such preserve but many more followed.[34] During the ensuing year Roosevelt used the bully pulpit to encourage other states to develop their own bird sanctuaries and forest reserves.

In 1904, after his decisive victory in the presidential election over Alton Parker, Roosevelt accelerated his campaign to preserve the United States' natural heritage. One of his first acts, just two months after his election, was to transfer federal forest reserves from the Department of the Interior to the Department of Agriculture; a month later, he announced reorganization of the Bureau of Forestry into the Forest Service and named Pinchot as its first director.[35] This bureaucratic shuffle took forestry decisions out of the hands of pro-business appointees who knew nothing about scientific forestry and put Pinchot and his army of scientific foresters in complete control of forest management policy. Pinchot used his enlarged budget and semiautonomous power to acquire control of grazing licenses, hydroelectric leases, even police summonses in national parks. In the process he added 20,000,000 acres to the national domain. One critic of Pinchot's policy wrote "that a man could ride from the Missouri River to the Pacific Ocean on Horse and need not once step a hoof outside government land."[36]

But those who celebrated—or feared—Pinchot's actions as a harbinger of setting aside vast areas of pristine wilderness discovered their assumptions to be wrong. Unlike Roosevelt, Pinchot was not a great admirer of Muir and others who were strong advocates of wildlife protection. He did not see the virtue in preserving forests simply for their aesthetic value or even as refuge for endangered species. Pinchot's plan was not to hold this land in pristine condition for the ages but rather to assure its scientific (i.e., efficient) use. This may have rankled Roosevelt, but he maintained his friendship and political alliance with Pinchot. He was, after all, of one mind with the president regarding the efficient use of forests and their conservation, if not preservation for their own sake, and he was a relentless and mostly successful bureaucratic infighter. Furthermore, his conservationist vision fit well with Roosevelt's idea that he was the caretaker of the United States' natural resources, and as such it was his responsibility to see that resources of the land were used for the benefit of the general public and not a few greedy monopolists.

In this same spirit—of protecting the United States' natural heritage from monopolists who exploited it for their own ends—on June 6, 1906, President Roosevelt signed the Antiquities Act into law. Like the Bureau of Corporations and the Forestry Transfer, it seemed innocuous, but the act excluded the Congress, and it became an unparalleled tool in the hands of the president to work his reformist will on a recalcitrant power structure. The act allowed for the president to designate historical landmarks, historic preservation structures, and other objects of scientific interest as national monuments. The preservationists involved had so craftily created the language of the legislation that it sounded inoffensive and whisked through the senate and the House that summer practically unaltered. With this new unencumbered power, Roosevelt circumvented Congress and confounded pro-development interests and halted plans for commercial development of numerous natural wonders like Devils Tower in the Black Hills of Wyoming and the Petrified Forests of Arizona.[37] The bill did not limit the amount of acreage the president could designate as a monument, and this provision allowed him to snatch the Grand Canyon—while it was the subject of a bitter debate between preservationists and developers—and put it safely under the protection of the federal government.[38]

During his second term, while Roosevelt used—some said overused—the power of the presidency to preserve the country's natural heritage, friction within his party developed between those who applauded Roosevelt's actions and those who felt he had stretched the legal limits of the office of president. The argument erupted in the last months of his presidency when the combined power of the major electric companies including General Electric and Westinghouse threatened to take control of sections of the country's major rivers to create hydroelectric power. Roosevelt had witnessed the abuses of oil, coal, and gas companies as they monopolized the energy sources of the country, at the end of the previous century, and feared that an electricity monopoly could do the same with water power. Whereas those fossil fuels would eventually be depleted, waterpower would not, and as the country became increasingly dependent on hydroelectric power, he did not want to see the management and ownership of this resource follow the same path as coal and oil.

Therefore, in the public interest, he authorized James Garfield, his sec-retary of interior to withdraw from private development over a million and a half acres of land along 16 rivers in a half dozen western states.[39] Pinchot defended the action as necessary in order to make detailed surveys of the land before development began. With William Howard Taft's inau-guration as president in 1909 and Garfield's departure, his replacement Richard Ballinger rescinded Garfield's order and declared that wholesale withdrawal of land without congressional approval was illegal and each case would have to be studied and approved by Congress. His action set off a firestorm between those who considered themselves Rooseveltian conservationists against those who favored a shift away from what they called Roosevelt's "Cowboy" methods. To them, Ballinger's decision manifested a more rational and responsible approach to executive manage-ment. To opponents of Ballinger's decision, including Pinchot, it repre-sented an attempt to turn the country's resources over to those who would harness them for their own profits at the cost of the average citizen.

But the struggle was over more than conservation. This conflict drew the battle lines between those Progressive Republicans who celebrated Roosevelt's reformist policies and those who were rankled at the imperious manner he had wielded presidential power in the name of reform. In the end the conservative wing of the party won out. Roosevelt and his fol-lowers were exiled from the party. Sensing an inroad to the Progressive vote in 1912, Democrats chose the Progressive New Jersey Governor Woodrow Wilson as their standard bearer. Progressive Republicans bolted their party and presented Roosevelt as a third party Progressive candidate. In the elec-tion, the voters chose a Progressive—either voting for Roosevelt or Wilson by a two to one margin over the more conservative candidate William Howard Taft. Despite this affirmation, a war, which saw government take unprecedented control of American life—including control over personal life decisions such as alcohol consumption—dwindled enthusiasm for

Progressivism by 1920, and Progressivism at the highest level of government remained dormant for over a decade. Nevertheless, under Teddy Roosevelt the Progressives had found a champion, and in fighting their cause he brought power to the presidency never seen in peacetime and changed the nature of the office forever.

NOTES

1. Theodore Roosevelt, "The Case against the Reactionaries: Speech Given at the Republican National Convention Chicago, June 17, 1912" in *The Wisdom of Theodore Roosevelt* (New York: Barnes and Noble Electronic Books, 2010), 14.

2. Edmund Morris, *Theodore Rex* (New York: Random House, 2001), 17.

3. Ibid., p. 43.

4. Ibid., p. 87.

5. Doris Kearns Goodwin, *The Bully Pulpit: Theodore Roosevelt, William Howard Taft, and the Golden Age of Journalism* (New York: Simon and Schuster, 2013), 297.

6. Morris, p. 89.

7. Ibid., pp. 90–2.

8. Morris, 313–316; Case #1904193 U.S. 197 U.S. *Supreme Court Northern Securities Co. v. United States*, 193 U.S. 197 (1904) *Northern Securities Co. v. United States* No. 277 Argued December 14, 15, 1903. Decided March 14, 1904 *Appeal from the Circuit Court of the United States for the District of Minnesota.*

9. Ibid.

10. Theodore Roosevelt, "First Annual Message December 3, 190," The American Presidency Project, University of California Santa Barbara, http://www.presidency.ucsb.edu/ws/?pid=29542 (Accessed August 18, 2014).

11. Johnson, p. 575.

12. Ibid., p. 576.

13. Keasrns-Goodwin, p. 462.

14. Johnson, pp. 588–9.

15. Goodwin, p. 311.

16. Ibid., p. 313.

17. Morris, p. 133.

18. Herbert Croly, *Marcus Alonzo Hanna; His Life and Work* (New York: Macmillan and Company, 1912), 399.

19. *New York World* (October 4, 1902): 1.

20. Goodwin, p. 315.

21. Walter T. K. Nugent, *Progressivism: A Very Short Introduction* (New York: Oxford Press, 2009), 38.

22. Douglass Brinkley, *The Wilderness Warrior* (New York: HarperCollins, 2009), 240.

23. Ibid., p. 409.

24. Ibid., p. 400.

25. Ibid., p. 399.

26. Ibid., p. 403.

27. Ibid., p. 308.

28. Ibid., p. 407.

29. Ibid., p. 410.

30. President Theodore Roosevelt, *Address to Congress*, December 3, 1901.

31. Kearns-Goodwin, p. 306.

32. Ibid., p. 422.

33. Ibid., pp. 425–6.

34. Ibid., pp. 492–4.

35. Ibid., p. 579.

36. *Vancouver Daily World* (March 30, 1909): 1.

37. Brinkley, pp. 642–7.

38. Ibid., pp. 754–5.

39. Kearns-Goodwin, p. 606.

CHAPTER 10

PROGRESSIVES AND FOREIGN POLICY

> America lives in the heart of every man everywhere who wishes to
> find a region where he will be free to work out his destiny as he
> chooses.
>
> — Woodrow Wilson[1]

When Theodore Roosevelt entered the White House in 1901, the Progressive president had inherited a country whose foreign policy had shifted abruptly from isolationism to dreams of empire. Just three years prior, the U.S. Navy had destroyed the Spanish fleet, and the army mopped up a war that had been going on in Cuba intermittently for 30 years. With armed forces halfway around the world in the Philippines, and with a military and diplomatic corps ready to fill the power vacuum left in the Caribbean by Spain's abrupt departure, the country announced to the world its presence as a power to be reckoned with. Progressive foreign policy, like its domestic policy, was guided by optimism and a faith in scientifically investigated and proven fact. And those facts—determined in part by the intellectually fashionable racism of the era—led many Progressives to the conclusion that the Anglo Saxon race had produced a superior society and the movement of all the world should be toward that ideal. Other races they believed were inferior and more prone to corruption, mismanagement, poor health care, and weak educational systems. Even the predominant interpretation of history taught at most universities usually carried a title such as the "Progress of Western Civilization," and the underlying thesis of these works was that society had steadily progressed westward from the Greeks, to the Romans, to the French, to the English, and finally to the Americans. The conclusion of this thesis was that there was no being on earth intellectually or socially superior to the educated, Christian, white male in the United States.

And with their advantages came the obligation to spread those benefits as far around the world as possible.

In 1899, McClure's magazine published a poem written by Englishman Rudyard Kipling that captured the sentiment and spirit that drove American expansionist ambition.

> Take up the White Man's burden—
> Send forth the best ye breed—
> Go, bind your sons to exile
> To serve your captives' need;
> To wait, in heavy harness,
> On fluttered folk and wild—
> Your new-caught sullen peoples,
> Half devil and half child.[2]

It was in this intellectual context that the United States entered the imperial rivalries at the turn of the century. In one sense this idea, with its subtle racism and its sense of social obligation can be described as typically Progressive, but in another sense it demonstrated the persistence of an idea as old as the Puritan founding fathers who strove to build in John Winthrop's words "A City on a Hill," an example to the world.

But the shining "City on a Hill" had been tarnished somewhat by the time that Roosevelt entered the White House, and his first foreign policy challenge was to address the growing military scandal in the Philippines where American soldiers were killing innocent civilians, burning villages of no strategic importance, and waterboarding suspected resistance leaders. Caught in the euphoria of their dramatic and decisive victory over Spain, most Americans did not notice that those Filipino rebels who had resisted Spain were continuing their struggle for independence against the United States, whom they did not view as liberators but rather as invaders. After three years of frustrating setbacks, the commanding general in the Philippines, Jacob Smith, ordered the burning of villages and the killing of anyone capable of carrying a weapon, whom he described as "anyone over ten years old." He also ordered the use of the "water-cure"—as waterboarding was called in those days—to extract information from captured guerillas. This practice, rooted in the Middle Ages, of forcing water down a person's throat to the point of drowning had already been universally condemned by the world community. When reports of these activities began to leak to congressional leaders and to the press, Americans were outraged. Leading the charge of the indignant was the newly formed Anti-Imperialist League, which counted leaders from a cross section of the United States, including Jane Addams, Andrew Carnegie, and Mark Twain. Formed to fight annexation of the Philippines, it leveled its anti-expansion weapons at the administration, as news of the atrocities in the Philippines spread. Outpacing the opposition, Roosevelt took action. He called for a full investigation of activities in the Philippines, declaring that while he intended to back up the army "in the heartiest fashion," he also intended to "see that the most vigorous care [be] exercised to detect and prevent any cruelty or brutality, and men who are guilty [of atrocities] be punished." And "Although the foe has resorted to treachery murder and torture against our men," nothing, he insisted, "can justify the use of torture or inhuman conduct of any kind on the part of the American Army."[3]

He also ordered the immediate court-martial of General Smith. Roosevelt's action, along with the news of the surrender of the leader of the resistance Miguel Malvar, took the wind out of the sails of the anti-imperialist movement and the voice from those who had protested American actions in the Philippines. The final end of criticism came when Henry Cabot Lodge rose in the senate and defended the administration. He admitted with sad regret that there may have been atrocities committed by American soldiers. But, he continued, "They have been provoked by horrors committed against them." And he began to recite a litany of outrages committed against Americans including having their eyes slashed, being burned alive, buried alive, dismembered with axes, and used as target practice while drowning. His Victorian propriety prevented him from including reports that the rebels often castrated captured Americans and gagged them with their own testicles. "Perhaps," he breathed a solemn pause, and then suggested that, "the action of the American soldier is not altogether without provocation."[4] Over the next few days a barrage of pro-administration articles appeared in (mostly Republican) newspapers, and the entire issue of American atrocities was quietly put to rest.

With the conflict and the scandal in the Philippines behind him, President Roosevelt could commence with the Progressive vision of civilizing inferior peoples of the world. The fact that the Filipinos had already been under the influence of Western culture for over 300 years probably did not enter his thought process. The man entrusted with the challenge of tutoring the Filipinos in responsible governing was William H. Taft. The transformation made by many Progressives from domestic reformers to international saviors is well illustrated by Taft's service in the Philippines. When appointed to the position in 1900 by President William McKinley, Taft was closely identified with the anti-imperialist wing of his party. Patient, capable, and full of goodwill, Taft seemed to capture and charm the Filipinos. They in turn seized his affection, and he embraced a people he referred to as "our little brown brothers." All the while, American soldiers in the battlefield mocked in campfire song, "he may be a brother of Big Bill Taft But he ain't no brother of mine."

Soon however, Taft began to move closer to the opinion of the average soldier on the ground. In a letter to Roosevelt in which he recommended delaying self-determination for the islands, Taft wrote, "Filipinos were the greatest liars it has ever been my fortune to meet." The educated minority he observed were "ambitious as Satan. And quite as unscrupulous." And the rest of the population—mostly peasants and tribesmen— were inferior to "the most ignorant negro," and "utterly unfit for self-government." He concluded that they would "need the training of at least fifty or a hundred years, before they even realize what Anglo-Saxon liberty is." Woodrow Wilson, although a Democrat, agreed. "Filipinos are children in matters of government and justice," and therefore, he decided, "They need to remain under the tutelage of the United States in order to learn the discipline of the law."

In contemplating the challenges for the United States in the international scene Wilson concluded

> It is by the widening of vision that nations, as men, grow and are made great. We need not fear the expanding scene. It was plain destiny that we should come to this, and if we have kept our ideals clean, unmarred, commanding through the great century and the moving scenes that made us a nation, we may keep them also through the century that shall see us a great power in the world. Let us put our leading characters at the front; let us pray that vision may come with power; let us ponder our duties like men of conscience and temper our ambitions like men who seek to serve, not to subdue, the world; let us lift our thoughts to the level of the great tasks that await us, and bring a great age in with the coming of our day of strength.[5]

Wilson voiced the opinion of Progressives in the Democratic Party who may have disagreed with Republicans on how to achieve Progressive goals domestically but were of one mind when it came to spreading their superior civilization to other parts of the world.

In Cuba things seemed to go more smoothly. With a provision in the treaty that allowed the United States to intervene at any time, Cuba proved unable to govern itself, and a perpetual lease on the strategic eastern coast of Cuba, transition to local powers seemed more reasonable. But before leaving Cuba, American Progressives placed their "civilizing" imprint on the island.

Progress in Cuba under General Leonard Wood's two-and-a-half years of administration had been remarkable. Wood, a trained surgeon, had transformed Cuba from one of the world's most pestilence-ridden countries to one of the healthiest. Through his draconian measures—public defecators were horsewhipped, privileged classes forced to pick up their own litter, and doors of houses resisting his sanitation crews smashed in—Cuba was free of yellow fever for the first time in two centuries. In addition, Wood supervised the construction of 3,000 new schools, modernized Havana's ancient sewage system, and established conduit for power and communication systems. In other words, he laid the foundation for an infrastructure for future American entrepreneurs.[6] Taft's and Wood's accomplishments in the Philippines and Cuba, respectively, reinforced Progressives' beliefs in their obligation to spread Anglo-Saxon civilization and government to the "less advanced" people of the world. Progressives' feeling could best be summed up by Roosevelt's speech at a Harvard commencement where in the process of chastening the Mugwump isolationists in his own party he heaped praise on his island administrators. Banging his fist into his open hand for emphasis he hailed, "Elihu Root . . . , Will Taft, and General Wood," who had sacrificed their careers to help "our weaker friends along the stony and difficult path of self-government." In another age General Wood, he declared, would be celebrated as "a hero mixed up with a sun god," for the miracles he performed in Cuba.[7] Although Cuba's upper class worried about the stability of a Cuban-led government, and its ability to sustain the pace of progress made under American occupation, Progressive leaders in Washington declared Cuba ready for self-government, and with little fanfare, sovereignty—with some caveats—was transferred to the new president Estrada Palma on May 20, 1902. The least problematic of the three new acquisitions was Puerto Rico. With the Foraker Act passed in 1900, civil government was established in the territory and in 1911 Puerto Ricans were granted all the rights of American citizens.

As the ink dried on agreements with Puerto Rico and Cuba, Roosevelt extended American power into the vacuum created in the Caribbean by Spain's sudden exodus. His first opportunity to flex American muscle in the region came in 1902 when Germany and England announced plans to send ships to block Venezuela's ports in response to Dictator Cipriano Castro's refusal to pay back loans made by the two countries. Although he disliked Castro and viewed the dictator as a typical example of Latin America's crude understanding of self-government, he loathed the thought that Germany would set its expansionist designs on the Caribbean. In response to the British and German blockade, he sent the navy under the command of the venerable admiral George Dewey into the Caribbean for maneuvers. After weeks of tense negotiations which brought the United States to the brink of war with Germany, the two European powers finally agreed to a negotiated settlement of the disputed debt. A similar financial crisis erupted in the Dominican Republic but with the precedent of Venezuela established the crisis was resolved more expeditiously. To avoid European interference, the Americans assumed control of Dominican customs houses and negotiated the debt with European bankers.

During the Santo Domingo crisis, Roosevelt formulated what became known as the Roosevelt Corollary to the Monroe Doctrine. The Monroe Doctrine, issued in 1823, stated that the United States would not accept European intervention in the Americas. Roosevelt realized that if nations in the Western Hemisphere continued to have chronic problems, such as the inability to repay foreign debt, they would become targets of European intervention. To preempt such action and to maintain regional stability, the president drafted his corollary: the United States would intervene in any Latin American country that manifested serious economic problems. The corollary announced that the United States would serve as the "policeman" of the Western Hemisphere.[8] Such a presumption of American authority and power bred resentment in the Western Hemisphere, but it reflected the Progressive sense of obligation to bring order and build models of effective government.

Beyond a doubt the greatest of Roosevelt's foreign policy achievements was the building of the Panama Canal, which was unquestionably the greatest commercial, political, and engineering accomplishment of the early twentieth century. It was also a clear expression of the Progressive view of the world, namely that some challenges are simply too great for one individual or company or private organization to accomplish, and in those cases government must take responsibility to see these projects to their conclusions. For over half a century there had been dreams of joining the great oceans of the world with a canal passing through the Isthmus of Panama. The first to take up the project were the French under a private corporation organized in 1882 by the genius behind the creation of the Suez Canal, Ferdinand Marie Vicomte de Lesseps. By 1889, defeated by mosquitoes, soft embankments, and de Leesseps's arrogant refusal to accept alternative designs for the canal, the *Compagnie Universelle du Canal Inter-oceanique* went bankrupt. By 1901, a new French company had been organized but by this time the United States had announced its presence as a world power with particular interest in the Caribbean. In a flourish of closed-door maneuvers, the U.S. senate approved a route through Panama, contingent upon Colombian approval. With suitors from France, England, and the United States at the door, Colombian leaders began to play the coquette in hopes of raising the benefits they would receive. In the background were a group of Panamanian politicians and business-men eager to close a deal with the United States and impatient with the intrigue of a corrupt Colombian government. Eager to move on the project, they reignited separatist sentiments that had been brewing in Panama for decades. Phillipe Bunau-Varilla, an engineer on the ill-fated French enterprise and a passionate believer in the canal, was hired by the Panama group to present their intentions to Washington and lobby for support. As talks with the government in Colombia stalled, Secretary of State John Hay wrote a memo to the president stating, "it is altogether likely that there will be an insurrection on the Isthmus against the regime of folly and graft that now rules in Bogota. It is for you to decide," he con-tinued, "whether you will 1) await the result, 2) take a hand in rescuing the Isthmus, from anarchy or (3) treat with Nicaragua" for an alternative canal route.[9]

New York political boss George Washington Plunket was unapologetic about accepting graft. "I saw my opportunities and I took em, . . ." he proclaimed. (Library of Congress)

Frustrated and angered by the Colombian government's decision to hold out for more concessions—which would never come—from the U.S. senate, the leaders in Panama on October 30, 1903, decided to declare the independence of the isthmus from Colombia. Citing a treaty written in 1846 that included American guarantees to secure the protection of the Panamanian railroad, Roosevelt ordered the U.S. Navy to Panama. Their presence prevented the Colombian army from entering Panama City and suppressing the rebellion. Hours after the successful revolution on November 4, and hours before the delegates form the new country of Panama arrived, Hay signed an agreement with the lobbyist Bunau-Varilla, who was now acting as temporary diplomat pleni-potentiary for the new country. The treaty gave the United States control in perpetuity of a narrow strip of the Isthmus of Panama where the canal would be completed. In return for granting sovereignty over a portion of their new country, the United States agreed to pay the government of Panama $10,000,000 plus an annual rental fee of $250,000.

When the newly appointed ministers from Panama arrived in Washington, they were aghast at the price paid for their independence, but Bunau-Varilla told them the treaty was final. Shortly after the signing Hay announced to the world, "The imperative demands of the interests of civili-zation required the president to put a stop to the incessant civil contests and bickerings which have been for so many years the curse of Panama."[10]

After waiting a few months to test the political winds (which over-whelmingly favored Roosevelt's actions), the senate passed, "An Act to Provide for the Temporary Governance of the Canal Zone at Panama, the Protection of the Works and Other Purposes." Upon signing the bill, Roosevelt announced, "I have taken possession of and now occupy on behalf of the United States the Canal Zone, the public land ceded by the Republic of Panama." Evoking the Progressive view of government's obli-gation to act in the interest of the people, he declared, "The possession of a territory fraught with such peculiar capacities as the Isthmus in question carries with it obligations to mankind. The course of events has shown that this canal cannot be built by private enterprise or by another nation than our own therefore it must be built by the United States."[11]

The canal project made the United States the unquestionable domi-nant power in the Caribbean. Influenced greatly by Alfred T. Mahan's, *The Influence of Sea Power Upon History: 1660–1783* (1890), Roosevelt understood that in order to maintain American power in the Caribbean and to impress upon the world the emergence of the United States as a world power, the size and strength of the navy would have to be increased radically. During his tenure as president, he built the U.S. Navy into one of the largest in the world, and it flexed its muscle not only in the Caribbean but elsewhere. In 1904, for example, when an insurgent tribe in Morocco led by Mohammed el Raisuli kidnapped an American citizen, Jon Perdicaris, in order to force the Sultan of Morocco to accept a list of demands, Roosevelt sent 16 warships on a "goodwill cruise" into the Medi-terranean. Accompanying the fleet was a curt message from the president issued through the State Department: "Perdicaris alive or Raisuli dead!" As the first of the warships steamed into Tangier harbor, booming cannons to announce their arrival, the Sultan declared he had come to terms with the insurgents and Perdicaris was released. Learning later that Perdicaris was not an American citizen in that he had renounced his citizenship in order to avoid the Civil War obligations, Roosevelt remained unflapped. Perdicaris was kidnapped because his attackers thought he was an American; therefore Roosevelt concluded the United States had to react as if Perdicaris were in fact an American. Needless to say a grateful—and apologetic—Perdicaris reapplied for citizenship. Shortly after the Perdicaris affair was settled, the appearance of the navy in the port of Constantinople convinced the Sultan Abd al Hamid's government that they ought to receive the American minister to Constantinople, John Laeishman, whom they had snubbed and also grant his request that American missionaries be given equal treatment and status as those from Europe.

Although noted for his aggressive foreign policy, Roosevelt was also a peacemaker. With the optimism of a true Progressive of the time, he firmly believed that reasonable men could avoid war through thoughtful negotiation. In 1904, war broke out between Russia and Japan. After a number of Japanese naval victories, Roosevelt offered his good offices to both sides to help settle their dispute. Both sides accepted, and the agreement reached at Portsmouth, New Hampshire, ended hostilities between the two nations and won for Roosevelt the Nobel Peace Prize in 1905. Roosevelt also arbitrated a dispute between France and Germany over the division of Morocco, which averted a conflict that could have exploded into a wider war.

As Roosevelt ended his tenure in the White House, he had left an indelible Progressive signature on American foreign policy. When he left office, the United States had one of the largest navies in the world, was building a canal that would unite the great oceans of the world and thus their people, and had become the policeman of the Caribbean. In the Roosevelt fashion it had been a rough and bumpy road, and many Americans took a collective sigh of relief when William Howard Taft took over the reins of power and foreign policy in 1909.

While governor of Philippines, Taft had gained a reputation as an affable leader who would be more inclined to negotiate than fight. After Taft brought the insurrection to a successful end in the Philippines and weathering the military atrocity, Roosevelt appointed him secretary of war. In that position he brought Cuba's first political crisis to a successful end by managing a peaceful transfer of power from ousted president Palma to an American governor and then to a Cuban president in 1909. Given Taft's resume, most observers believed the short era of American adventurism might be over. But Taft had his own ideas on expanding the nascent American empire. His views can best be summarized by his statement to Congress made in 1912. "The diplomacy of the present administration," he declared, "has sought to respond to modern ideas of commercial intercourse. This policy has been characterized as substituting dollars for bullets. It is one that appeals alike to idealistic humanitarian sentiments, to the dictates of sound policy and strategy, and to legitimate commercial aims."[12] More committed to the expansion of influence through foreign trade than by a display of military power, Taft pursued a program known as "dollar diplomacy" that encouraged U.S. investments in South and Central America, the Caribbean, and the Far East. He also believed that the military was a tool of economic diplomacy. For example, after the overthrow of Nicaraguan dictator Jose Santos Zelaya in December, 1909, he sent 2,700 U.S. Marines to Nicaragua to stabilize the new conservative, pro-U.S. regime when it was threatened by a more radical anti-American contingent. He also believed that American capitalism was an essential tool of diplomacy. For example, when Honduras seemed likely to default on its unsupportable debt to England, which raised the possibility of an English invasion, Taft encouraged American bankers to invest in Honduras in order to relieve the nation of its financial obligations to England. However, his program aimed at seeking commercial advantages in Central America aggravated the existing ill will that had been generated by Roosevelt's military interventions in Panama and Santa Domingo. The bad relations between the United States and other American nations to the south continued to brew when the fourth Pan-American Conference convened in 1910 in Buenos Aires and participants discussed ways to curtail U.S. commercial penetration, influence, and intervention. In 1910 when revolution broke out in Mexico, Taft—again viewing the military as a tool of his economic diplomacy—ordered 2,000 troops to the Mexican border to stand ready to intervene to protect U.S. investments. But when Congress raised vehement opposition, Taft recalled the troops and left the situation in Mexico for his successor Woodrow Wilson to handle.

Wilson not only held Progressive views on foreign affairs, he had taught them to his students at Princeton, and now as president would teach those values to the world. "We are chosen," he declared, "and prominently chosen to show the way to nations of the world how they should walk in the paths of liberty." His first pupil in the classroom of nations was Mexico, where in 1910 a revolution designed to overthrow the aged dictator Porfirio Diaz pushed the country to the brink of chaos and civil war. Out of the turmoil emerged the hero of the landed class, Victor Huerta, who had murdered the popular Francisco Madera and took control of Mexico at about the same time Wilson became president. Populists rebelled against Huerta's dictatorship and in the name of their slain leader launched a civil war against him and his followers. Although most European nations supported Huerta as the legitimate leader of Mexico, Wilson's politics of morality would not allow him to support a "government of butchers." After prohibiting the sale of arms to Huerta's government, Wilson threw his support to the rebel leader, Venustiano Carranza, who immediately in a burst of patriotic fervor and political sagacity declined. Wilson for all his knowledge as a political scientist and historian could not measure the strength of Mexican nationalism and the harm that his offer would do to Carranza.

Rejected by Carranza, Wilson pursued Huerta's downfall on his own. Landing troops first in Tampico and afterwards in Veracruz, the U.S. invasion disrupted the Huerta government sufficiently to allow Carranza to take control of the country. Bruised by Carranza's rejection, Wilson for a while supported the bandit revolutionaries Pancho Villa and Emilio Zapata, but soon he rejected this flight from reality and recognized Carranza. Miffed at the U.S. rejection, Villa launched raids against the United States, and for two years American forces under General John "Black Jack" Pershing pursued Villa unsuccessfully along and sometimes inside the Mexican border. When the smoke finally settled, it was obvious that Mexican American relations had sunk to their lowest level in 70 years.

Events in Mexico distracted Wilson from the drama that was occurring across the Atlantic. For a century, aside from two small wars, Europe had been at peace, but for the last quarter of that century many had been spoiling for war. Expanding populations, increasing international trade, neocolonialism, and emerging nationalism were all combining to strain the

European nations' tolerance for one another. The industrial revolution that had provided miracles of production found its way into armaments, and soon every major industrial power of Europe was boasting of its new weapons such as long-range Howitzer cannons, machine guns, and steel-plated warships. And as the new century opened, even the new invention, the airplane was being redesigned as a war machine. As added insurance, the major powers of Europe entered into secret alliances to ensure their advantage if war should break out. The excuse to put these new inventions and alliances to the test came in July of 1914 when the Archduke Francis Ferdinand of Austria, while visiting Serbia, was shot by a Serbian nationalist. Austria demanded concessions that would have smothered emerging Serbia nationalism. Serbia, although much weaker than Austria, bravely rejected the ultimatum knowing that a strong Russia stood by in their support. Austria was aware of Russian support but did not back down because they knew they enjoyed German support. The Russians were not afraid of the Germans because they secretly had an alliance with the English and the French. The Germans were not afraid of this alliance because they had a war plan which would put them in Paris six weeks before the Russians could even mobilize the eastern front. With all the parties convinced of their advantages, they went to peace discussions in August with no intention of peace on their mind. Soon all of Europe was at war, and it would become a world war since European nations had spent most of the nineteenth century extending their influence around the earth.

Wilson looked from afar with a feeling of hope and superiority—hope that the war world bring old regimes crashing down and the superiority of knowing that American ideas of democracy would prevail in a new order. For Wilson to become the creator of this new order at the end of the conflagration, the United States must remain above the war, yet also be prepared for war. Americans, he reminded his fellow citizens, must remain neutral in thought and deed.

Wilson resisted early pressure to enter the war on the side of England and France, and he entered the 1916 election with the slogan, "He has kept us out of war," and he could promise American mothers (although they could not yet vote) that he would not send their sons to die on a foreign battlefield. Accelerating events and pressures soon made that promise an empty one. Slowly Wilson became pushed to the view that the moral thing to do was not stay above the fracas but to join the war against the reactionary forces of Germany. Wilson and key members of his inner circle favored England in principle because of long-standing cultural and commercial ties, and the English shrewdly played on anti-German sentiment in the United States and supported the circulation of news of German atrocities to help shape public opinion. The greatest persuasion for Wilson, however, was the German use of submarines.

The Americans had declared themselves neutral and had declared their right to trade with all belligerents. Geographic reality complicated this outward claim of neutrality. England was physically closer to the United States than Germany, and there was no belligerent nation situated between England and the North American continent. Consequently, American products flowed freely to English ports. On the other hand, delivering goods to Germany's single port of Bremen became a tricky maneuver. After crossing the Atlantic, American ships had to navigate the North Sea, which the British had successfully blockaded. During the first year of the war, trade with England increased as trade with Germany fell dramatically. When England had spent all they could, they began to borrow from American banks and the American economy boomed. To counteract British naval advantage, the Germans developed the submarine, which they patrolled off the coast of England.

On May 7, 1915, the Germans sank the British luxury liner *Lusitania* killing 128 Americans. Disregarding the fact that that the Lusitania flew the British flag and carried weapons, which made it a legitimate target and that the Germans had warned Americans in newspaper notices to stay off British ships entering war zones, Americans were outraged. The rage was fueled by attacks on other ships that resulted in the loss of American lives. In March 1916 when the *Sussex*, a French ferry boat carrying passengers was sunk, an enraged Wilson issued an ultimatum threatening war with Germany if they continued to sink unarmed ships without warning. The doves in Germany still had the upper hand, and Germany promised not to sink any more nonmilitary ships without warning. As tensions seemed to be easing, however, Wilson and the United States discovered that the Germans had offered the Mexicans an alliance that in the event of war with the United States, if Mexico would attack the United States, Germany would provide guns, troops, and money to recover its lost territory in Texas, New Mexico, and Arizona. Americans who conveniently suffered from historic amnesia were shocked to learn that the

In April 1917, President Woodrow Wilson, asked Congress for a declaration of war against Germany. Many historians agree that American entry into World War I brought an end (at least for the immediate future) to the Progressive Era. (National Archives)

Germans tried to persuade the Mexicans to attack and that they would ever consider such an offer.

Finally in early 1917, with the land war stalled and costs in lives and treasure mounting, the German hawks prevailed, reasoning that the United States was, by virtue of trade with Britain de facto already in the war. They advocated ignoring the U.S. ultimatum regarding the use of submarines, arguing that with the use of submarines they could strangle British trade and end the war before the United States could mobilize. The hawks prevailed and the German government announced to the world that they would reinstitute this policy effective January 31, 1917. It did not take long for an incident and a cause for war to emerge and on April 2, 1917, the United States entered the Great War.

Some say that the "Great War," as it was called, ended Progressivism. Others call it the "Flowering of Progressivism." If by Progressive government one means the use of government bureaucracy to order, organize, and protect individuals then, in fact, the latter definition is true.

Overnight, hundreds of bureaucracies were created to coordinate the war effort. Bernard Baruch, a Wall Street wizard, headed up the War Industries Board, which coordinated production and distribution across the country. Herbert Hoover headed the Food Administration Board, which mobilized both consumers and producers of food. Huge publicity campaigns encouraged families to buy liberty bonds, eat and drink less, and plant Victory gardens.

The Fuel Administration was created to develop and implement energy conservation, and a Committee on Public Information was formed to explain to people how to think about the war. Knowing that Americans were not eager to enter this conflict, Wilson commissioned California publicist George M. Creel to launch a major propaganda battle for "the minds of men." And for those not persuaded by Creel's propaganda army, dubbed "four minute men" for their prepared speeches, which they delivered in theaters in four minute before the beginning of a show; Congress passed the Espionage and Sedition Acts, which made it a federal offense to speak against the war, denounce the draft, complain about wartime taxes, or say anything derogatory about the war effort. To shore up an unprepared army, in May of 1917 Congress passed the Selective Service Act, which initiated the first draft since the Civil War. Over 24 million men registered for the draft of which 3 million would eventually serve.

Upon arriving in Europe, Americans soldiers soon discovered the horrors of trench warfare. For four years, Germans, Frenchmen, and Englishmen had been slaughtering each other at close range along a line that ran from the northeastern corner of France almost to the border of Switzerland. For four years men had been living, fighting, and dying in trenches six to eight feet high. Battles were comprised of young men running, bayoneted rifle in hand against a trench protected with machine guns. The men kept coming until the machine gun barrels melted or warped, and then they jumped over barbed wire into the trench where they engaged in hand to hand combat with their enemy. Victory meant moving the trench line back into enemy territory a few yards. Over the course of the war over 15,000 miles of trenches were dug and over 4 million young men died. One battle emphasized the horror of it all. At the Somme River a million men died in just over a month of fighting. When the battle finally ended, the British generals could boast that they had gained seven miles of territory.

By the time the Americans arrived, both sides had been bled white. Like two heavyweights in a terribly close battle in the last round, one side was simply waiting for the other to collapse. The fresh young troops from the United States, though inexperienced and undisciplined, marked the difference. In the spring of 1918, the Germans were 50 miles from Paris, by September the weight of the new American troops proved overwhelming and the tired and battered German army was in retreat. The U.S. Navy also contributed to the cause by developing a convoy system that rendered the submarines ineffectual. But by far the greatest contribution of the Americans was the propaganda value of Wilson's Fourteen Points. From the moment his country entered the war, Wilson began to envision the peaceful, prosperous world that would follow. Although his Fourteen Points called for self-determination of peoples and anticolonial demands, they also included a call to return to the status quo antebellum, no recrimination, recognition of national indemnities, and open treaties openly arrived at. With their army in retreat, a seemingly endless flow of fresh young troops arriving on the other side, the vast production power of the United States now enlisted on the Allied side, and food supplies and civilian morale growing low, the Germans decided to sue for a peace based on Wilson's proposal.

Much to Wilson's surprise, and the Germans' dismay, the Allied forces of Europe had no intention of using Wilson's Fourteen Points as an outline for peace. Disappointed but determined, Wilson held tenaciously to each of his principles until it was chipped away by the vindictive victors. Finally, only one remained, the League of Nations, which Wilson refused to relinquish. Meanwhile, the victorious nations ighored a century of growing animosity and declared Germany the sole perpetrator of the Great War and as such obligated to pay reparations. No one was sure what the war cost, but an immediate down payment of $30 billion seemed adequate for the moment. The German diplomats were horrified. They left Versailles without signing the treaty, and the duty of conveying the treaty fell on two German clerks who upon returning to their homeland were assassinated.

Back in the United States, Wilson discovered that his countrymen were eager to forget the war "to end all wars" and get on with the business of peace. The treaty that Wilson brought home from Versailles with his beloved League of Nations still intact was rejected by the senate, and

Wilson wore himself out traveling back and forth across the country trying to rally support for his League.

The United States that the young American soldiers came home to had changed radically in a short two years. Industries which prospered during the war years had altered the demography of the country. Women had entered factories doing men's jobs. Mexicans crossed the borders in droves to fill the demand for semiskilled workers. Blacks left the farms of the South in great numbers seeking higher paying jobs in the North. They brought their art with them. Jazz and Blues made their way up the Mississippi River all the way to Chicago and then east on the rails to New York City. Women went back to their homes after the war, but blacks did not return to the South. Their "great migration" of 1917 and 1918 continued. It would change the complexion of large cities of the United States and set the stage for greater migrations in the future. Many whites reacted violently to the presence of newly arrived African Americans. Race riots in Chicago and other urban areas of the North signaled a troubled future for cities growing with an influx of black southerners.

For Americans, the Great War started and ended quickly, and there were many manifestations at home that the war fever, which the government had generated had not had enough time to dissipate. The year 1919 became one of the most violent domestic years on record as a wave of violence broke out in the form of race riots, labor unrest, bombings, political terrorism, and lynching across the country. In Florida, whites burned the entire black town of Rosewood and those that were not killed scattered never to return again.

The government responded to the violence by blaming the Reds, and A. Mitchell Palmer, the attorney general, began a campaign against political radicals. He launched raids across the country that saw the arrest or deportation of thousands of people, some innocent and some not, but none were given due process. Over the course of a few months in late 1919 and early 1920, raids against radicals occurred in over 30 cities, over 4,000 people were taken into custody, and hundreds of immigrants with radical ties as moderate as belonging to the Socialist party were deported. In New York State, five such socialists who had been elected to office were refused their seats in the legislature and expelled from the country.

Americans quickly grew tired of this abuse of power, and politicians across the country railed against the Palmer raids. It became one of the issues leading to Democratic defeats in the November, 1920, elections. The man who would lead the Republicans, Warren Harding had, as senator, led his state in denouncing the actions of the attorney general. He won the ensuing presidential election by promising to return the country to "normalcy."

Meanwhile, Wilson continued traveling across the country campaigning for his League of Nations. In the midst of this crusade he suffered a debilitating stroke, and like his battered body, the Progressive movement also for the moment became paralyzed. For over two decades, the Progressive movement had done much to improve government and make it responsive to the challenges of the new century. But as the second decade of the century came to an end, the movement seemed to have lost its vitality, and new forces were emerging in both parties. One indication of this change was the successful passage of the Eighteenth Amendment, which made temperance the law of the land. An ironic legacy of prohibition is that although it is generally viewed as reactionary, it captured many aspects of the Progressive mentality. It saw government as an instrument for social change, it believed in legislation to make people behave better, and it was slightly racist, for it was premised on the belief the new waves of immigrants in the North and the poor black farmers in the South were the ones that abused alcohol and in turn their wives and families and caused crime. In 1920, Americans, weary of campaigns at home and abroad, elected a man who promised to let them rest awhile and to be normal for a while. And the United States entered a new era of prosperity and frivolity freed from the clutches of Progressives who had hoped to redeem them.

NOTES

1. Woodrow Wilson, Chicago Speech, April 8, 1912, "Voices of Freedom Exchange," http://www.voicesoffreedom.us/voices/woodrowwilson/woodrow wilson.htm (accessed September 8, 2014).

2. Rudyard Kipling, "The White Man's Burden," *McClure's Magazine* (February, 1899): 290.

3. Edmund Morris, *Theodore Rex* (New York: Random House, 2001), 100–101.

4. Ibid., p. 104.

5. *Atlantic Monthly* 90, no. 6 (December 1901): 732–34.

6. Morris, pp. 104–05.

7. Ibid., p. 117.

8. "President Theodore Roosevelt and Foreign Policy," Miller Center, University of Virginia, http://millercenter.org/president/roosevelt/essays/biography/5 (accessed 15 July 2014).

9. Morris, pp. 238–40.

10. Morgan, p. 295.

11. Ibid., p. 302.

12. Address to Congress, 1912.

ANALYTICAL ESSAYS

COUNTERFACTUAL ESSAY: THE ELECTION OF 1896
What if Bryan Had Won in 1896?

The presidential campaign of 1896 became one of the great watershed elections in American political history. The Democrats and Populists, united behind William Jennings Bryan, campaigned for the coining of silver to expand a tight money market. The Republicans countered with a platform that called for maintaining the gold standard in order to protect the country's international economic integrity, thus ensuring an increase in trade and jobs.

Often dubbed the "battle of the standards," the campaign represented much more than that. It marked the climax of a decade's long political struggle between the farmers, especially those of the South and plains states, against Northeastern railroad and banking interests whose meteoric growth in the post-Civil War era had transformed the economy. Unable to understand or control the complexities of the newly emerging industrial capitalist society, farmers sought a panacea in the government purchase and coining of silver. They believed that making silver legal tender would increase the supply of money which in turn would drive up the prices of their crops while devaluing money that (the always indebted) farmers had borrowed. They also believed that the inflationary result of coining silver would stimulate the economy, which had been in a relatively stagnant recovery since the great depression of 1893. In their attempt to win the White House in 1896, midwestern and southern Populists suppressed their innate distrust of foreigners and city dwellers and formed an uneasy alliance with Democrats who had rejected the conservative "gold" wing of their party and embraced the immigrant urban working class as their new base.

The campaign became a grand battle over the future direction of the country. Reduced to its simplest explanation, the contest was between those who wanted to return to a simpler Jeffersonian view of a country of farmers and shopkeepers and those who embraced the Hamiltonian vision of a highly centralized efficient national economy that would dominate world markets. In the end, the Democratic-Populist alliance of farmers and urban labor never materialized. The Republican strategy broke the alliance by suggesting to workers that inflation was not the solution to their economic woes. What good, they asked, would a paycheck twice as big do if rent and food increased threefold? Signs in various European languages also appeared on factory bulletin boards shortly before the election announcing to workers that if the Democratic candidate Bryan won the election, the factory would close. Democrats had hoped that workers voting for their self-interest would propel Bryan into the White House. Workers did indeed vote for their self-interest, but in the end they decided their interests were more closely linked to the success of the industrial capitalists not farmers. McKinley won by the largest majority of popular votes since 1872.

The election heralded a great turning point in American history. With support of the working class in the urban Northeast, Republicans handed Democrats their most crushing defeat since the Civil War. As the final results came in, it became clear that the Democrats had become a regional party centered in the South and plains states and that Republicans would dominate national politics for the next 50 years.

But what if a majority of workers had viewed the economic world otherwise? What if they had come to see the common interest they shared with the farmers? What if the urban socialist ideas of owning industry had found common ground with the Populist urge to control industry? What if the coalition held together long enough to elect William Jennings Bryan president? Would the world have been different? Probably not, but it is certain that the United States would have been on a different path at least for the next four years. Let us take a look at what might have been.

With assurances from Great Britain and France that bi-mentalism would not harm the United States's credit worthiness in their country, Bryan and his Democratic-Populist coalition in Congress almost immediately passed a bill, which authorized the coining of silver at a ratio of 16 to1. The mints in Philadelphia and San Francisco had hardly begun coining the new silver when new supplies of gold from discoveries in Alaska and Africa began to flood into the monetary system. These discoveries along with a new smelting process for extracting gold from low-grade mines dramatically increased the money supply to levels that Populists had been demanding. But then, with silver supplementing the gold supply, inflation, which had slowly increased from −2 percent in 1895 to 0 percent in 1896 soared to 10 percent in 1897, and international bankers began to eye American currency with some skepticism.

With the silver debate settled, Bryan turned his energy to the tariff issue. In their platform, Republicans proposed—in the name of protectionism—raising the tariff to all-time highs. President Bryan had run on a platform of lowering the tariffs in order to increase exportation of agricultural products and at the same time make European products cheaper for the American worker. Remaining true to his campaign promise, Bryan urged the Congress to drastically reduce the tariffs. With import duties at an all-time low, the industrial countries of Europe began to dump products onto the American markets. Soon overwhelmed by the competition from lower priced, and often better, products, American factories began closing and laying off workers. Unemployment numbers soon began to drift back to levels of the 1893 depression. At the same time, because of increased money in circulation, inflation continued and economists reported that the country was suffering a heretofore unheard of phenomenon: inflation and depression occurring at the same time. They dubbed the new phenomenon "stagflation."

Although personally Bryan probably held no dislike for people of color, the realities of his new coalition demanded that he support ideas on race that may not have been his own. No president in this era could be considered a champion of the African American cause in the South, but Bryan proved less an advocate than his predecessors. For fear of offending his southern populist support, he refused Booker T. Washington's invitations to speak at Tuskegee Institute. In his first year in office, he signed a segregation bill designed to strengthen the Supreme Court decision of the previous year, *Plessy vs. Ferguson*, which had decided that separate but equal facilities were within the constitutional guidelines of the Fourteenth Amendment. At the urging of western Democrats and Populists, Bryan also signed a bill that expanded the Chinese Exclusion Act to include all Asian people.

The Democratic-Populist coalition in Congress also passed a law calling for government ownership of the railroads. Administration of the railroads was initially put under the control of the Department of the Post Office, but that massive transportation system proved too unwieldy for the post office bureaucracy and Congress spent the next year debating the makeup of the new Department of Transportation, which they proposed as a cabinet level office. Meanwhile without clear direction, the railroad system began to deteriorate. The cost of transportation fell, but the cost of running the industry rose. Roads were left unrepaired, schedules were no longer kept, and strikes (organized without fear of military intervention) increased. Eventually Bryan called on James J. Hill to be the acting director of an ad hoc railroad commission and the system slowly improved.

In foreign affairs, Bryan found himself in a perplexing situation. As a fundamental Christian, he took the Bible's admonition "Thou shalt not kill," literally. Therefore, initially, despite demands by many influential Americans including a number of important journalists such as William Randolph Hearst and politicians such as Theodore Roosevelt to join the struggle to free Cuba from the corrupt regime of Spain, Bryan resisted getting involved in the conflict. He even remained steadfast in his decision when the battleship Maine blew up in Havana Harbor. While most blamed the Spanish, Bryan called for restraint and refused to act until a commission investigating the accident had been completed. But soon his own belief that the United States had an obligation to spread democracy trumped his pacifist instincts, and he decided to enter the conflict. In his declaration of war speech to Congress, Bryan stated, "Universal peace cannot come until justice is enthroned throughout the world. Until the right has triumphed in every land and love reigns in every heart, government must, as a last resort, appeal to force."[1]

Suddenly, with the defeat of Spain, Bryan found himself and his country the de facto rulers of Spain's abandoned colonies. Fearful of falling into the trap of imperialism, he resisted sending a military governor to supervise Cuba's transition to a republic. Instead, he supported a junta of generals, who had led the successful campaign against Spain. He also resisted pressure from many quarters to take possession of Puerto Rico and recognized that island as an independent country. Finally he refused to send the military to the Philippines, where insurrectionists were attempting to create a coalition government. There were many in Congress who opposed these provisions in the Paris treaty that left the country devoid of the fruits of victory, but a coalition of Midwest isolationists and anti-imperialists prevailed and the treaty passed by the thinnest of margins. In his last year in office, Bryan condemned the European incursion into China in 1900 to put down a nativist rebellion. He declared that the western nations outside of sending missionaries to China should avoid supporting interests, especially commercial ones, in China at the cost of war with those historically peaceful people.

As the new century opened and a new presidential campaign began, it appeared that Bryan would join the long list (since 1876) of one-term presidents. Due to a harsh monetary policy, which included rescinding the Silver Act, inflation had lowered from a high of 11 percent in 1898 to around 7 percent by 1900. Unemployment hovered around 16 percent, and although the trains were once again running on time, farmers complained about price increases implemented by Commissioner Hill. As the summer of 1900 approached, it seemed clear that despite these setbacks, the Democrats would nominate William Jennings Bryan and the Republicans once again would turn to William McKinley who came within a hairbreadth of winning the 1896 campaign. McKinley's running mate Garret Hobart had died in 1897 and so this time McKinley ran with Governor Theodore Roosevelt of New York, who had become a national figure as a result of his heroics as a leader of a group of troops in Cuba known as the Rough Riders. Roosevelt had also attracted attention for his outspoken criticism of Bryan's foreign policy. He had advocated a takeover of Puerto Rico and occupation of Cuba and the Philippines. Most Americans agreed with Roosevelt, who crisscrossed the country speaking as a surrogate for McKinley, who remained at home and held weekly news conferences on his back porch with reporters. Beleaguered by high unemployment, inflation, and a directionless foreign policy Bryan was defeated in 1900.

DEFINING MOMENTS
Establishing the Forestry Service and the Shirtwaist Company Fire

Two very different but equally defining moments of the Progressive Era were the establishment of the Department of Forestry and Progressive response to the Shirtwaist Company factory fire in New York City. In both of these occasions, Progressives demonstrated their willingness to enlist the power of the government—in one case local, the other federal—to fight for the common good against forces too powerful to be overcome by individual effort.

Gifford Pinchot and the Bureau of Forestry

Along with his concern for preservation of natural resources, President Theodore Roosevelt also understood the need for land reclamation in the West. In his first address to the U.S. Congress, he stated that along with the forests, water problems were "the most vital internal questions of the United States."[2] The early settlers of the West, he observed, settled near rivers and streams, which they could channel for their own use. But vast land areas of the West that were not near water could only be made arable through judicious policies of damming and rechanneling water. Partly as a result of Roosevelt's persuasive power and partly the collective will of those who saw the great possibilities of making the vast arid lands of the West economically profitable, the 1902 Congress passed the New-lands Act that created the Bureau of Reclamation.[3]

Roosevelt's closest confident and ally on issues related to the judicious use of resources including land reclamation was Gifford Pinchot. Although he celebrated his French roots, Pinchot was born in Connecticut in 1866. He attended Yale and after graduation spent a year at the French National Forestry School at which time he decided to dedicate his life to *forest conservation*, a word that he coined and to him meant the wise use of national resources not necessarily their preservation at all cost.[4]

In 1898, President McKinley appointed Pinchot as head of the Division of Forestry, and he remained in that position under Roosevelt. Pinchot's pragmatic and utilitarian view of forest conservation fit well with Roosevelt's idea that he was the caretaker of the United States' natural resources, and as such it was his responsibility to see that resources of the land were used for the benefit of the general public not a few greedy monopolists.

Two months after his 1904 election, Roosevelt transferred Federal Forest Reserves from the Department of the Interior's General Land Office (GLO) to the Department of Agriculture's Bureau of Forestry, and he announced the reorganization of the Bureau of Forestry into the Forest Service, naming Pinchot as its first director.[5] This bureaucratic shuffle, which took control of forestry land out of the hands of the GLO helped define the president's Progressive agenda. Pinchot and his army of scientific foresters then determined forest management policy. This promised that in the future decisions regarding use of national forests would be based on scientific evidence that would benefit the greater public good. Judgments affecting national forest use would no longer be made by the GLO's pro-business appointees, who knew nothing or cared little about threats to the natural environment. Nor would they be based on the impassioned arguments of preservationists such as John Muir and the Sierra Club. In the future, under the direction of Pinchot, resolutions determining the use of forest lands would be based on hard scientific fact, or so they argued.

Pinchot used his enlarged budget and semiautonomous power to acquire control of grazing licenses, hydroelectric leases, and even police summonses in National Parks. In the process he added 20,000,000 acres to the national domain and proportionally increased the revenue of the forest service budget. One critic of Pinchot's policy wrote "that a man could ride from the Missouri River to the Pacific Ocean on horse and need not once step a hoof outside government land."[6] Pinchot's plan was not to hold this land in pristine condition for the ages but rather to assure its scientific (i.e., efficient) use. Roosevelt supported Pinchot categorically and often boasted about how smart he was to have Pinchot running the forest service out of Agriculture not Interior. Roosevelt believed that under Pinchot's stewardship, the U.S. Forest Service made sure that all forest reserves contributed to the permanent prosperity of the people who depended on them. While some western entrepreneurs berated his policies as socialist, the president argued that his far-sighted planning guaranteed future jobs to stockmen, miners, lumbermen, railroad employees, and small ranchers. If western forests were destroyed by unrestricted mining and lumbering, there would be no water and the burgeoning cities of the West would soon become ghost towns.[7] On the other hand, Pinchot's cold scientific analysis of conservation at times disappointed the preservationists like John Muir. For example in 1907, when the city of San Francisco applied to the federal government for permission to dam the Hetch Hetchy Valley in order to establish a stable source of electricity and water for the growing city, preservationists objected and lobbied in vain for Roosevelt and Pinchot's support. John Muir wrote,

> That anyone would try to destroy [Hetch Hetchy Valley] seems; incredible; but sad experience shows that there are people good enough and bad enough for anything.
>
> The proponents of the dam scheme bring forward a lot of bad arguments to prove that the only righteous thing to do with the people's parks is to destroy them bit by bit as they are able. Their arguments are curiously like those of the devil, devised for the destruction of the first garden. . . . These temple destroyers, devotees of ravaging commercialism, seem to have a perfect contempt for Nature, and, instead of lifting their eyes to the God of the mountains, lift them to the Almighty Dollar.[8]

But at the urging of Pinchot, whose natural and social scientists in the forestry service had carefully studied the pros and cons of damming Hetch Hetchy, Roosevelt did not support his friend Muir. And in 1908, Secretary of the Interior James R. Garfield granted San Francisco the rights to develop the Tuolumne River, which ran through the valley. Although that decision was delayed by five years of debate in the Congress, the forestry service recommendations became law and the Progressive philosophy that the government power aided by scientific study judiciously applied was the principle means of carrying out the common good over private interest—as exemplified by the forestry service—prevailed.

Triangle Shirtwaist Company Factory Fire

On March 25, 1911, a fire broke out in the Triangle Shirtwaist Company factory. It marked a sad ending to what had been a triumphant story for the young girls who defied the collective wisdom of those who insisted that women—especially immigrant women—could not be organized, and their victory inspired the entire garment industry. The young women braved starvation, physical violence, and jail time, but with the support a group of actively concerned middle and upper class women, the girls won a small victory over factory owners who conceded to their demands for a modest wage increase, fewer working hours, and better working conditions.

Joy from the small victory over management soon turned to anguish when barely a year after the strike ended, a factory fire broke out that killed

145 of the young female workers. The Triangle Shirtwaist Company factory operated on the top three floors of a building that sat on the edge of Washington Park. Shortly before quitting time on March 25, 1911, a fire broke out. The girls ran to the elevators only to discover that three of the four elevators did not work. When the frightened girls ran to the two stairwells they could not open the doors. A later investigation revealed that the doors remained locked during working hours to prevent employees from sneaking out early or from stealing materials. For a few minutes they lined up in front of the one serviceable elevator. But as smoke engulfed them, the girls panicked. They ran to the fire escape, but the passage was so narrow it would have taken hours for all of them to pass down this stairwell. As the smoke rose, they squeezed, pulled, and tore at each other to gain access to the narrow stairwell and the single elevator that slowly rose and descended bringing only a precious few to safety. In a last desperate act, many jumped from the windows. Their bodies fell on the fire hoses, making it difficult for the men fighting the fire. Also, the fire company ladders reached only seven floors, one short of the factory. In one case, a life net was unfurled to catch the jumpers, but three girls jumped at the same time, ripping the net and leaving the girls' bodies crushed on the sidewalk. Within 18 minutes, it was all over. Forty-nine workers had burned to death in the building or been suffocated by smoke, 36 were dead in the elevator shaft, and 58 girls had died leaping from the inferno. The event became more tragic after investigators revealed that most of the deaths were preventable. Fire Chief Edward Croker blamed the high casualty count on insufficient fire escapes and stairways, a lack of sprinklers, and the fact that doors had been sealed shut. "This calamity is just what I have been predicting," he said. "I have been advocating and agitating that fire escapes be put on buildings just such as this. This large loss of life is due to this neglect." [9] The factory owners were indicted on charges of negligence, but a jury failed to convict them.

In the aftermath of the conflagration, the International Ladies Garment Workers Union (ILGWU) organized a march on April 5 down New York's Fifth Avenue to protest the conditions that had led to the fire; it was attended by 80,000 people. The same women who had supported the factory girls in the previous year's strikes returned to join in the funeral march and to collect funds for the survivors. They vowed to pressure for safety laws in the factories, and in October the city government passed the

Sullivan-Hoey Fire Prevention Law, which established safety guidelines for factories. Although passed, the laws were not rigidly enforced. Pointing to this fact and recalling the Shirtwaist fire "where corpses of young girls were piled up like cordwood," Women's Trade Union League founder Rhetta Childe Dorr urged women to fight more passionately for the right to vote. "Only through voting," she declared, "could women push for political solutions to municipal problems."[10]

In the second decade of the twentieth century, appeals such as Dorr's had an ever increasing resonance among middle class women. Reform-minded women came to realize that the methods of their Federations—rooted in antebellum strategies designed to raise consciousness and consciences among those in power—would not suffice, and they could not affect real reform until they wielded the power of the ballot. During the 1910s and the 1920s, women's public activity moved from the "municipal housekeeping" of the 1890s to the development of formidable state and national lobbies that secured legislation that could effectively address major social problems. Women's political pressure groups advocated numerous social reforms, including workman's compensation for victims of industrial accidents, better education, adequate nutrition, and inspections of factories and tenement houses. As historian Paula Baker has pointed out, "Progressive era women passed on to the state the work of social policy that they found increasingly unmanageable [and] social policy—formerly the province of women's voluntary work—became public policy."[11]

PERSPECTIVES ESSAY

Were Progressives Racists?

The Progressive movement began in an era when racism had become a scientifically accepted theory. The academic world celebrated sociologists, anthropologists, and biologists who documented and asserted that white Anglo Saxons stood at the highest level on the evolutionary scale and other races followed with blacks being the lowest, possibly even more closely related to distant less human biological relatives. Some scientists even suggested the blacks had suffered from an arrested development or that slavery had somehow stifled the African march of progress. Others simply concluded that blacks were genetically inferior Caucasians who would eventually evolve to the higher levels of white civilization. Even the most prestigious of academic journals published erroneous theories on race. The American Economic Association, for example, which represented one of the most progressive of the new social sciences, published an article in 1896 by Frederick L. Hoffman entitled "Race Traits and Tendencies of the American Negro," in which he described blacks as a "serious hindrance to the progress of the white race."[12] Progressives placed great faith in the new social sciences and most accepted the purportedly objective scientific data on race as dogma.

It is not fair to say that every Progressive was a racist. There were many —historian Arthur Link described them as advanced Progressives—who resisted racial stereotyping and the assertion that a racial hierarchy existed. Indeed, a distinctly different opinion emerged among some Progressives like Jane Addams, whose work in settlement houses and schools had given her an appreciation of immigrant cultures. And although this era has been described as the "nadir of the African American experience," the age also witnessed the birth of the National Association for the Advancement of Colored People (NAACP), which marked the beginning of the modern civil rights movement.

On the other hand, the overwhelming majority of Progressives accepted racist theory as axiomatic and acted accordingly. For example, although Progressives championed democratic principles and expressed an unyielding faith in the power of the vote, most remained sanguine in the face of the systematic disenfranchisement of blacks in the South. Neither insurgent Republicans nor northern Democrats, who championed direct election of senators and other progressive political reforms, spoke out vigorously in the interest of blacks or against encroachments upon democratic practices in the South. Indeed, they apparently were willing to accept these practices in order to gain support for other cherished political reforms.[13] Southern Progressives supported disenfranchisement of blacks in order to remove a supposedly corruptible element from the election process and thus ensure clean government run by the best men. In 1912, even rebellious Republicans who formed a new more liberal Progressive Party abandoned the cause of the black voters in the South. Theodore Roosevelt, the leader of the insurgents, declared that his new party's plan "with respect to the Negro," was "to try for the gradual re-enfranchisement of the worthy colored man of the South by frankly giving the leadership of our movement to the wisest and justest [sic] white men of the South." He made this declaration in spite of the fact that the black vote in Maryland had given him his margin of victory over William Howard Taft in the 1912 primaries.[14]

Progressives tried to compensate for their lack of action in the South on behalf of blacks by concentrating on reforming southern education, which ironically further exposed their racism. Progressive educators championed the cause of industrial education that would allow blacks to assume a subordinate though productive place in southern society.[15] Southern university leaders active in the educational wing of the Progressive movement cast themselves as disinterested technocrats committed to promoting economic vitality and political tranquility in the South. They wrote articles, speeches, and treatises that promoted technical education for blacks and liberal education for whites. Southern Progressives replaced the image of blacks as beasts of burden with a paternalistic counterimage that likened them to dependent children. For example, in discussing the alleged problem of intemperance, one Progressive educator suggested that "under the fairest conditions, this child-race, so clogged by appetite and passion, finds it difficult to get on well in the world." He postulated that blacks had been morally and intellectually stunted by slavery and were thus capable of improvement only under the guidance of liberal-minded Southerners. Another educator reminded fellow reformers that they must recognize, "the momentous fact that the Negro is a child race, at least two thousand years behind the Anglo-Saxon in its development."[16]

The establishment of distinct learning tracks for whites and blacks also anticipated segregation of learning facilities, which Southern Progressives enthusiastically accepted. Samuel Mitchell, president of the University of South Carolina and deeply involved in the movement for Progressive education in the South, praised educational leaders in the state of Mississippi for their "heroism in bearing the burden of a dual system of public education" for whites and blacks. He described Mississippi's system as a model for the South, applauding it for providing the "capital, initiative, [and] brains" to educate the masses separately.[17]

Walter Barnard Hill, chancellor of the University of Georgia from 1899 to 1906 and a strong proponent of university modernization, claimed that—despite the protest of black intellectuals like W. E. B. Du Bois and William Trotter—the majority of blacks agreed with the Progressive educational plan for the new South, which included segregation. "Intelligent Negroes," he observed "accepted the wisdom of separate schooling on the premise that integrated education would threaten a blending of the races ... between the higher types of their people and the lower types of the white race."[18] Despite good intentions, racism determined the course of educational reform in the South. Consequently, as one historian has concluded, "the history of the progressive educational movement in the South is virtually inseparable from the history of 'Jim Crow' segregation."[19]

Not only African Americans but Asians and southern Europeans also felt the sting of racism from Progressive quarters. During the presidential campaign of 1912, the *Progressive Bulletin* attacked Woodrow Wilson, who, the paper claimed, "refers Chinese immigrants to white—"and finds "Chinese immigrants ... more desirable than the white people." They pointed out that their candidate, Theodore Roosevelt, advocated "renewing the Chinese Exclusion Act and extending its provisions to the island territory of the United States" in order to reduce the threat of the "yellow peril."[20] The same publication also referred to southern Europeans as "hearty 'hunkies' and 'dagoes' " who felt that "they are working to make America rich and that their services should be appreciated, but," the *Progressive Bulletin* questioned, "are they?"[21]

Racism also found its way into the foreign policy decisions of the Progressives. In the wake of victory over Spain and the occupation of Cuba, Puerto Rico, and the Philippines, journalist William Allen White spoke for most Progressives when he declared "Only Anglo-Saxons can govern themselves ... It is the Anglo-Saxon's manifest destiny to go forth as a world conqueror."[22] Progressives took on responsibility to govern the newly acquired regions because, as one historian has pointed out, "They readily accepted the notion that the little brown brother was a ward of the United States, not fit for self-government."

It is clear that racial prejudice tainted both Progressive domestic and foreign policy. They simply could not resist the racist theories that permeated the climate of opinion of the era. Pragmatic to the end, Progressives believed that the end justified the means; and if it was necessary to curtail African American rights, or to restrict the immigration from less democratic societies, or to install military governors in conquered territories, then so be it. For all these actions—in the mind of many Progressives—were being done for the greater good and the expansion of democratic principles. While Progressives articulated some of the best aspirations of Americans at the time, they could not escape the era's racism, which denied dignity and equal access for people of color to fundamental tools of advancement such as home loans, employment, and a college education and made segregation—either de jure in the South or de facto in the North—the norm for another half century.

Populist Convention of 1892. Was a Third Party Necessary?

In early July 1892, delegates of the People's Party gathered in Omaha, Nebraska. They came to protest common grievances, nominate a president, and save the country that one delegate pronounced to be "on the verge of moral, political, and material ruin!" They were angry and at deep odds with the new industrial oligarchy that seemed to be controlling the nation. They hoped to wrest power from the new industrial giants through political action even though one of their leading candidates for president of the United States believed that the country would have to have a "bloody revolution before [the] plutocracy of wealth surrender [ed]," even as gun smoke hovered over the city of Homestead, Pennsylvania, where workers and citizens faced federal troops in a dangerous stand-off. Still, those gathered in Omaha held faith in the political process and hoped for a vigorous yet peaceful revolution at the ballot box.

The disparate groups of farmers, industrial workers, Greenbackers, nativists, and others disagreed on many issues, but fear of the political power that the new economic giants—particularly the railroads and the banks—wielded compelled them into an uneasy alliance. Raucous disagreement so prevalent at the conventions of the era was almost nonexistent in Omaha as harmony and goodwill prevailed. Six months prior in St. Louis the two most contrasting groups: organized labor, mostly urban and partly immigrant with socialist tendencies, met with representatives of the farmers, who were mostly suspicious of both foreigners and city folk, and self-proclaimed small capitalists, who were wary of socialism. At St. Louis major differences were ironed out, and the meeting ended with the promise of a united front and platform to be ratified in Omaha. A writer for the *New York Times* observed, "there is not the slightest evidence of discord, and there seems a general resolve all around to make this convention a harmonious gathering . . ., [despite] the heterogeneous elements that go to make up those various political and industrial orders, and have heretofore refused to assimilate into any great political organization." The journalist advised those political groups that predicted the Populist Party's quick dissolution over issues of principle should know that "the Peoples Party platform is already practically agreed upon."[23] Throughout the night at the Millard Hotel on the eve of the convention, boisterous delegates sang campaign songs in celebration and anticipation of the great work they were about to undertake.

The delegates to the Omaha meeting convened with a sense of mission and purpose. The only major hitch had been that their chosen leader, Walter Gresham, declined to take up the banner. Gresham, a savvy political veteran and until recently an earnest Republican, would have been the perfect candidate for the new party that some accused of socialist leanings. A lawyer from Croydan, Indiana, he was present at the birth of the Republican Party. In 1856 he crossed the country as an advocate of the Republican ticket, and in 1860 he had been elected to Congress as a Republican from a strongly Democratic district. In Congress, as chairman of the committee on military affairs, he did much to prepare the Indiana troops for service in the federal army. After returning from war as a hero, he practiced law at New Albany, Indiana. In 1869 President Grant appointed him to the district court. Later he served as postmaster general, and in 1888, at the Republican National Convention, supporters nominated him for president, but he lost to Benjamin Harrison. Over the next few years Gresham, a midwesterner, saw his party become increasingly under the control of northeasterners who supported the interests of big business at the cost of farmers. His public dissension from Grand Old Party (GOP) political positions caught the attention of leaders within the newly emerging Populist Party, and in the spring of 1892, a group of Populist delegates, personal friends of Gresham, visited him in Chicago to persuade him to run for president under their party's banner. One reporter noted, that a "great wave of enthusiasm spread through the convention when rumors began to spread that Gresham would accept the nomination." Delegates smelled victory in the fall with Gresham at the head of their ticket. They believed that his willingness to abandon the Republicans marked the beginning of the disintegration of that party. To the disappointment of many at the convention, in the end Gresham demurred. Citing personal reasons, including his financial responsibilities to his family and the family farm, he declined the honor.[24]

The convention opened on the fourth of July, and the delegates noted the auspicious symbolism of the date, for they truly believed that they were participating in the birth of a new political movement that would rescue the country from the grasp of the corporate giants who were squeezing the life blood out of the people. The convention also began on an ominous note. While the delegates were gathering to find political, but above all peaceful, solutions to the challenges facing their country, a thousand miles to the east workers and local supporters were engaged in a bloody war with the mercenaries of capitalist plant owners outside the gates of the Carnegie Steel Works near Pittsburgh. Omaha and Pittsburgh provided stark contrasts to the expressions of hope and desire for major change that permeated the political air of 1892.

Standing firmly on one leg and swinging his crutch with an extended arm, H. L. Loucks of South Dakota, the party's permanent chairman, waved the great assemblage to order. The fire of his speech, said a local reporter, riled the crowd into a frenzy. He told the crowd that they were there to start a revolution, "not of bullets but one of education and the ballot." He warned that the republic was in great danger, but (to the roar of the crowd) he affirmed the great "mass of wealth producers had gathered and will be successful in changing the government."[25]

As the cheering from Loucks's speech subsided and the convention came back to order, General William Jackson Armstrong, inspector general under General Ulysses S. Grant, was given the floor, and again the crowd broke into great cheers when Armstrong derided those who talked about the "sacredness of the financial systems," and declared, "The only sacred thing in the world is humanity the only thing deserving of rights is man."

The din continued when Marion Cannon of California took the podium. Harnessing the collective anger of the delegates against for the railroads, Cannon brought the delegates again to a roaring voice of protest when he declared, "We tell those railroad operators that the people will own those railroads yet! We meet in the midst of a nation on the verge of moral, political, and material ruin! caused by avaricious corporate giants," but Cannon warned the corporate elite that "wealth belongs to

he who creates it." Bringing the diverse convention delegates to their feet
again, he averred, "The interest of rural and civil labor are the same [and]
the time has come when either the railroad corporations will own the
people or the people will own the railroads."

One of the most electrifying speakers of the day was James "Cyclone"
Davis, who appeared as a biblical prophet as he ascended the platform in
a long Prince Albert coat that draped his 6'3" frame. Addressing the delegates, he declared with moral certitude that the People's Party platform
stood firmly and solely on Jeffersonian principles.[26] Ignatius Donnelly,
the sage of Niningen, also gave a long speech. Terence Powderly, the
president of the Knights of Labor, was also invited to speak, but declined,
saying his voice was not equal to the task.

Mary Lease then rose to speak. When she told the delegates that their
country no longer had a government of the people, by the people, and
for the people, but a government "of Wall Street, by Wall Street, and for
Wall Street," they responded with shouts of "you tell them sister!" She
concluded by displaying a piece of paper purporting to be a telegram from
President Benjamin Harrison accepting the Populist nomination and the
crowd roared in disdainful laughter. Sealing the solidarity of the movement, John G. Maugherham of Indiana, a one-legged Union veteran of
the Civil War brought the crowd once again to their feet with a vigorous
speech that closed by inviting Southern veterans to come up and shake
hands and bury the past. At that moment a spontaneous procession of veterans, both Union and Confederate began winding through the hall to the
rhythm of the band playing "Marching through Georgia."[27]

During the afternoon session the convention took on the air of a camp
meeting as Georgia delegate Thomas H. Branch, Chairman of the Resolutions Committee, read the platform proper. He read each plank with the
cadence of a country preacher, and when he dramatized with dire warning
the ruin of the country if it were not adopted, the delegates responded with
a loud and decisive "Amen!" After the platform passed unanimously, the
hall broke out in a great uproar. Several delegates lifted Branch to their
shoulders and marched him in the air around the hall creating an
impromptu parade. Other delegates stood on their chairs cheering, waving
coats, fans, and banners in the air. Some paraded with placards with
various epitaphs including "Congress—not the people—be damned!"
The demonstration went on for more than half an hour while the band

played "Yankee Doodle" then "Dixie" in a continuous cycle. Women who—much to the chagrin of Susan B. Anthony who was there—collectively did not demand a suffrage plank in the platform joined the parade and were embraced and hailed as "Sister!"[28]

With Gresham out of the picture, the convention settled on James B. Weaver as their candidate. Weaver hailed from Iowa where his family had moved to homestead in 1842 when he was a child. He entered the Civil War as a lieutenant and after participating in the battles at Fort Donnellson, Shiloh, and Corinth mustered out at the end of the war as a brigadier general. After the war he became involved in Republican politics but soon became disenchanted with the party, which seemed to be becoming increasingly under the control of big business at the expense of farmers and small businessmen. He joined the newly formed Greenback Party, which advocated the coining of silver, the eight-hour work day, the taxation of money earned on interest, and a graduated income tax. All those Greenback positions were embraced by the Populist Party at their convention. Weaver was elected to Congress as a member of the Greenback Party and accepted its nomination for president in 1880. In 1891, he joined the movement to create the Populist Party and thereafter became the unanimous favorite to serve as the standard bearer for the party after Gresham bowed out. In order to seal the bond of unity and to bring an end to the bloody shirt politics of the post-Civil War era, the delegates nominated James G. Field, a former Confederate general from Virginia.

Weaver ran a vigorous campaign in the fall and received 1,027, 329 votes. He won all the electoral votes of Colorado, Kansas, Idaho, and Nevada and a portion of the votes of Oregon and North Dakota. The party did well among farmers of the Southwest and the Great Plains and had moderate success in the South, where they faced an uphill battle against strongly entrenched Bourbon Democrats. Weaver's campaign marked the strongest third party showing up to that time and many looked hopefully at the election as a harbinger of future electoral success and a realignment of the political order.

The failed campaign in a sense was successful since Weaver's candidacy gave a voice to the hundreds of thousands of workers and farmers who had felt economically and politically marginalized by the new industrial economy. And while some did indeed pick up arms against the new industrial order, many thousands more—because of the Populist campaign—held onto their faith in the political process. Watching from a distance at the proceedings in Omaha, an editorialist for the *New York Times* described the Populists as "nothing more than Socialists in disguise. While [socialist author of *Looking Backward*] Edward Bellamy was not honored at Omaha," he observed, his ideas were advanced by hundreds of the delegates, who consider Bellamy "their guiding star." His observation is only correct if it is accurate to collectively describe all disgruntled people who feel disconnected from the political and economic system as socialists. In 1892 many people were angry at the system but only a portion of them were socialists. It was a bloody era in American political history. Deadly riots had broken out in cities across the country; three presidents had been assassinated within 32 years. Myriad political motives and persuasions brought the delegates to Omaha.

The Populists lost the election of 1892 and by 1896 their political strength had been "stolen" by a group of insurgents within the Democratic Party. But they left an important legacy. By giving a political voice to those who were angered to the point of violence, they helped keep the country from greater bloodshed and reinforced for a majority of Americans the belief that ballots not bullets provide the most effective means of political change.

PRIMARY DOCUMENT ESSAY

The Octopus in Political Cartoons

The image of the octopus as a rapacious, frightening creature that devoured all within its grasp had already been fixated in the American mind when G. F. Keller's drawing, "The Curse of California," originally appeared in *The Wasp* in 1882. Since there were no known versions of this animal depicted in political cartoons prior to 1870, it is reasonable to assume that its fearsome image may be traced to Jules Verne's, *20,000 Leagues under the Sea* (1870). Although when first translated into English, Verne's octopus became a giant squid, in the original French it appears as *poulpe*, which is usually translated as octopus. The creature made its first appearance as an editorial cartoon in 1871 in European magazines that decried the new imperialism spreading through Europe. In 1881 the octopus first appeared in this country when Thomas Nast used it as a symbol for the threat of Roman Catholicism to American democracy. A year later, Keller applied the image to the expanding railroad monopoly in California.

THE CURSE OF CALIFORNIA.

G. F. Keller. "The Curse of California." *The Wasp* 9, no. 316 (August 19, 1882): 520–21.

In Keller's drawing, the head and eyes of the voracious creature belong to Leland Stanford and Mark Hopkins, two of the founders of the Central Pacific Railroad. Although Hopkins had died in 1878, his image remains as part of the brain and eyes of the monster. Stanford served as the president of Central Pacific and later of the Southern Pacific railroad when it took control of the Central Pacific. The tentacles, which extend from the head and capture its victims are depicted as freight rates. Caught in these tentacles is every major facet of California's economic life, including wheat farmers, fruit growers, miners, lumber workers, as well as the traditional transportation industries of stagecoach and ocean vessels. Even federal bonds, representing the finances of the U.S. government, are caught in the clutches of the railroad octopus.

In 1901 the image became verbalized when Frank Norris used the metaphoric octopus as the title for his book on the Southern Pacific Railroad. In the final pages of the novel Norris laments, "Yes, the railroad had prevailed. The ranches had been seized in the tentacles of the octopus; the iniquitous burden of extortionate freight rates had been imposed like a yoke of iron."

By the turn of the century, the image of the octopus in political cartoons had become ubiquitous. It had been used to describe the railroads, Wall Street, and urban bosses, among others seen as a threat to American economic and political life. The image endured in political cartoons at least until the 1930s because of the powerful image it portrayed to the American public. Not only does the octopus represent a dangerous insatiable creature that may actually exist, but with all of its tentacles extending from one large bulbous head, it also reminds the public of the interconnectedness of the economic and political world in which they live and the dangers inherent in allowing one entity to control it all.

NOTES

1. William Jennings Bryan, "First Speech Against Imperialism." Extract from speech delivered at Trans-Mississippi Exposition, Omaha, NE, June 14, 1898, http://www.trinityhistory.org/AmH/Bryan.pdf

2. President Theodore Roosevelt, *Address to Congress* (December 3, 1901).

3. Douglas Brinkley, *Wilderness Warrior: President Roosevelt and the Crusade for America* (New York: HarperCollins, 2009), 432–36.

4. Ibid., pp. 340–41.

5. Ibid., p. 579.

6. *Vancouver Daily World* (March 30, 1909): 1.

7. Brinkley, pp. 663–64.

8. John Muir, *The Yosemite* (New York: Century, 1912), 255–257, 260–262

9. *The New York Tribune* (March 26, 1911): 1.

10. *New York Times*, "Fire Story for Suffrage" (December 27, 1914): 7.

11. Baker, p. 644.

12. Walter Willcox and Mark Aldrich, "Progressive Economists and Scientific Racism: Black Americans, 1895–1910," *Phylon* 40, no. 1 (1st Qtr., 1979), 1–14: 8.

13. Howard W. Allen, Aage R. Clausen, and Jerome M. Clubb, "Political Reform and Negro Rights in the Senate, 1909–1915," *The Journal of Southern History* 37, no. 2 (May 1971), 191–212: 199.

14. William E. Leuchtenburg "Progressivism and Imperialism: The Progressive Movement and American Foreign Policy, 1898–1916," *The Mississippi Valley Historical Review* 39, no. 3 (December 1952), 483–504: 498–499.

15. Michael Dennis, "The Skillful Use of Higher Education to Protect White Supremacy," *The Journal of Blacks in Higher Education*, no. 32 (Summer 2001), 115–123: 117.

16. Michael Dennis, "Schooling along the Color Line: Progressives and the Education of Blacks in the New South," *The Journal of Negro Education* 67, no. 2 (Spring 1998), 142–56: 144.

17. Ibid., p. 146.

18. Ibid., p. 144.

19. Ibid., p. 155.

20. Leuchtenberg, p. 499.

21. Ibid., p. 500.

22. Leuchtenberg, p. 486.

23. *New York Times* (June 30, 1892): 1.

24. *New York Times* (June 17, 1892): 1.

25. *New York Times* (July 5, 1892): 5.

26. *Texas Historical Association Online*, https://www.tshaonline.org/, June 7, 2013.

27. *The Advocate* (Meridian Kansas), July 6, 1892, p. 5.

28. Ibid.

Biographical Essays

MARY HARRIS "MOTHER" JONES

"Pray for the Dead and Fight Like Hell for the Living"

A West Virginia district attorney called her "the most dangerous woman in America." But Clarence Darrow declared her "one of the most forceful and picturesque figures of the American labor movement." She was at the forefront of almost every labor conflict of the late nineteenth and the early twentieth centuries. She witnessed the great railroad strike of 1877, organized the coal workers of Pennsylvania in 1899, and led a march of factory worker's children from Philadelphia to the doorstep of President Theodore Roosevelt's home on Oyster Bay. She was arrested in West Virginia in 1912 and at the age of 72 arrested again during the great steel strike of 1919. Through her fiery and inspiring speeches and sometimes through her mere presence, Mary Harris became Mother Jones, "the incarnation of labor's struggle." Her iconic power continues to the present in the form a left-leaning magazine that bears her name.

"I was born in the city of Cork, Ireland in 1830." So begins her autobiography, a book that is part fact and part fancy consciously designed to augment her carefully designed public image. Mary Harris's life actually began according to church records around 1837, probably in the summer, in Cork, Ireland. In 1845 her simple life, like the life of hundreds of thousands of her countrymen, was disrupted by a fungus that ravished the potato fields of Ireland. English politicians remained deaf to the cries for help that rang from the Irish coast. Most of them agreed that the plight was an example of Irish indolence, and many warned that sending free grain to the potato-starved Irish would lower the price of wheat on international markets and thus disrupt the British economy. In the winter of 1847, as thousands were dying of starvation and thousands more were being evicted from their homes, over 200,000 Irish chose to risk the dangers of the sea over certain death in their homeland and fled to the United States and Canada.[1] Mary Harris's family was among the migrants, and they survived the journey that killed one out of every 10 who attempted it. Eventually they settled in Toronto. In Canada she received a normal school education, and at the age of 23 left her family to take a teaching position at a Catholic school in Monroe, Michigan. A year later, she moved to Chicago for a short time and then on to Memphis, where in 1860 she met and after a brief courtship married George Jones, an iron moulder. Over the course of the next six years Mary had four children, and despite the Civil War and General U. S. Grant's occupation of the city, the family settled into a life of domestic tranquility that was not disrupted until two years after the war when yellow fever struck. The disease wiped out Mary's family taking each of her children and then finally her husband.

After burying her family, she volunteered to nurse the sick, and after the plague ran its deadly course, she escaped the grief of Memphis by returning to Chicago. There she earned her living as a dressmaker. She worked for the rich who lived in palatial mansions along Lake Shore drive. It pained her to see "the shivering wretches, jobless and hungry walking along the frozen lakefront" in plain view of her wealthy employers who "seemed not to notice or care."[2] During these years in Chicago, Mary Jones began to see life through the lenses of class struggle. In solidarity with the working class, she attended labor union rallies, visited scenes of labor unrest, and became converted to that movement.[3] She also began a lifelong friendship with fellow Irishman Terrence Powderly, the new leader of the Knights of Labor, then the most powerful union of the late nineteenth century.

The stage was set for the emergence of the Mother Jones of history and legend in 1894, when Jacob Coxey organized a march on Washington to demand that the government create jobs for workers, who were suffering in the second year of a great economic depression. Coxey called his movement the "Commonwealers," but newspapers soon dubbed the marchers "Coxey's army" as they traveled across the country supported by donations from well wishers. Mary Jones joined the men, and along the way she collected funds, and food, and boosted the morale of the men with her fiery speeches. A newspaper reporter noted her actions and dubbed her the "mother of the commonwealers." Coxey's crusade failed, but it put Mother Jones on the road where she remained for the next 30 years.[4]

In 1890, mine workers organized into the United Mine Workers of America (UMW), and Mother Jones, who Eugene V. Debs called "a modern day Joan of Arc," became their champion. UMW leader John Brophy recalled

> She had complete disregard for danger or hardship and would go wherever she thought she was needed. Wherever people were in trouble she showed up to lead the fight with tireless devotion. With all this she was no fanatic. She had a lively sense of humor. She could tell wonderful stories usually at the expense of some boss, for she couldn't resist the temptation to agitate even in a joke and she exuded a warm friendliness and human sympathy.[5]

She became one of a handful of UMW organizers that crossed the country as needed. She earned $500 a year for her services. It was hardly enough to pay for rental of halls and other expenses connected to rallies, but she struggled on. Her speeches were captivating, passionate, and often comical. She included herself and her own experiences both real and imagined in her speeches, and wherever she went large crowds listened and then joined the unions.[6]

In 1902 mill girls went on strike in Appalachia. The girls worked with razor sharp knives, breathing air heavy with dust for 10 hours a day, for $3 a week. "Oh we do wish Mother Jones would come and help us with our strike," one girl told a reporter. "They say that strikers always win when they have Mother Jones to help them." Mother Jones did not appear at that strike, and the disheartened girls returned to work. But she did not forget the appeal and a year late organized what became known as the Children's Crusade. "I am going to show Wall Street the flesh and blood from which it squeezes its wealth," she declared. One hundred boys and girls, some with maimed or missing limbs from factory accidents, followed her on a march from Philadelphia to New York City. After arriving on Wall Street, the crusade continued out to Sagamore Hill, the home of Theodore Roosevelt. The president refused to meet with them, but an aide accepted a letter from Mother Jones that addressed the president as "Our Father," and asked him to help, "These children raked by cruel toil beneath the iron wheels of greed." In 1912 she crisscrossed West Virginia working feverously, often entering mining towns where other organizers feared to go. At one rally she warned the governor that if he did not rid "Paint Creek and Cabin Creek [mines] of these god damn . . . mine guard thugs there is going to be one hell of a lot of bloodletting in these hills."

She railed against owners with biblical epithets convincing workers that they were "doing God's holy work . . . putting the fear of God into the robbers." Mother Jones continued to actively work for the UMW until 1920s, when at the age of 86 she finally rested on a friend's farm in Adelphi, Maryland. But retirement did not silence her. She continued to speak out in support of unions and decry the greed of capitalists until she died on November 30, 1930, at the age of 93. Historians have noted that working class protests gave a sense of immediacy to Progressives' concern for social justice and the desire to expand what Herbert Croly called the "Promise of American Life" to all citizens.[7] In this era, no voice rang out more clearly or passionately for the rights of the working class than that of Mother Jones, who even carried her campaign to the doorstep of President Roosevelt. Analyzing the legacy of Mother Jones, her recent biographer Elliot Gorn wrote, "out of nothing but courage, passion and commitment, she created a unique voice, a prophetic voice, and raised it to the cause of renewing America's democratic promise."[8]

EUGENE V. DEBS (1855–1926)

> He is a man of much personal charm and impressive personality, which . . . make him a dangerous man . . .
>
> —Warren Harding

Eugene Victor Debs was born on November 5, 1855, in Terre Haute, Indiana, to Jean Daniel and Marguerite Debs, who had recently emigrated from the Alsace region of France. Debs dropped out of school at the age of 14 and began working at various jobs as a laborer in a railroad car shop. Although he took other jobs and even returned to school at night, his early days as a railroad worker connected him to his destiny, which began to unfold at the age of 20, when he joined the Brotherhood of Locomotive Firemen (BLF). In 1878 he became the editor of the Union's monthly *Fireman's Magazine*. In 1880, although only 25 years old, his brother workers elected him grand secretary and treasurer of the BLF and chief editor of their magazine. For the next 15 years he served the brotherhood as an officer and editor. At the same time he served the greater community of Terre Haute as city clerk and also as their representative in the State General Assembly.

His tenure at the BLF witnessed the consolidation of railroad corporations and their increasing economic power. In order to create a counterbalance to the emerging corporate giants, Debs attempted to transform the BLF from a relatively conservative mutual aid society into a more militant and organized union designed to advocate for workers' rights. Frustrated in his attempt to transform the BLF, in 1893 Debs organized the American Railway Union (ARU), one of the first industrial unions for unskilled workers in the United States. In 1894, the union struck against the Great Northern Railways and won most of its demands. Following the success of that strike and the notoriety it brought to the union, Debs and the ARU were drawn into the great Pullman Strike in Chicago. Despite Debs's warning that it was the wrong struggle at the wrong time, he relented to the demands of the workers and other ARU leaders and led his union into the fight. In the end, the collective power of the railroad corporations, underwritten by the muscle of the federal courts, President Grover Cleveland, and the army defeated the ARU. When the Army was brought in under the guise of ensuring the movement of the U.S. mail, violence broke out. Thirteen strikers were killed, hundreds injured, and over $80 million worth of property was damaged. Despite a passionate and able defense launched by Clarence Darrow, who had quit his position as a railroad corporation lawyer to defend him, Debs was found guilty of violating a judicial injunction against the ARU and sentenced to nine months in a federal prison. The path that began with the failed struggle against the Pullman Company and ended with a prison sentence became Debs's road to Damascus. Several years later he wrote that while in prison

> I began to read and think and dissect the anatomy of the system in which workingmen, however organized, could be shattered and battered and splintered at a single stroke. The writings of Bellamy and Blatchford early appealed to me. *The Cooperative Commonwealth* of Gronlund also impressed me, but the writings of Kautsky were so clear and conclusive that I readily grasped, not merely his argument, but also caught the spirit of his socialist utterance—and I thank him and all who helped me out of darkness into light.

Victor Burger, the socialist mayor of Milwaukee, also visited Debs in prison and left him with a copy of Karl Marx's *Das Kapital*. Nine months later Debs walked out of prison a convinced socialist and championed that cause for the rest of his life. Years later in another speech he recalled his conversion to socialism:

> It was the day of days for me. I remember it well. It was like passing from midnight darkness to the noontide light of day. It came almost like a flash and found me ready. It must have been in such a flash that great, seething, throbbing Russia, prepared by centuries of slavery and tears and martyrdom, was transformed from a dark continent to a land of living light.

Throughout the next decade, Debs supported the political aims of the Socialist Party. Although he paid homage to the political process, even running as the socialist candidate for president four different times from 1904 to 1920, he became increasingly disillusioned with politics, and shortly after his first run for the presidency, Debs along with Bill Haywood, leader of the Western Federation of Miners (WFM), and other labor leaders created a new union, which they called the Industrial Workers of the World (IWW). Abandoning the tactic of political compromise at their inaugural convention, this new union declared itself to be "the economic organization of the working class, without affiliation with any political party, founded on the principle of class struggle." They affirmed but one object and one purpose: "to bring the workers of this country into the possession of the full value of the product of their toil." Adding to the enthusiasm of the moment, in his speech to the convention Debs declared that, "it would be impossible to shrink from [the call of the IWW] without betraying the working class."

In the first decades of the twentieth century, Debs became the charismatic voice of the labor movement. He was a great speaker who interjected the message of Christian charity into his demands for worker justice. "The Almighty marks the passage of time upon the dial of the universe"; he once declared to a crowded courtroom, "and though no bell may beat the glad tidings, the look-out knows that the midnight is passing— that relief and rest are close at hand." He railed against those factory owners who in the course of their quest "for Mammon" had created industrial dungeons that consume the "bodies and souls [of women and children]."

He eschewed the label of Prophet. He urged his listeners to take control of their own destiny. He refused to "be a Moses to lead you into the

Promised Land." "Because," he warned, "if I could lead you into it, some-
one else could lead you out of it."

When World War I broke out, Debs railed against the capitalists' war
being fought with workers' lives. It disheartened him to see how quickly
many socialists had abandoned the banner of international worker solidarity for the flag of their country. He spoke out loudly and passionately
against the war. In Canton, Ohio, on June 16, 1918, he declared,

> They have always taught and trained you to believe it to be your patriotic
> duty to go to war and to have yourselves slaughtered at their command.
> But in all the history of the world you, the people, have never had a voice
> in declaring war, and strange as it certainly appears, no war by any nation
> in any age has ever been declared by the people. They are continually talk-
> ing about your patriotic duty. It is not their but your patriotic duty that they
> are concerned about. There is a decided difference. Their patriotic duty
> never takes them to the firing line or chucks them into the trenches.
>
> And here let me emphasize the fact—and it cannot be repeated too
> often—that the working class who fight all the battles, the working class
> who make the supreme sacrifices, the working class who freely shed their
> blood and furnish the corpses, have never yet had a voice in either declaring
> war or making peace. It is the ruling class that invariably does both. They
> alone declare war and they alone make peace.

After this speech against the war, President Woodrow Wilson declared
Debs a traitor to his country, and two weeks later Debs was arrested for
undermining the Selective Service Act. During his trial Debs called no
witnesses for his defense. He simply asked that he be allowed to personally
address the court. "Your Honor," he began,

> I have stated in this court that I am opposed to the form of our present
> government; that I am opposed to the social system in which we live; that
> I believe in the change of both but by perfectly peaceable and orderly
> means. . . .
>
> I am thinking this morning of the men in the mills and factories; I am
> thinking of the women who, for a paltry wage, are compelled to work out
> their lives; of the little children who, in this system, are robbed of their
> childhood, and in their early, tender years, are seized in the remorseless

grasp of Mammon, and forced into the industrial dungeons, there to feed the machines while they themselves are being starved body and soul. . . .

Your honor, I ask no mercy, I plead for no immunity. I realize that finally the right must prevail. I never more fully comprehended than now the great struggle between the powers of greed on the one hand and upon the other the rising hosts of freedom.

Debs concluded with a phrase for which he will be best remembered and which best defines his lifetime mission:

Your Honor, years ago I recognized my kinship with all living beings, and I made up my mind that I was not one bit better than the meanest on earth. I said then, and I say now, that while there is a lower class, I am in it, and while there is a criminal element, I am of it, and while there is a soul in prison, I am not free.

Debs was sentenced to prison for 10 years. A few months later the war ended and Attorney General A. Mitchell Palmer tried to persuade President Wilson to grant the ailing Debs a pardon. In 1920 Debs was nominated as the socialist candidate for president and while running a campaign from prison garnered close to a million votes. But Wilson remained unforgiving and unrelenting. In January 1921, Palmer tried again. He sent a memo to Wilson who was now leaving office and recommended a pardon for Debs. Wilson returned the memo with the word *Denied* scrawled across it.

The day before Christmas Eve in 1921, President Warren G. Harding commuted Debs's sentence to time served. Refusing to give Debs a pardon, the White House issued a statement declaring

There is no question of his [Debs's] guilt. . . . He was by no means as rabid and outspoken in his expressions as many others, and but for his prominence and the resulting far-reaching effect of his words, very probably might not have received the sentence he did. He is an old man, not strong physically. He is a man of much personal charm and impressive personality, which qualifications make him a dangerous man calculated to mislead the unthinking and affording excuse for those with criminal intent.

Debs returned home to Terre Haute, Indiana, where he was greeted by a crowd of over 50,000 well wishers. Shortly after his release, he was invited to the White House where a smiling President Harding told him, "Well, I've heard so damned much about you, Mr. Debs, that I am now glad to meet you personally." A year later he was nominated for the Nobel Peace Prize, a fitting capstone to a man who through peaceful means struggled for social justice his entire life. The great heart of Debs failed him on October 20, 1926. At Debs's his eulogy, writer Heywood Broun noted, "That old man with the burning eyes actually believe[d] that there can be such a thing as the brotherhood of man. And that's not the funniest part of it. As long as he [was] around I believe[d] it myself."

RAY STANNARD BAKER

Ray Stannard Baker, born in 1870 and raised in LaCroix, Wisconsin, was a member of the elite reporting team at *McClure's* when the magazine made its mark as the leading investigative journal in the country. He went to Michigan Agricultural College (later Michigan State University) and then on to the University of Michigan Law School. But he was soon drawn to writing and to the English department, and after graduating he went to work for the *Chicago Record*. Shortly thereafter the plight of the industrial worker captured his attention. In March 1894 he went to Massillon, Ohio, to cover the Coxey's Army march. He arrived objective and indifferent to the quixotic campaign, but as he got to know the men and walk with them, his attitude changed. He "began to know some of them as Joe, and Bill and George." Soon they were talking about "their homes in Iowa, and Colorado, and Illinois, and Chicago, and Pittsburgh, and the real problems they had to meet." Baker's empathetic presentation of the marchers drew the interest of readers, and although skeptics had predicted that the ill-supplied activists would dissipate in a few days from hunger and cold, they did not. At every scheduled stop—thanks to Baker's empathetic articles—their appearance brought an impromptu committee, sometimes led by a city official, who replenished their supplies with enough to get them to their next destination. The manifestation of solidarity might never had occurred had the people in the towns along the way to Washington not read about "Coxey's army" in the newspaper, and this demonstrated power of the press left a lasting impression on Baker. After six weeks they ended up in the nation's capital. Massive crowds thronged the streets, and as the procession headed toward the Capitol portico, a large mounted police guard awaited them. As the marchers spread out on the lawn, Baker reported, "the police seemed to lose their heads completely as they dashed into the crowds on their horses and slashed out with their clubs." When Coxey gained the Capitol steps and began to talk to the crowd, he was arrested for trespassing. "Coxey's eventful march from Massillon to the marble steps of the national capitol closed today in riot and bloodshed," Baker recorded, "leaving in its wake public works bills, no nearer passage today than they were a month ago."[9]

After his return to Chicago he was sent to cover the Pullman Strike. The Pullman Company managers had requested and received a federal injunction against the ARU boycott, and over the objection of Illinois governor, Peter Altgeld, federal troops were sent in. The presence of the troops provoked the crowd to violence. When they began to overturn and burn boxcars, the federal troops opened fire. Dozens were killed and wounded, and Eugene Debs, president of the ARU, was jailed. Baker witnessed the violence and reported that federal troops fired into the crowd with no warning, killing, and wounding innocent spectators. While most newspapers blamed the strikers and created the impression that federal troops saved Chicago from anarchy, Baker carefully recounted what he had observed, and reported that no strikers had appeared to participate in the violence and that it was mainly the work of outside provocateurs. When the Pullman Strike ended, so did editorial interest in labor issues at the *Record* and Baker's bosses relegated him to stories of murder, arson, and robberies, which stifled his enthusiasm for reporting. During those months he began submitting article after article to *McClure's* and when finally invited to join the staff there, he left for New York immediately. Writing to his father he said, "New York is a magnificent old town, never worked so hard in my life as I am doing now." He also got along well with his fellow writers. Ida Tarbell called him a "capital team worker who had curiosity, and appreciation of the facts." Phillips wrote that "he had a joyous laugh which was more revealing of his healthy inner self than anything else about him." His cheerful and balanced personality probably proved a helpful counterbalance to publisher McClure's volatile and often mercurial personality.[10]

For McClure's newly formatted investigative magazine, Baker went to the anthracite coal mines of Pennsylvania where a bitter strike had been broken. He went into the homes of those who had gone back to work, both union and nonunion men. He discovered in the process the horrible conditions of the mines, the corruption of some mine owners and union leaders both, and the dangers that men faced when they returned to work not only in the mines but on their way to the mines at the hands of those trying to continue the strike. One of the most poignant interviews came from a mother whose son was seriously beaten by strikers when he tried to return to work. "As we mentioned her son," Baker wrote, "she flushed and said she had nothing to say about him, but finally she did. He might better be dead because he has brought disgrace on the family," she said. He and all his brothers had been members of the union and had come out when the strike was called, but John went back to work. "He deserved all he got" his mother sighed, for "he wasn't raised scab." "None of the family visited or paid attention to him." Baker commented, "Such a story as this gives a faint idea of the meaning of a strike in the coal fields."[11]

Baker continued his investigative reporting for *McClure's* for the next five years. In the spring of 1904 he went to Colorado to report on the mine workers' strike that had erupted into a full-scale labor war between the WFM and the Cripple Creek Mine Owners Association (CCMOA). Baker carefully traced the history of the conflict from its origins in the 1890s and exposed the "corruption and bribery on the part of the corporations and violence on the part of the strikers." President Roosevelt commented that he found the article to be absolutely correct and justified his own reluctance to intervene. [12]

Bakers relationship with *McClure's* magazine came to an end in 1906, when along with the rest of the investigative staff at *McClure's*, Baker decided to part ways with his publisher and start a new journal. The decision was made in part because of editorial and business disagreements with Sam McClure, and in part from a growing sense that the reading public had become fatigued with investigative journalism that President Roosevelt had recently dubbed "muckraking." Many Progressives came to the defense of Baker and his associates, Ida Tarbell and Lincoln Steffens, calling them "the loftiest of living patriots ... and soldiers of the common good." But the journalists knew the president had correctly gauged the change in public sentiment, and they set out to create a journal that reflected the changing mood of the reading public.

With combined stock realized from their share in *McClure's*, Tarbell, Steffens, Baker, and John Phillips, McClure's original partner, created a new magazine they called *The American Magazine*. They promised readers "a monthly book of fiction, humor, sentiment, and joyous reading, which will be wholesome, hopeful, stimulating, uplifting [with] human interest on every page."[13]

Baker abandoned his hard-hitting journalism of the *McClure's* years. Under the pseudonym David Grayson, he began a series based on a simple living country gentleman full of folk stories and wisdom that attracted millions of avid readers, who idolized the fictional philosopher farmer who found happiness and truth in farming, schoolhouse meetings, country fairs, and conversations with neighbors. "David Grayson" clubs sprang up in all sections of the country. Even the urbane Lincoln Steffens was impressed, telling Baker, "I never realized there was in you such a sense of beauty, so much fine philosophic wisdom, and most wonderful of all—serenity."[14]

Despite the success of the Grayson articles, Baker did not abandon his investigative instincts. Soon he began a series on San Francisco's recovery from the earthquake of 1906, and then he began extensive travels through the North and South in order to "get at the facts" of African American life prejudice and segregation. The series of articles he wrote for the *American* along with two he had previously written for *McClure's* on lynching became a book entitled *Following the Color Line* (1908), the first book by a prominent journalist to explore the racial divide in the United States. Three decades later in preparing *An American Dilemma: The Negro Problem and Modern Democracy* (1944), Karl Gunnar Myrdal relied on Baker's articles as a major source for his groundbreaking work on race relations in the United States.

Politically, Baker remained a Progressive. After feeling betrayed by Roosevelt's muckraker's speech, he flirted briefly with socialism, but returned to the mainstream political fold in 1912, when he supported Woodrow Wilson for the presidency. The political relationship developed into a close friendship, and in 1918 Baker joined Wilson at the Versailles peace conference as an advisor. In the ensuing decade he wrote extensively on Wilson's internationalism. He also wrote an eight volume biography of Wilson, for which he won the Pulitzer Prize in 1940. Baker spent the last years of his life teaching and writing in Amherst, Massachusetts, where he died of a heart attack in 1949. In his long and prolific career Baker excelled as investigative journalist, political commentator, folk philosopher, and biographer. During the Progressive Era his hard-hitting

journalism provided credible sources and encouragement to all Progressives including President Roosevelt. He truly was as defenders of the so-
called muckrakers affirmed, "a soldier of the common good."

HENRY FLAGLER

Henry Flagler, cofounder and—according to John D. Rockefeller—the
genius behind the Standard Oil trust was vilified by reformers who fought
to eliminate the abuses of large corporations. Although they scorned
him, Progressives shared many characteristics with their nemesis Flagler,
who is often revered as the "father" of modern Florida and was affection-
ately called "Uncle Henry" by workers who built his Florida Empire of
hotels and railroads. Like his Progressive challengers, Flagler had great
faith in the advancement of humanity and in the wonders of science to
bring about a new and better civilization. On the other hand Flagler did
not share the Progressive faith in the capabilities of government. Rather
he believed that well-managed and humanely directed business enterprises
provided the best means of harnessing the powers of the new century for
the common good.

Flagler was born the son of a Presbyterian minister, Isaac Flagler, in
Hopewell, New York. His mother, Elizabeth Morrison Harness, had been
a widow with a son and stepson when she married Isaac, and Henry would
be one of a family that eventually grew to 10 children. His birth date, January 2, 1830, marked the start of the decade in which railroads began to
alter the U.S. landscape and to drive an economy that made Flagler and
others fabulously wealthy in the latter half of the century. At the age of
14 after finishing the eighth grade, Flagler left home to seek his fortune.
Working on canals and railroads to pay his transportation and living costs,
he arrived in Republic, Ohio, where he went to work in the store of Lamon
G. Harkness, his mother's brother-in-law from her first marriage. Young
Henry started in the store as a clerk working for $5.00 a month plus room
and board. Five years later he was earning $400 a month and managing
the sales staff. He also married the boss' daughter, Mary Harkness. Soon
he became managing partner with Lamon Harkness in a grain business.
In 1862, after paying his $300 bounty to avoid service in the Civil War,
he partnered with his brother-in-law in the creation of a salt mining company. At this point the burgeoning Flagler fortune collapsed, when the

Civil War curtailed the distribution and sale of salt leaving Flagler with a failed business and $50,000 in debt.

Flagler redirected his energies into the rapidly expanding grain futures market, which brought him to Cleveland where he met John D. Rockefeller, who also traded futures. Flagler soon became successful enough to repay his debts and to accumulate enough money to look for other investments. By the mid 1860s, oil had become the new fascination for investors. Before the process of refining had been developed, oil came almost exclusively from whales, making it a luxury affordable only to the more fortunate. The refining process developed a decade earlier had made oil a universally accessible product, and demand had skyrocketed. In this pre-internal combustion engine era, oil was refined into kerosene—the gasoline by-product usually discarded into the local river—and sold in gallon cans in general stores. It fueled stoves, lamps, and heating devices. Soon Cleveland, because of its geographic advantages including railroad trunk lines and access to the Great Lakes, became the oil refining center of the country. Observing the success of this new industry, Rockefeller partnered with a chemist, Samuel Andrews, to create a small refinery and profit from the rapidly expanding mass market for oil. In need of capital, he approached Flagler, who was able to borrow $100,000 from his Harkness family relatives. Not only did Flagler have connections to capital, but he also had a better idea on how to profit from this newly emerging industry. Instead of building a small refinery and competing with other small producers, Flagler proposed controlling all facets of the industry from production, to marketing, to distribution. He also suggested a system of rebates to contracted buyers, which allowed them to underprice their competitors. Eventually Flagler's strategy drove most competitors out of their own business and into the massive vertically organized system devised by Flagler. By 1892, the Rockefeller, Flagler, and Andrews Oil Company became the Standard Oil Company with control of over 90 percent of the country's petroleum market. When John D. Rockefeller was asked if the Standard Oil Company was the result of his thinking, he answered, "No, sir. I wish I had the brains to think of it. It was Henry M. Flagler."[15]

In 1878 Flagler visited St. Augustine, Florida, in hope of improving his wife's health, which had been slowly deteriorating since the difficult birth of their third child, Harry, in 1870. St. Augustine, a Spanish colony until

1821, consisted of small eighteenth century Mediterranean houses and shops that lined its three main streets. A grand castillo constructed in the late seventeenth century anchored the northern end of the town. The Spanish colonial architecture as well as the local residents' striking Mediterranean features, all seemed quite quaint and exotic to northern visitors of the late nineteenth century, and many rich Northerners took advantage of cheap land prices to build large mansions south of the plaza. One of these wealthy Northerners, Franklin Smith, built a concrete form house—designed to replicate the mythical Zorayda castle—where Flagler stayed on his visit. Flagler was fascinated by it all. He was especially taken by the reenactment of Ponce de Leon's 1513 landing, which had become an annual tradition in St. Augustine. Despite St. Augustine's appeal, and pleas from his wife who seemed to be thriving in the pleasant weather, Flagler returned to New York and his business. Within a year his wife, Mary, died and within two years he married Ida Alice Shourds—his wife's nurse and companion. Possibly realizing after Mary's death the fragility of life, or possibly at Shourds's insistence, Flagler began to remove himself from the daily business of the Standard Oil Company and spent increasingly more time in St. Augustine.

In 1882, he moved to St. Augustine, but at the age of 52 his active mind could not slip into the easy retirement that his fortune allowed. Rather, he began dreaming of the possibilities that existed in the new frontier of Florida. Envisioning an empire of hotels connected by train to the North, he hired the famous architectural firm of Career and Hastings to plan a complex of grand hotels. He was determined to build a resort town that accentuated the Spanish colonial ambience of the city, so before they began, he sent his architects to southern Spain to make sketches of buildings there. The end products were the *Ponce de Leon* hotel adorned with two replicas of the great Giralda tower of Seville and the *Alcazar* with interior gardens that recreated the wonders of the Alhambra fountains in Granada. He also purchased and renovated a third hotel, which he named the *Cordoba*. The *Ponce de Leon* boasted interior work and windows designed by Tiffany and an electric light system powered by a plant designed by Thomas Edison. The *Alcazar* boasted the largest indoor swimming pool in the world. To bring clients to his hotels Flagler developed a railroad southward. At the time the railroad lines from the north ended in Jacksonville. Negotiating a generous deal from the Florida legislature, he received land and right of way all along the Florida coast, and he began building his railroad while selling excess land granted by the government to orange growers.

The *Ponce de Leon* opened in 1888. In an age when workers' wages averaged between $10 to $15 a week, the cost of a room at the *Ponce de Leon* was about $85 a day. And guests usually stayed for the season, which extended from New Year's until Easter. Reservations at the *Ponce de Leon* were restricted to those who appeared on the *New York Social Register* or carried letters of recommendation from someone who was included in the *Register*. Guests arrived at the Flagler train station in their personal cars pulled by Flagler's Florida East Coast locomotives. At the station they were met by horse-driven carriages, which brought them to the hotel. After uncoupling the private dining, lounge, and sleeping cars of their wealthy passengers, the locomotives returned north with boxcars full of oranges. Flagler continued his development southward with a hotel in Ormond Beach just north of Daytona. Eventually the Flagler enterprise arrived in Palm Beach, where in 1894, Flagler's construction crews completed train service and the 1,150 room hotel *Royal Poinciana*.

That same year, his second wife Ida Alice Shourds was institutionalized. After a whirlwind marriage and elevation to the country's highest social circles, the simple Philadelphia girl suffered a complete mental collapse from the pressure of living under the disdainful eyes and critical opinions of the high society crowd that accompanied Flagler. Commenting on Flagler's companions, the *Chicago Tribune* reported, "The wonder of the century is the growth of the fortunes of the Standard Oil crowd, as they are known the Rockefellers, the Flagler's and their associates." The *New York Times* noted Standard Oil's elite are ". . . the most powerful, the most resourceful and the most daring combination of capitalists the country has ever known." And they all gathered at Flagler's sumptuous Palm Beach Hotels to spend the winter months. The opening of the season shortly after New Year's Day and the closing in early April were major events on the national social calendar. In 1895 he decided to extend his railroad to the end of the peninsula and in doing so created the city of Miami, which in 1896 grew from a wilderness of less than 25 families to a town of over 500—almost all Flagler's workers. That same year the small village declared itself an incorporated city. Some wanted to call the new city "Flagler" but the name of the local river, an Indian word for *sweet water*, prevailed. A decade later, the population reached 10,000 people, almost all employed by Flagler or a Flagler-associated enterprise.

In 1901, the members of the Florida Legislature—many of whom were elected thanks to generous campaign contributions from Flagler—passed a new law allowing divorce from an institutionalized spouse. That same year Flagler divorced Ida Alice Shrouds and married 34-year-old Mary Lilly Kinnan, whom he had met 10 years earlier at the Newport, Rhode Island, regatta. As a wedding present, he built the White Hall in Palm Beach, possibly the United States' most magnificent mansion. As Flagler became settled in Palm Beach, it became a magnet for wealthiest and most influential Americans. In 1905 at the age of 78 years, when most men at the time—if they were still alive—were enjoying quiet retirement, Flagler announced a new project: a railroad to the sea that would connect the island of Key West—then Florida's largest city—to the mainland.

Building the railroad cost Flagler most of his fortune and several lives, but it did what it was designed to do; it connected Key West to the mainland. Although it was washed out by a hurricane and bankrupted in 1935, the railroad bed provided the foundation for a permanent highway which continues to be the island city's only land link to the rest of the continent. On January 22, 1912, the "Flagler Special" with 82-year-old "Uncle Henry" aboard arrived in Key West to the shouts of citizens, the blaring of a band, and the chorus of children. "I can hear the children but cannot see them," Flagler remarked. A year late Flagler died from complications that developed after a terrible fall in his mansion in Palm Beach. His body was transported to St. Augustine, where it laid in state in the rotunda of the grand hotel *Ponce De Leon*. For hours people waited to pass by and say their last goodbye to Florida's premier developer.

Flagler wrote his own epitaph when he once told Richard Edmonds of the *Manufacturers Record* that he believed that he could probably have been one of the richest men in the world if he cared to confine his work to money making. But he preferred to carry out his Florida scheme, because, as he told the reporter, he "believed that in this way [he] could do more good for humanity than in anything else [he] could undertake since [he] was opening limitless possibilities for profitable work for thousands of people who were settling along the east coast of Florida." Hubris also drove the multimillionaire. As he told James Ingraham, president of Flagler's Land Holding Company in Florida, "I wanted to see if a plain

American could not succeed where the Spaniard, the Frenchmen, and the Englishmen had failed."

GEORGE WASHINGTON PLUNKETT OF TAMMANY HALL

At the end of the nineteenth century a great object of concern for reformers was corruption in local government. The meteoric growth of cities in the second half of the nineteenth century had turned local politics from a dignified public service into a lucrative enterprise, as political leaders earned large kickbacks from competing contractors and huge profits speculating on land they knew was destined for public projects. Many reformers represented established urban families of the past, who—in their view of the universe—had run more orderly and gentlemanly administrations. They fumed over the realization that they had lost power to "inferiors" who had been able to harness the political clout of the new immigrant masses. They hoped to regain their lost power and apply new principles of social science and management to create a more orderly system of urban government.

Not everyone viewed the political world in a similar vein. Many saw the urban bosses, who emerged in the latter half of the nineteenth century as their saviors, filling a void in social services that former administrations failed to recognize. One product of the new urban politics was the "ward heeler," a man assigned to a district or ward of the city whose primary responsibility was to deliver votes on Election Day. In the process of creating this legion of loyal voters, the ward heeler brought the face of local government to the doorstep of every resident in his district. If a man— temporarily out of work—needed food for his family, the ward heeler got him credit at the local grocery, or if he needed a few bushels of coal, he might do the same. Those merchants who were reluctant knew that the ward heeler might send a fire or building inspector to their business if they refused, so they begrudgingly offered credit to their less fortunate neighbors. Other times, a needy family might find a box of clothes on their doorstep or a bag of groceries compliments of the local ward heeler. An unemployed worker also knew he could often depend on his ward heeler to find him a job. In a practical way, urban bosses through their army of ward heelers addressed the social needs of the expanding city population, and in the process built a political structure bonded by a chain of loyalty that began at individual doorsteps and wound its way around neighborhoods, voting districts, and all the way to city hall.

One of the most notorious of these urban dynasties was New York's Tammany Hall, which controlled or was a major force in New York politics from the late eighteenth century to the mid-twentieth century. Originally established as a counterforce to the power of the federalists in the late eighteenth century, the Tammany Hall Democrats gained power during the nineteenth century by becoming the voice for the growing number of immigrants entering the city. It reached its pinnacle of power in the late nineteenth century under Boss William Tweed. During his years of ascendancy, the city of New York expanded geographically into the Upper East and West Sides of Manhattan, and New Yorkers also witnessed a grand transformation of the built environment. The Brooklyn Bridge was begun, land was set aside for the Metropolitan Museum of Art, orphanages and almshouses were constructed, and social services expanded. All of these enterprises benefited the people of the city but not as much as they benefited Tweed who controlled all the contracts connected to these projects.

Tweed maintained an uneven but cooperative relationship with the rich elite of the city. Some tolerated him because they too benefited from his many expansion projects and others because of his and Tammany Hall's ability to maintain tranquility among the immigrants. However, a small group of reformers with the *New York Times* on their side began a campaign against the corrupt hold Tweed had on the city, and with the help of testimony from disgruntled associates, they began to tear down the protective wall Tweed had built around himself. Tweed was arrested and tried in 1872. He died in Ludlow Street Jail, in 1878, and political reformers took over the city and state governments. The high point of the early reform movement came in 1894 after a police scandal investigation ended at Tammany Hall's doorstep and a committee comprising the city's richest men—including J. P. Morgan, Cornelius Vanderbilt, Abram Hewitt, and Elihu Root—organized to break the stranglehold that Tammany had on the city. They defeated the Tammany Hall candidate that year but their control was short lived, and by the turn of the century Tammany Hall politicos had regained power and continued to be a force in New York politics for another half century.

In 1905 William Riordon recorded and published the thoughts and random comments of George Washington Plunkett—one of Tammany's most powerful leaders from the 1870s through 1905. During this period he was Tammany leader of the Fifteenth Assembly district and chairman of the Elections Committee of Tammany Hall. He also held the offices of state senator, assemblyman, police magistrate, county supervisor, and alderman and boasted that he had filled four public offices in one year and drew salaries from three of them at the same time. While he was in the assembly and the state senate, he was one of its most influential members and introduced bills that provided for the outlying parks of New York City, the Harlem River Speedway, the Washington Bridge, the 155th Street Viaduct, the grading of Eighth Avenue north of Fifty-seventh Street, additions to the Museum of Natural History, the West Side Court, and many other important public improvements. Plunkett had no formal office space but rather he presided over his domain from a bootblack stand in the county courthouse, where he listened to voters, pontificated, and politicked. William L. Riordon often attended Plunkett's sessions and recorded his comments on government, graft, political theory, and patronage. He published this collection in 1905. What Plunkett revealed in his random comments and reflections provides a window into the mind of a successful Tammany operative and also the political landscape of New York at the end of the nineteenth century. What emerges is a complex picture of a city boss that does not fit well into the facile description provide by reformers at the time.

For example, reformers accused political bosses of enriching themselves through graft—a generic term that came to mean any funds a politician took illegally outside of his allotted salary. In response Plunkett scoffed, "Everybody is talkin'.[sic] these days about Tammany men growin'.[sic] rich on graft, but nobody thinks of drawin' [sic] the distinction between honest graft and dishonest graft." He admitted that many men had grown rich in politics. "I hae.[sic] myself." He admitted, "I've made a big fortune out of the game, and I'm gettin'.[sic] richer every day, but I've not gone in for dishonest graft—blackmailin'.[sic] gamblers, saloonkeepers, disorderly people, etc.—and neither has any of the men who have made big fortunes in politics.[sic]" He maintained that there was such a thing as "honest graft." As an example he said if his party is in power and he learns of a piece of vacant land that is marked for public improvement,

"I go to that place and I buy up all the land I can in the neighborhood. Then the board ... makes its plan public, and there is a rush to get my land, which nobody cared particular for before. Ain't [*sic*] it perfectly honest to charge a good price and make a profit on my investment and foresight?"[16]

This was not dishonest, Plunkett declared, he simply, "seen ... opportunities and ... took 'em. [*sic*]"

He also advised against young politicians wasting time practicing public speaking. The practical route to political power was not becoming a fine orator he advised but rather demonstrating an ability to deliver votes, which he described as a "marketable commodity." When he decided to go into politics he did not make a speech at the local district hall, he pointed out, he simply went to a friend and asked if he would support him, then he went to visit

Two young men in the flat next to mine who were school friends. I went to them and they agreed to stand by me. ... And so it went on like a snowball rollin' [*sic*]down a hill I worked the flat-house that I lived in from the basement to the top floor, and I got about a dozen young men to follow me. Then I tackled the next house and so on down the block and around the corner. Before long I had sixty men back of me, and formed the George Washington Plunkitt Association. What did the district leader say then when I called at headquarters? I didn't have to call at headquarters. He came after me and said: "George, what do you want? If you don't see what you want, ask for it. Wouldn't you like to have a job or two in the departments for your friends?" I said: "I'll think it over; I haven't yet decided what the George Washington Plunkitt Association will do in the next campaign."

He also scoffed at the notion held by college-educated Progressives that scientific study would bring neighborhood improvement and grateful voters would turn out corrupt politicians in favor of reformers who brought real improvement to their lives. "There's only one way to hold a district," he advised, "you must study human nature and act accordin'.[*sic*] You can't study human nature in books," he counseled, "books is [*sic*]a hindrance more than anything else. If you have been to college," he warned, "so much the worse for you. You'll have to unlearn all you learned before you can get right down to human nature, and unlearnin'[*sic*] takes a lot of time. To learn real human nature," he observed "you have to go among the people, see them and be seen. I know every man, woman, and child in the Fifteenth District," he boasted,

except them [sic] that's been born this summer—and I know some of them, too. I know what they like and what they don't like, what they are strong at and what they are weak in, and I reach them by approachin' [sic] at the right side.

For instance, here's how I gather in the young men. I hear of a young feller that's proud of his voice, thinks that he can sing fine. I ask him to come around to Washington Hall and join our Glee Club. He comes and sings, and he's a follower of Plunkitt for life. Another young feller gains a reputation as a baseball player in a vacant lot. I bring him into our baseball club. That fixes him. You'll find him workin' [sic] for my ticket at the polls next election day. Then there's the feller that likes rowin' [sic] on the river, the young feller that makes a name as a waltzer [sic] on his block, the young feller that's handy with his dukes—I rope them all in by givin' [sic] them opportunities to show themselves off. I don't trouble them with political arguments. I just study human nature and act accordin [sic]

He also belied the use of pamphlets, speeches, and promises. "They don't get votes," he warned "but helping people when you can does." In order "to hold a grip on your district" he advised the aspiring politician "to go right down among the poor families and help them in the different ways they need help," For example

If there's a fire in Ninth, Tenth, or Eleventh Avenue . . . any hour of the day or night, I'm usually there with some of my election district captains as soon as the fire engines. If a family is burned out I don't ask whether they are Republicans or Democrats, and I don't refer them to the Charity Organization Society, which would investigate their case in a month or two and decide they were worthy of help about the time they are dead from starvation. I just get quarters for them, buy clothes for them if their clothes were burned up, and fix them up till they get things runnin'[sic] again. It's philanthropy, but it's politics, too—mighty good politics. Who can tell how many votes one of these fires bring me? The poor are the most grateful people in the world, and, let me tell you, they have more friends in their neighborhoods than the rich have in theirs.

To the sociologists who maintain that government bureaucracy needs to include social service facilities he replied "If there's a family in my district in want I know it before the charitable societies do, and me and my men are first on the ground." Because of this system, he bragged, "the poor look up to George W. Plunkitt as a father, come to him in trouble—and don't forget him on election day." He also boasted that he, "can always get a job for a deservin' [sic] man." He knew "every big employer in the district and in the whole city, for that matter, and they ain't [sic] in the habit of sayin' [sic] no to me when I ask them for a job."

He defended himself and his colleagues against the accusations of reformers who labeled machine politicians as corrupt swindlers who lived well and did little for the people. "No other politician in New York or elsewhere," he swore, worked harder than a Tammany district leader. "As a rule, he has no business or occupation other than politics. He plays politics every day and night in the year, and his headquarters bears the inscription, 'Never closed.'"

> Everybody in the district knows him. Everybody knows where to find him, and nearly everybody goes to him for assistance of one sort or another, especially the poor of the tenements.
>
> He is always obliging. He will go to the police courts to put in a good word for the "drunks and disorderlies" [sic] or pay their fines, if a good word is not effective. He will attend christenings, weddings, and funerals. He will feed the hungry and help bury the dead.

Plunkett continued, "He [the political operative], has learned how to reach the hearts of the great mass of voters. He does not bother about reaching their heads. It is his belief that arguments and campaign literature have never gained votes." He seeks direct contact with the people, and he "does them good turns when he can, and relies on their not forgetting him on Election Day. His heart is always in his work," Plunkett affirmed, because "his subsistence depends on its results."

Riordon concluded his book with a schedule from a typical workday for Plunkett:

> 2 A.M.: Aroused from sleep by the ringing Of his doorbell; went to the door and found a bartender, who asked him to go to the police station and ball out a saloon-keeper who had been arrested for violating the excise law. Furnished bail and returned to bed at three o'clock.
>
> 6 A.M.: Awakened by fire engines passing his house. Hastened to the scene of the fire, according to the custom of the Tammany district leaders,

to give assistance to the fire sufferers, if needed. Met several of his election district captains who are always under orders to look out for fires, which are considered great vote-getters. Found several tenants who had been burned out, took them to a hotel, supplied them with clothes, fed them, and arranged temporary quarters for them until they could rent and furnish new apartments.

8:30 A.M.: Went to the police court to look after his constituents. Found six "drunks." Secured the discharge of four by a timely word with the judge, and paid the fines of two.

9 A.M.: Appeared in the Municipal District Court. Directed one of his district captains to act as counsel for a widow against whom dispossess proceedings had been instituted and obtained an extension of time. Paid the rent of a poor family about to be dispossessed and gave them a dollar for food.

11 A.M.: At home again. Found four men waiting for him. One had been discharged by the Metropolitan Rail way Company for neglect of duty, and wanted the district leader to fix things. Another wanted a job on the road. The third sought a place on the Subway and the fourth, a plumber, was looking for work with the Consolidated Gas Company. The district leader spent nearly three hours fixing things for the four men, and succeeded in each case.

3 P.M.: Attended the funeral of an Italian as far as the ferry. Hurried back to make his appearance at the funeral of a Hebrew constituent. Went conspicuously to the front both in the Catholic church and the synagogue, and later attended the Hebrew confirmation ceremonies in the synagogue.

7 P.M.: Went to district headquarters and presided over a meeting of election district captains. Each captain submitted a list of all the voters in his district, reported on their attitude toward Tammany, suggested who might be won over and how they could be won, told who were in need, and who were in trouble of any kind and the best way to reach them. District leader took notes and gave orders.

8 P.M.: Went to a church fair. Took chances on everything, bought ice cream for the young girls and the children. Kissed the little ones, flattered their mother: and took their fathers out for something down at the comer.

9 P.M.: At the clubhouse again. Spent $10 on tickets for a church excursion and promised a subscription for a new church bell. Bought tickets for a baseball game to be played by two nines from his district. Listened to the complaints of a dozen pushcart peddlers who said they were persecuted by the police and assured them he would go to Police Headquarter: in the morning and see about it.

10:30 P.M.: Attended a Hebrew wedding reception and dance. Had previously sent a handsome wedding present to the bride.

12 P.M.: In bed.

"That is the actual record of one day in the life of Plunkitt." Riordon reported. "He does some of the same things every day, but his life is not so monotonous as to be wearisome."[17] For his part, Plunkett noted that, "some papers complain that the bosses get rich while devotin' [sic] their lives to the interests of the city." But "What of it?" he asked "If opportunities for turnin' [sic] an honest dollar comes their 'way, why shouldn't they take advantage of them, just as I have done?" Reasserting his philosophy that "there is honest graft and dishonest graft." Plunkett affirmed that "the bosses go in for the former. There is so much of it in this big town that they would be fools to go in for dishonest graft." Considered a crude form of favor-based politics by some, hailed as a practical approach to social problems in a growing city by others, the historic contribution of urban bosses remains a debated subject in U.S. history. Plunkett's own words add fodder to the debate as they condemn, yet at the same time exculpate his intentions and actions. While he explains that he dedicated his career to helping his fellow human beings, he admits that his political activities provided, "Opportunities [for his own enrichment] and. [he] took 'em. [sic]."

VICTORIA WOODHULL

No one lived the struggle for women's equality more passionately or daringly than Victoria Woodhull. In an age that celebrated child bearing and homemaking as the highest aspirations of womanhood, Woodhull became the first woman to occupy a seat on the New York Stock Exchange and the first woman to run for president of the United States. She also published her own journal that advocated equal rights for woman, sexual freedom, social reform, and denounced the injustices of the capitalist system. Woodhull was born in Homer, Ohio, on September 2, 1838. Her mother Roxanna Buckman Claflin contributed to the family income by telling fortunes and helping people communicate with the dead. Her father had a well-known traveling medicine show. Claiming to have created an elixir that cured cancer, he dubbed himself "Dr. R. B. Claffin, American King of Cancer."

Victoria, a chronically ill child, was under the care of Dr. Canning Woodhull, whom she married in 1853 at the age of 15. The couple had two children: a daughter Zula Maude and a son Byron, who suffered from mental disabilities. She blamed her son's frailties on complications related to her husband's alcoholism. Weary of both his drinking and his philandering, she eventually divorced him. Years later she reflected, "Rude contact with facts chased my visions and dreams quickly away, and in their stead I beheld the horrors, the corruption, the evils, and hypocrisy of society, and as I stood among them, a young wife, a great wail of agony went out from my soul."[18] She divorced her husband in an age when women were expected to forbear in quiet suffering the agonies of a bad marriage. Many states outlawed divorce, and in states where it was permitted judges—who consulted the Bible more frequently than common law— were given great leeway in deciding cases, which invariably ended in favor of the husband. For example, in one case in New York a victim of severe spousal beatings was told by the judge "one or two acts of cruel treatment" were not proper grounds for divorce and that the wife "should not seek on slight provocation to dissolve that sacred tie which binds her to her husband for life, for better or worse."[19] But in the face of public scrutiny and disdain for divorce, Woodhull stood firm in her belief that she had the same right to the pursuit of happiness as any man.

In 1866, she married James Harvey Blood, and they moved, along with her sister Tenny, to New York. There, she and her sister worked as clairvoyants and spiritualists. They were befriended by recently widowed Cornelius Vanderbilt, who became impressed with their intelligence and paranormal powers. He set them up in business on Wall Street, and they were so successful that within a short time they opened their own brokerage house and had a seat on the New York Stock Exchange. They also started a newspaper, *Woodhull and Claflin's Weekly*, in which Woodhull began to express her developing political ideas on suffrage, free love, birth control, social reform, and labor. The journal also published the first English translation of Karl Marx's *The Communist Manifesto*. Impressed with Marx's synthesis, Woodhull joined the International Workingmen's Association, also known as the First International and wrote and lectured on their behalf. However, the regard did not reciprocate, and Karl Marx, who approved of the expulsion of all Americans from the International in 1872 publicly criticized Woodhull's views.

After attending a number of suffragist meetings, she became convinced of the cause and in 1871 persuaded a sympathetic congressman, Benjamin Butler, to arrange for her to speak before the House Judiciary Committee, where she argued that by virtue of the Fourteenth and Fifteenth Amendments, women had already won the right to vote. She challenged the House Committee to create legislation that would enable enforcement of those rights.[20] Although she failed to convince the congressmen, her appearance elevated her importance in the women's suffrage movement. However, she soon lost the support of Elizabeth Cady Stanton and Susan B. Anthony, who disdained her love of the limelight and her radical stands on free love. Susan B. Anthony even advised a group of British suffragists not to meet with Woodhull whom she regarded as "lewd and indecent."[21] The final collapse of her relationship with the leading suffragists of the era came in 1872 when she organized the Equal Rights Party and presented herself as a candidate for president of the United States and was able to get on the ballot in several states.

Around the time of the presidential election—which Grant won handily—came one of the defining points of her life, but it had little to do with the campaign. In response to attacks for her statements on free love and divorce, she declared her critics "hypocrites," who "preach against free love openly, but practice it secretly." To affirm her accusations she published in 1872—a few days before the presidential election—an exposé that revealed an affair between the leading evangelical preacher of the time Henry Ward Beecher—whom she labeled "an adulterous hypocrite"—and the wife of one of his most ardent supporters. She charged that, in the late 1860s, Beecher had conducted an affair with Elizabeth Tilton, wife of Theodore Tilton. Both were members of Beecher's Plymouth Church. Mr. Tilton was also editor of the journal *Independent*, which Beecher had formerly directed. In the same issue Woodhull also revealed that a leading New York stockbroker Luther Chalis had used alcohol to seduce two underaged girls at a masquerade party. A few days after the stories were published—on Election Day—Woodhull found herself in the Ludlow Street Jail, New York City's federal prison. The charge was that she had sent pornographic material—the description of the affair—through the mail. The articles precipitated several court cases including a libel suit by Chalis. But the two cases that captured national attention were Theodore Tilton's suit against Beecher for "alienation of affection"—a sensationalized trial that ended in a hung jury—and Woodhull's pornography trial.

Woodhull's prosecution had been spearheaded by the nation's self-appointed morality sheriff, Anthony Comstock, who pursued the case relentlessly. The trial became a national sensation not only because of the lurid details but also because it reflected sexual tensions percolating in the late nineteenth century, when new science was challenging Victorian ideas of sexuality. On one side were the evangelical Christians with their distrust of the flesh. The counterpoint was a collection of newly emerging nineteenth century "notions of the body, nerves, health, and the relation of mind and body; and an emerging sensibility that placed sex at the center of life." The new view was especially predominant in the city. In Woodhull's home of New York for example, "sex seemed in the air, everywhere—in conversation, in print, on the streets. Prostitution was brazenly open. Newspapers advertised sexually enhancing medications and implements as well as contraceptive devices and abortionists' addresses."[22]

Despite the fact that Comstock's crusade threatened their concern for freedom of speech, the press, and expression, health reformers, women's rights leaders, reporters, editors, and the broader public—disgusted with the open flaunting of previously unmentionable sexual issues—were willing to tolerate the persecution of Woodhull. Those who feared the challenges to their traditional views on marriage and sex focused their anxieties on Woodhull, and attacks on her were immediate and acrimonious. Harriet Beecher Stowe, sister of the disgraced minister, called her a "vile jailbird" and an "impudent witch." Cartoonist Thomas Nast touched a collective nerve when he drew the picture of a young, haggard woman dragging two poorly clothed children and fending off a drunken husband exclaiming, "get thee behind me (Mrs) Satan, I'd rather travel the hardest path of matrimony than follow your footsteps." The cartoon included a caricature of Woodhull depicted as Satan carrying a sign proclaiming "free love."[23]

Victoria Woodhull was eventually acquitted, but her American career was crushed by the battle. Facing diminished resources, a shrinking audience, and serious illness, she hung on for several years, lecturing throughout the nation and publishing her weekly. She eventually found her way back to traditional religion and divorced James Harvey Blood. In 1877 she was close to bankruptcy, and on what was rumored to be money paid by Vanderbilt heirs to her and her sister for their silence about their relationship with the recently deceased magnate, she and her sister migrated to England. She made her first public appearance there on December 4, 1877, at St. James's Hall in London, where she delivered a lecture entitled, "The Human Body, the Temple of God." She abandoned her free love philosophy of the past and married a proper British banker and philanthropist John Biddulph Martin. From 1892 until 1907, with Martin's financial support and under her new name, she published a magazine, *The Humanitarian.* Topics included woman's suffrage, health, eugenics, politics, and popular science. After her husband's death in 1897 she continued his philanthropic work and became a principle donor in the purchase of Sulgrave Manor, George Washington's ancestral home, which she gave to the Anglo American Association. Among her many philanthropic enterprises, she became a great promoter of Anglo American relations, and in February, 1914, she offered on behalf of the Women's Aerial League of England—a group that she helped organize—a prize of $5,000 and a trophy for the first aviator who would make a flight across the Atlantic in either direction between any point on the American continent and the British Isles. Victoria Woodhull Martin, editor, philanthropist, and mistress of Bredon North, Martin's country estate in Worcestershire, died at the age of 80 in 1927 far removed from the time, place, and philosophy that had made her—in the minds of many—one of the most notorious women in the United States.

RANDOLPH BOURNE

Randolph Silliman Bourne was a physically weak, hunchbacked, and unattractive man, but he had a character and intellect strong enough to withstand the full force of American patriotism and enthusiastic war fervor that flooded the country during World War I. He was born in Bloomfield, New Jersey, a suburb of New York, on May 30, 1886. The goddess Hygeia never smiled on him. His face was disfigured by an inept use of forceps at birth and at the age of 5 a battle with spinal tuberculosis left him a hunchback. He never reached five feet of height. The great economic depression of 1893 took away his materially comfortable middle-class life as well as his father, and he and his mother had to live off the charity of a prosperous but parsimonious uncle. His excellent school record won him admission to Princeton in 1903, but he could not afford to go, and his mother needed his financial support, so he went to work earning money with the only saleable talents he possessed. He tuned pianos, cut piano rolls, and became a session player at a New York recording studio. Utilizing his literary talent, he earned extra income proofreading.

By 1909 the family financial situation had improved to the point where he could finally attend college and that fall he entered Columbia University where Charles Beard was developing his theory of the economic influence on United States history and philosopher John Dewey was working on his pioneering ideas on democracy and education. Both men had a tremendous influence on shaping Bourne's ideas on democracy and the threat of industrial capitalism to its preservation. While an undergraduate at Columbia, Bourne also began his literary career publishing articles in *Dial*, *Atlantic Monthly*, *North American Review*, *The Masses*, and other opinion-forming magazines. His first book, *Youth and Life*, a collection of his magazine essays, was published the year he graduated from Columbia in 1913. Following graduation, with a fellowship for travel abroad, Bourne left for Europe. He journeyed throughout the continent until the threat of war drove him back to the United States, where he settled in Greenwich Village and continued writing for a number of magazines including the *New Republic*, a progressive liberal magazine started by Herbert Croly, Walter Lippman, and Walter Weyl in 1914. Bourne helped set the editorial tone of the magazine, which called for a strong central government, acting in the public interest to control the abuses of industrial capitalism.

Bourne had witnessed firsthand the forces that had spun out of control and exploded in Europe, and upon returning to the United States, he became an outspoken critic of the war. He railed against Wilson's "phony neutrality," which, he predicted, would eventually drag the United States into the conflict. He warned that the new industrialized nature of war by necessity turned governments to totalitarianism. "War is the Health of the State," he declared. Bourne became contemptuous of the weak logic of those who surrendered their principles to join the national call to arms. He decried those "pragmatic thinkers," like his former mentor Dewey and his new colleagues at the *New Republic*, whose liberal universe included a powerful but honorable government, which could support the war without losing the moral imperative that compelled them to enter the conflict. He called those naïve who believed that ethical motives and principles could harness the amoral force of unleashed militarism.

Bourne remained steadfast in his conviction that militarism destroyed democracy, even though it brought upon him the wrath of his former colleagues and friends, who had been caught up in Wilson's idealistic call to make the "world safe for democracy." Bourne scoffed at those who believed Wilson's promise that the Great War would create a new world order in which armed conflict would become obsolete. Bourne's resistance cost him dearly. As intellectuals and purveyors of public opinion increasingly fell into line and marched to the drumbeat of war, Bourne became the target of insufferable levels of attack. The *New Republic* stopped publishing his work. The *Seven Arts*, a magazine he helped create, collapsed when financial support dried up, and the *Dial*—his last great hope for an oasis of sanity—removed him from the editorial board. "I feel very much secluded from the world, very much out of touch with my times," Bourne lamented to one of his few remaining friends. "The magazines I write for die violent deaths, and all my thoughts are unprintable." Historian Robert Westbrook has cogently observed that "Bourne disturbed the peace of John Dewey and other intellectuals supporting Woodrow Wilson's crusade to make the world safe for democracy, and they made him pay for it."

Despite his personal anguish, he maintained his faith in a better future, and when the war finally ended, he hoped that peace would allow rationality to return and the madness that had led to so much destruction of life and property, and had caused him so much personal pain, would finally be tempered. In a letter to his mother he exulted in the armistice that had been declared. "Now that the war is over," he rejoiced, "people can speak freely and [once again] we can dare to think. It's like coming out of a nightmare."

Unfortunately for Bourne he did not see that day come. The influenza epidemic that had killed over 600,000 Americans silenced the passionate yet reasonable voice of 32-year-old Randolph Bourne on December 22, 1918. Bourne's spirit continued to survive. An institute for peace studies bears his name (The Randolph Bourne Institute), and his writings and ideas continue to serve as inspiration and philosophic support for those who carry on the campaign for noninterventionist foreign policy and the search for more peaceful resolutions to conflict. Bourne remains an inspiration for those who believe that war indeed "is the health of the state."[24]

NOTES

1. Elliot Gorn, *Mother Jones: The Most Dangerous Woman in America* (New York: Hill and Wang, 2001), 15–7.

2. Ibid., pp. 42–3.

3. Ibid., p. 49.

4. Ibid., p. 63.

5. Ibid., pp. 74–5.

6. Ibid., p. 82.

7. For example see Nell Irvin Painter, *Standing at Armageddon: A Grassroots History of the Progressive Era* (New York: W. W. Norton, 2008).

8. Gorn, p. 303.

9. Doris Kearns Goodwin, *The Bully Pulpit: Theodore Roosevelt, William Howard Taft and the Golden Age of Journalism* (New York: Simon and Schuster, 2013), 185–7.

10. Ibid., pp. 188–9.

11. Ray Stannard Baker, "The Right to Work: The Story of the Non-Striking Miners," *McClure's Magazine*, January 1903: 334.

12. Kearns Goodwin, pp. 402–3.

13. Ibid., p. 491.

14. Ibid., p. 493.

15. Edwin Lefevre, in "Flagler and Florida" from *Everybody's Magazine*, XXII (February, 1910) p. 183.

16. All of the Plunkett quotes that follow come from George Washington Plunkett, *Plunkett of Tammany Hall: A Series of Very Plain Talks on Very Practical Politics, Delivered by Ex-senator George Washington Plunkett, the Tammany Philosopher, from His Rostrum—the New York County Court House Bootblack Stand*, Recorded by William L. Riordon (1905) Gutenberg Project, http://www.gutenberg.org/files/2810/2810-h/2810-h.htm. *Release Date: December 29, 2008 [EBook #2810]* Last Updated: February 7, 2013.

17. Ibid., Chapter 23, np.

18. "Victoria Woodhull Quotes," http://www.brainyquote.com/quotes/quotes/v/victoriawo312237.html#HIGtpjGzvWLgC3s7.99 (August 8, 2014).

19. Adam Goodheart, "Divorce, Antebellum Style" Opinionator Blog, *New York Times*, March 18, 2011, http://opinionator.blogs.nytimes.com/2011/03/18/divorce-antebellum-style/?_php=true&_type=blogs&_r=0

20. Victoria Woodhull, *Constitutional Equality, The Logical Results of the Fourteenth and Fifteenth Amendments, Which Not Only Declare Who Are Citizens but Also Defends Their Rights One of Which Is the Right to Vote Without Regard to Sex* (New York: Journeymen Printers, 1870).

21. "Victoria Woodhull," http://www.highplainschautauqua.org/victoria-woodhull-.aspx (August 8, 2014).

22. Helen Lefkowitz Horowitz, "Victoria Woodhull, Anthony Comstock, and Conflict over Sex in the United States in the1870s," *The Journal of American History*, Vol. 87, No. 2 (September 2000), 403–434: 404.

23. *Harpers Weekly*, http://www.harpweek.com/09cartoon/BrowseByDateCartoon.asp?Month=February&Date=17

24. All quotes come from: Jeff Riggenbach "Randolph Bourne 1886–1918" http://randolphbourne.org/rbbio.html (August 7, 2014).

PRIMARY DOCUMENTS

DOCUMENT 1
Jacob Riis Describes Life among the Urban Poor (1890)

An extraordinarily gifted photographer, Jacob Riis focused much of his attention on capturing the plight of the country's poor. In a series of publications, but most notably this one of 1890, Riis published photographs and accompanying text showing the horrible conditions of the poor living in New York City's tenements. Riis converted his photographs to lantern slides and used them for talks he gave to enlighten the middle class especially about the need to discover the poor and help them. An excerpt of his book, How the Other Half Lives, *appears next. Riis's work shocked the nation and led to calls for poor relief, sanitation and health care reform, and greater workers' rights.*

The dread of advancing cholera, with the guilty knowledge of the harvest field that awaited the plague in New York's slums, pricked the conscience of the community into action soon after the close of the war. A citizens' movement resulted in the organization of a Board of Health and the adoption of the "Tenement-House Act" of 1867, the first step toward remedial legislation. A thorough canvass of the tenements had been begun already in the previous year; but the cholera first, and next a scourge of smallpox, delayed the work, while emphasizing the need of it, so that it was 1869 before it got fairly under way and began to tell. The dark bedroom fell under the ban first. In that year the Board ordered the cutting of more than forty-six thousand windows in interior rooms, chiefly for ventilation—for little or no light was to be had from the dark hallways. Air-shafts were unknown. The saw had a job all that summer; by early fall nearly all the orders had been carried out. Not without opposition; obstacles were thrown in the way of the officials on the one side by the owners of the tenements, who saw in every order to repair or clean up only an item of added expense to diminish their income from the rent; on the other side by the tenants themselves, who had sunk, after a generation of unavailing protest, to the level of their surroundings, and were at last content to remain there. The tenements had bred their Nemesis, a proletariat ready and able to avenge the wrongs of their crowds. Already it taxed the city heavily for the support of its jails and charities. The basis of opposition, curiously enough was the same at both extremes; owner and tenant alike considered official interference an infringement of personal rights, and a hardship. It took long years of weary labor to make good the claim of the sunlight to such corners of the dens as it could reach at all. Not until five years after did the department succeed at last in ousting the "cave-dwellers" and closing some five hundred and fifty cellars south of Houston Street, many of them below tide-water, that had been used as living apartments. In many instances the police had to drag the tenants out by force.

The work went on; but the need of it only grew with the effort. The Sanitarians were following up an evil that grew faster than they went; like a fire, it could only be headed off, not chased, with success. Official reports, read in the churches in 1879, characterized the younger criminals as Victims of low social conditions of life and unhealthy, overcrowded lodgings, brought up in "an atmosphere of actual darkness, moral and physical." This after the saw had been busy in the dark corners ten years! "If we could see the air breathed by these poor creatures in their tenements," said a well-known physician, "it would show itself to be fouler than the mud of the gutters." Little improvement was apparent despite all that had been done. "The new tenements, that have been recently built, have been usually as badly planned as the old, with dark and unhealthy rooms, often over wet cellars, where extreme overcrowding is permitted," was the verdict of one authority. These are the houses that to-day perpetuate the worst traditions of the past, and they are counted by thousands. The Five Points had been cleansed, as far as the immediate neighborhood was concerned, but the Mulberry Street Bend was fast outdoing it in foulness not a stone's threw away, and new centres of corruption were continually springing up and getting the upper hand whenever vigilance was relaxed for ever so short a time. It is one of the curses of the tenement-house system that the worst houses exercise a levelling influence upon all the rest, just as one bad boy in a schoolroom will spoil the whole class. It is one of the ways the evil that was "the result of forgetfulness of the poor," as the Council of Hygiene mildly put it, has of avenging itself.

The determined effort to head it off by laying a strong hand upon the tenement builders that has been the chief business of the Health Board of recent years, dates from this period. The era of the air-shaft has not solved the problem of housing the poor, but it has made good use of limited opportunities. Over the new houses sanitary law exercises full control. But the old remain. They cannot be summarily torn down, though in extreme cases the authorities can order them cleared. The outrageous overcrowding, too, remains. It is characteristic of the tenements. Poverty, their badge and typical condition, invites—compels it. All efforts to abate it result only in temporary relief. As long as they exist it will exist with them. And the tenements will exist in New York forever.

To-day, what is a tenement? The law defines it as a house "occupied by three or more families, living independently and doing their cooking on the premises; or by more than two families on a floor, so living and cooking and having a common right in the halls, stairways, yards, etc." That is the legal meaning, and includes flats and apartment-houses, with which we have nothing to do. In its narrower sense the typical tenement was thus described when last arraigned before the bar of public justice: "It is generally a brick building from four to six stories high on the street, frequently with a store on the first floor which, when used for the sale of liquor, has a side opening for the benefit of the inmates and to evade the Sunday law; four families occupy each floor, and a set of rooms consists of one or two dark closets, used as bedrooms, with a living room twelve feet by ten. The staircase is too often a dark well in the centre of the house, and no direct through ventilation is possible, each family being separated from the other by partitions. Frequently the rear of the lot is occupied by another building of three stories high with two families on a floor." The picture is nearly as true to-day as ten years ago, and will be for a long time to come. The dim light admitted by the air-shaft shines upon greater crowds than ever. Tenements are still "good property," and the poverty of the poor man his destruction. A barrack down town where he has to live because he is poor brings in a third more rent than a decent flat house in

Harlem. The statement once made a sensation that between seventy and eighty children had been found in one tenement. It no longer excites even passing attention, when the sanitary police report counting 101 adults and 91 children in a Crosby Street house, one of twins, built together. The children in the other, if I am not mistaken, numbered 89, a total of 180 for two tenements! Or when a midnight inspection in Mulberry Street unearths a hundred and fifty "lodgers" sleeping on filthy floors in two buildings. Spite of brown-stone trimmings, plate-glass and mosaic vestibule floors, the water does not rise in summer to the second story, while the beer flows unchecked to the all-night picnics on the roof. The saloon with the side-door and the landlord divide the prosperity of the place between them, and the tenant, in sullen submission, foots the bills.

Where are the tenements of to-day? Say rather: where are they not? In fifty years they have crept up from the Fourth Ward slums and the Five Points the whole length of the island, and have polluted the Annexed District to the Westchester line. Crowding all the lower wards, wherever business leaves a foot of ground unclaimed; strung along both rivers, like ball and chain tied to the foot of every street, and filling up Harlem with their restless, pent-up multitudes, they hold within their clutch the wealth and business of New York, hold them at their mercy in the day of mob-rule and wrath. The bullet-proof shutters, the stacks of hand-grenades, and the Gatling guns of the Sub-Treasury are tacit admissions of the fact and of the quality of the mercy expected. The tenements to-day are New York, harboring three-fourths of its population. When another generation shall have doubled the census of our city, and to that vast army of workers, held captive by poverty, the very name of home shall be as a bitter mockery, what will the harvest be?

Source: Jacob Riis, *How the Other Half Lives* (New York: Charles Scribner's Sons, 1890).

DOCUMENT 2
William Jennings Bryan: Cross of Gold Speech (1896)

At the Democratic National Convention on July 8, 1896, William Jennings Bryan, a young congressman from Nebraska known as "the boy orator from the Platte" electrified the convention with one of the most famous and memorable

speeches in American political history. With his plea for a plank supporting silver,
Bryan rallied the insurgents of the Democratic Party who defeated the old guard
"Gold" Democrats and nominated Bryan as their candidate for president. Follow-
ing are excerpts from that speech.

I would be presumptuous, indeed, to present myself against the distinguished gentlemen to whom you have listened if this were but a measuring
of ability; but this is not a contest among persons. The humblest citizen
in all the land when clad in the armor of a righteous cause is stronger
than all the whole hosts of error that they can bring. I come to speak to
you in defense of a cause as holy as the cause of liberty—the cause of
humanity.

When you come before us and tell us that we shall disturb your business
interests, we reply that you have disturbed our business interests by your
action. We say to you that you have made too limited in its application
the definition of a businessman. The man who is employed for wages is as
much a businessman as his employer. The attorney in a country town is
as much a businessman as the corporation counsel in a great metropolis.
The merchant at the crossroads store is as much a businessman as the merchant of New York. The farmer who goes forth in the morning and toils all
day, begins in the spring and toils all summer, and by the application of
brain and muscle to the natural resources of this country creates wealth,
is as much a businessman as the man who goes upon the Board of Trade
and bets upon the price of grain. The miners who go 1,000 feet into the
earth or climb 2,000 feet upon the cliffs and bring forth from their hiding
places the precious metals to be poured in the channels of trade are as
much businessmen as the few financial magnates who in a backroom corner the money of the world.

You come to us and tell us that the great cities are in favor of the gold
standard. I tell you that the great cities rest upon these broad and fertile
prairies. Burn down your cities and leave our farms, and your cities will
spring up again as if by magic. But destroy our farms and the grass will grow
in the streets of every city in the country.

If they dare to come out in the open field and defend the gold standard
as a good thing, we shall fight them to the uttermost, having behind us the
producing masses of the nation and the world. Having behind us the commercial interests and the laboring interests and all the toiling masses, we

shall answer their demands for a gold standard by saying to them, you shall not press down upon the brow of labor this crown of thorns. You shall not crucify mankind upon a cross of gold.

Source: Official Proceedings of the Democratic National Convention Held in Chicago, Illinois, July 7, 8, 9, 10, and 11, 1896 (Logansport, IN, 1896), 226–234.

DOCUMENT 3
Progressive Party Platform (1912)

By the end of the nineteenth century, a large cross section of Americans, including professionals such a lawyers, teachers, social workers, and doctors, became increasingly concerned and angry over the injustices perpetrated by the new corporate system and the corruption in government. In response, they began to organize politically to reform governments at all levels and then to get those governments to address social and economic inequities. Urged on by journalists whom Teddy Roosevelt called "muckrakers," these groups fought for laws that protected children and women in the workplace, regulated trusts, protected natural resources, brought professional standards to the various professions, and more. Although these groups usually worked locally, and each had its particular cause, they collectively became known as and prided themselves as Progressives. In 1901 fate—in the form of the assassination of William McKinley and the succession of Teddy Roosevelt to the presidency—gave these largely local movements a national leader. Over the next eight years, Roosevelt supported much of the Progressive agenda. In 1912, when Roosevelt was denied the nomination of his party after a four-year hiatus from the White House, his supporters in a third-party movement, the Progressive Party, nominated him as their presidential candidate. Roosevelt lost the election, but much of what the Progressives called for in their 1912 platform became realized in the ensuing decades.

The conscience of the people, in a time of grave national problems, has called into being a new party, born of the nation's sense of justice. We of the Progressive party here dedicate ourselves to the fulfillment of the duty laid upon us by our fathers to maintain the government of the people, by the people and for the people whose foundations they laid.

This country belongs to the people who inhabit it. Its resources, its business, its institutions and its laws should be utilized, maintained or altered in whatever manner will best promote the general interest.

It is time to set the public welfare in the first place.

The National Progressive party, committed to the principles of government by a self-controlled democracy expressing its will through representatives of the people, pledges itself to secure such alterations in the fundamental law of the several States and of the United States as shall insure the representative character of the government.

In particular, the party declares for direct primaries for the nomination of State and National officers, for nation-wide preferential primaries for candidates for the presidency; for the direct election of United States Senators by the people; and we urge on the States the policy of the short ballot, with responsibility to the people secured by the initiative, referendum and recall.

. . . equal suffrage to men and women alike.

. . . all campaign contributions and expenditures, and detailed publicity of both before as well as after primaries and elections.

. . . the registration of lobbyists; publicity of committee hearings except on foreign affairs, and recording of all votes in committee.

. . . We believe that the issuance of injunctions in cases arising out of labor disputes should be prohibited when such injunctions would not apply when no labor disputes existed.

. . . the conservation of human resources through an enlightened measure of social and industrial justice.

. . . Effective legislation looking to the prevention of industrial accidents, occupational diseases, overwork, involuntary unemployment, and other injurious effects incident to modern industry;

. . . minimum safety and health standards for the various occupations, and the exercise of the public authority of State and Nation, including the Federal Control over interstate commerce, and the taxing power, to maintain such standards;

. . . The prohibition of child labor;

. . . Minimum wage standards for working women, to provide a "living wage" in all industrial occupations;

. . . One days rest in seven for all wage workers;

. . . The eight hour day in continuous twenty-four hour industries;

. . . The abolition of the convict contract labor system;

. . . The protection of home life against the hazards of sickness, irregular employment and old age through the adoption of a system of social insurance adapted to American use;

... The development of the creative labor power of America by lifting the last load of illiteracy from American youth and establishing continuation schools for industrial education under public control and encouraging agricultural education and demonstration in rural schools;

... We pledge our party to foster the development of agricultural credit and cooperation, the teaching of agriculture in schools, agricultural college extension, the use of mechanical power on the farm, and to re-establish the Country Life Commission, thus directly promoting the welfare of the farmers, and bringing the benefits of better farming, better business and better living within their reach.

... We favor the union of all the existing agencies of the Federal Government dealing with the public health into a single national health service.

The natural resources of the Nation must be promptly developed and generously used to supply the peoples needs, but we cannot safely allow them to be wasted, exploited, monopolized or controlled against the general good. We heartily favor the policy of conservation, and we pledge our party to protect the National forests without hindering their legitimate use for the benefit of all the people.

Agricultural lands in the National forests are, and should remain, open to the genuine settler.

We believe that the remaining forests, coal and oil lands, water powers and other natural resources still in State or National control (except agricultural lands) are more likely to be wisely conserved and utilized for the general welfare if held in the public hands.

The people of the United States are swindled out of many millions of dollars every year, through worthless investments. The plain people, the wage earner and the men and women with small savings, have no way of knowing the merit of concerns sending out highly colored prospectuses offering stock for sale, prospectuses that make big returns seem certain and fortunes easily within grasp.

We hold it to be the duty of the Government to protect its people from this kind of piracy. We, therefore, demand wise, carefully thought out legislation that will give us such Governmental supervision over this matter as will furnish to the people of the United States this much-needed protection, and we pledge ourselves thereto.

Conclusion

On these principles and on the recognized desirability of uniting the Progressive forces of the Nation into an organization which shall unequivocally represent the Progressive spirit and policy we appeal for the support of all American citizens, without regard to previous political affiliation.

Source: Platform of the Progressive Party, Adopted at Its First National Convention, Chicago, August 7, 1912 (New York City: Progressive National Committee, 1912).

DOCUMENT 4
Justice John Marshall Harlan's Dissent to *Plessy vs. Ferguson* Decision (1896)

In a landmark case that made segregation legal, the U.S. Supreme Court upheld a Louisiana law providing for racial segregation on railroads. The effect of the decision was to encourage further legislation to institute racial segregation in all public places and activities, which occurred rapidly following the decision. Southerners invoked the decision as having legitimized the entrenchment of segregation practices in the South. Justice John Marshall Harlan, in his prescient dissent in Plessy, anticipated the arguments that led to the decision's reversal 60 years later.

By the Louisiana statute the validity of which is here involved, all railway companies (other than street-railroad companies) carry passengers in that state are required to have separate but equal accommodations for white and colored persons, "by providing two or more passenger coaches for each passenger train, or by dividing the passenger coaches by a partition so as to secure separate accommodations." Under this statute, no colored person is permitted to occupy a seat in a coach assigned to white persons; nor any white person to occupy a seat in a coach assigned to colored persons. The managers of the railroad are not allowed to exercise any discretion in the premises, but are required to assign each passenger to some coach or compartment set apart for the exclusive use of his race. If a passenger insists upon going into a coach or compartment not set apart for persons of his race, he is subject to be fined, or to be imprisoned in the parish jail. Penalties are prescribed for the refusal or neglect of the officers, directors, conductors, and employees of railroad companies to comply with the provisions of the act.

The thirteenth amendment does not permit the withholding or the deprivation of any right necessarily inhering in freedom. It not only struck down the institution of slavery as previously existing in the United States, but it prevents the imposition of any burdens or disabilities that constitute badges of slavery or servitude. It decreed universal civil freedom in this country.

Finally, and to the end that no citizen should be denied, on account of his race, the privilege of participating in the political control of his country, it was declared by the fifteenth amendment that "the right of citizens of the United States to vote shall not be denied or abridged by the United States or by any state on account of race, color or previous condition of servitude."

These notable additions to the fundamental law were welcomed by the friends of liberty throughout the world.

It is one thing for railroad carriers to furnish, or to be required by law to furnish, equal accommodations for all whom they are under a legal duty to carry. It is quite another thing for government to forbid citizens of the white and black races from traveling in the same public conveyance and to punish officers of railroad companies for permitting persons of the two races to occupy the same passenger coach. If a state can prescribe, as a rule of civil conduct, that whites and blacks shall not travel as passengers in the same railroad coach, why may it not so regulate the use of the streets of its cities and towns as to compel white citizens to keep on one side of a street and black citizens to keep on the other? Why may it not, upon like grounds, punish whites and blacks who ride together in street cars or in open vehicles on a public road or street? Why may it not require sheriffs to assign whites to one side of a court room and blacks to the other? And why may it not also prohibit the commingling of the two races in the galleries of legislative halls or in public assemblages convened for the consideration of the political questions of the day? Further, if this statute of Louisiana is consistent with the personal liberty of citizens, why may not the state require the separation in railroad coaches of native and naturalized citizens of the United States or of Protestants and Roman Catholics?

The answer given at the argument to these questions was that regulations of the kind they suggest would be unreasonable, and could not, therefore, stand before the law.

The white race deems itself to be the dominant race in this country. And so it is, in prestige, in achievements, in education, in wealth, and in power. So, I doubt not, it will continue to be for all time, if it remains true to its great heritage and holds fast to the principles of constitutional liberty. But in view of the constitution, in the eye of the law, there is in this country no superior, dominant, ruling class of citizens. There is no caste here. Our constitution is color-blind and neither knows nor tolerates classes among citizens. In respect of civil rights, all citizens are equal before the law. The humblest is the peer of the most powerful. The law regards man as man and takes no account of his surroundings or of his color when his civil rights as guaranteed by the supreme law of the land are involved. It is therefore to be regretted that this high tribunal, the final expositor of the fundamental law of the land, has reached the conclusion that it is competent for a state to regulate the enjoyment by citizens of their civil rights solely upon the basis of race.

In my opinion, the judgment this day rendered will, in time, prove to be quite as pernicious as the decision made by this tribunal in the Dred Scott Case.

I am of opinion that the state of Louisiana is inconsistent with the personal liberty of citizens, white and black, in that state, and hostile to both the spirit and letter of the constitution of the United States. If laws of like character should be enacted in the several states of the Union, the effect would be in the highest degree mischievous. Slavery, as an institution tolerated by law, would, it is true, have disappeared from our country; but there would remain a power in the states, by sinister legislation, to interfere with the full enjoyment of the blessings of freedom, to regulate civil rights, common to all citizens, upon the basis of race, and to place in a condition of legal inferiority a large body of American citizens, now constituting a part of the political community, called the "People of the United States," for whom, and by whom through representatives, our government is administered. Such a system is inconsistent with the guaranty given by the constitution to each state of a republican form of government, and may be stricken down by congressional action, or by the courts in the discharge of their solemn duty to maintain the supreme law of the land, anything in the constitution or laws of any state to the contrary notwithstanding.

For the reason stated, I am constrained to withhold my assent from the opinion and judgment of the majority.

Source: 163 U.S. 537 (1896).

DOCUMENT 5
Booker T. Washington Delivers the 1895 Atlanta Compromise Speech

On September 18, 1895, African American leader Booker T. Washington spoke before a predominantly white audience at the Cotton States and International Exposition in Atlanta. Some organizers of the event questioned whether their fellow Southerners were ready for such a departure from accepted decorum. But others insisted on having the black man address the white audience in order to show northern whites that a new more racially tolerant South was emerging. The speech, which became known as the Atlanta Compromise, reverberated over the decades. Hailed by some, condemned by others, it marked nonetheless a defining moment in the history of Civil Rights in the United States. Following are excerpts from that speech.

One-third of the population of the South is of the Negro race. No enterprise seeking the material, civil, or moral welfare of this section can disregard this element of our population and reach the highest success. I but convey to you, Mr. President and Directors, the sentiment of the masses of my race when I say that in no way have the value and manhood of the American Negro been more fittingly and generously recognized than by the managers of this magnificent Exposition at every stage of its progress. It is a recognition that will do more to cement the friendship of the two races than any occurrence since the dawn of our freedom.

Not only this, but the opportunity here afforded will awaken among us a new era of industrial progress. Ignorant and inexperienced, it is not strange that in the first years of our new life we began at the top instead of at the bottom; that a seat in Congress or the state legislature was more sought than real estate or industrial skill; that the political convention or stump speaking had more attractions than starting a dairy farm or truck garden . . .

To those of my race who depend on bettering their condition in a foreign land or who underestimate the importance of cultivating friendly relations with the Southern white man, who is their next-door neighbor, I would say: "Cast down your bucket where you are"—cast it down in making friends in every manly way of the people of all races by whom we are surrounded.

Cast it down in agriculture, mechanics, in commerce, in domestic service, and in the professions. And in this connection it is well to bear in mind that whatever other sins the South may be called to bear, when it comes to business, pure and simple, it is in the South that the Negro is given a man's chance in the commercial world . . .

Our greatest danger is that in the great leap from slavery to freedom we may overlook the fact that the masses of us are to live by the productions of our hands, and fail to keep in mind that we shall prosper in proportion as we learn to dignify and glorify common labour, and put brains and skill into the common occupations of life; shall prosper in proportion as we learn to draw the line between the superficial and the substantial, the ornamental gewgaws of life and the useful. No race can prosper till it learns that there is as much dignity in tilling a field as in writing a poem. It is at the bottom of life we must begin, and not at the top. Nor should we permit our grievances to overshadow our opportunities.

To those of the white race who look to the incoming of those of foreign birth and strange tongue and habits for the prosperity of the South, were I permitted I would repeat what I say to my own race, "Cast down your bucket where you are."

. . . we shall stand by you with a devotion that no foreigner can approach, ready to lay down our lives, if need be, in defense of yours, interlacing our industrial, commercial, civil, and religious life with yours in a way that shall make the interests of both races one. In all things that are purely social we can be as separate as the fingers, yet one as the hand in all things essential to mutual progress.

Source: Daniel Murray Pamphlet Collection, Library of Congress. Available online at http://hdl.loc.gov/loc.rbc/lcrbmrp.t0c15.

DOCUMENT 6
W. E. B. Du Bois, *The Philadelphia Negro* (1899)

In this seminal work on blacks in Philadelphia, Du Bois established himself as the preeminent sociologist in the country. In the following section he describes how the urban black working-class community found entertainment.

The most innocent amusements of this class are the balls and cake-walks, although they are accompanied by much drinking, and are attended by white and black prostitutes, the cake-walk is a rhythmic promenade or slow dance, and when well done is pretty and quite innocent. Excursions are frequent in summer, and are accompanied often by much fighting and drinking. The mass of the laboring Negroes get their amusement in connection with the churches. There are suppers, fairs, concerts, socials and the like. Dancing is forbidden by most of the churches, and many of the stricter sort would not think of going to balls or theatres. The younger set, however, dance, although the parents seldom accompany them, and the hours kept are late, making it often a dissipation. Secret societies and social clubs add to these amusements by balls and suppers, and there are numbers of parties at private houses. This class also patronizes frequent excursions given by churches and Sunday schools and secret societies; they are usually well conducted, but cost a great deal more than is necessary. The money wasted in excursions above what would be necessary for a day's outing and plenty of recreation, would foot up many thousand dollars in a season.

Source: W. E. B. Du Bois, *The Philadelphia Negro: A Social Study* (New York: Schocken Books, 1899), 220.

DOCUMENT 7
Upton Sinclair Exposes the Meat Industry (1906)

In 1906 Upton Sinclair was a young socialist who set out to write a novel exposing the abuses of the meatpacking industry committed against immigrant workers. In the process of telling Americans about the horrible conditions under which the workers suffered, he also revealed the disgusting practices in Chicago's meat processing plants. He included stories of rats and sometimes workers' fingers being ground up with the sausage. The book became an immediate best seller and turned many people into vegetarians, at least for a time. Theodore Roosevelt was so sickened by what he read that he demanded and got the passage of a Federal Meat Inspection Bill. Following is an excerpt from the book, which remains the most popular and powerful piece of fiction associated with the Progressive Era.

They passed down the busy street that led to the yards. It was still early morning, and everything was at its high tide of activity. A steady stream of employees was pouring through the gate—employees of the higher sort, at this hour, clerks and stenographers and such. For the women there were waiting big two-horse wagons, which set off at a gallop as fast as they were filled. In the distance there was heard again the lowing of the cattle, a sound as of a far-off ocean calling. They followed it this time, as eager as children in sight of a circus menagerie—which, indeed, the scene a good deal resembled. They crossed the railroad tracks, and then on each side of the street were the pens full of cattle; they would have stopped to look, but Jokubas hurried them on, to where there was a stairway and a raised gallery, from which everything could be seen. Here they stood, staring, breathless with wonder.

There is over a square mile of space in the yards, and more than half of it is occupied by cattle pens; north and south as far as the eye can reach there stretches a sea of pens. And they were all filled—so many cattle no one had ever dreamed existed in the world. Red cattle, black, white, and yellow cattle; old cattle and young cattle; great bellowing bulls and little calves not an hour born; meek-eyed milch cows and fierce, long-horned Texas steers. The sound of them here was as of all the barnyards of the universe; and as for counting them—it would have taken all day simply to count the pens. Here and there ran long alleys, blocked at intervals by gates; and Jokubas told them that the number of these gates was twenty-five thousand. Jokubas had recently been reading a newspaper article which was full of statistics such as that, and he was very proud as he repeated them and made his guests cry out with wonder. Jurgis too had a little of this sense of pride. Had he not just gotten a job, and become a sharer in all this activity, a cog in this marvelous machine?

Here and there about the alleys galloped men upon horse-back, booted, and carrying long whips; they were very busy, calling to each other, and to those who were driving the cattle. They were drovers and stock-raisers, who had come from far states, and brokers and commission-merchants, and buyers for all the big packing houses. Here and there they would stop to inspect a bunch of cattle, and there would be a parley, brief and businesslike. The buyer would nod or drop his whip, and that would mean a bargain; and he would note it in his little book, along with hundreds of others he had made that morning. Then Jokubas pointed out the place where the cattle were driven to be weighed upon a great scale that would weigh a hundred thousand pounds at once and record it automatically. It was near to the east entrance that they stood, and all along this east side of the yards ran the railroad tracks, into which the cars were run, loaded with cattle. All night long this had been going on, and now the pens were full; by tonight they would all be empty, and the same thing would be done again.

"And what will become of all these creatures?" cried Teta Elzbieta.

"By tonight," Jokubas answered, "they will all be killed and cut up; and over there on the other side of the packing houses are more railroad tracks, were the cars come to take them away."

There were two hundred and fifty miles of track within the yards, their guide went on to tell them. They brought about ten thousand head of cattle every day, and as many hogs, and half as many sheep—which meant some eight or ten million live creatures turned into food every year. One stood and watched, and little by little caught the drift of the tide, as it set in the direction of the packing houses. There were groups of cattle being driven to the chutes, which were roadways about fifteen feet wide, raised high above the pens. In these chutes the stream of animals was continuous; it was quite uncanny to watch them, pressing on to their fate, all unsuspicious—a very river of death. Our friends were not poetical, and the sight suggested to them no metaphors of human destiny; they thought only of the wonderful efficiency of it all. The chutes into which the hogs went climbed high up—to the very top of the distant buildings, and Jokubas explained that the hogs went up by the power of their own legs, and then their weight carried them back through all the processes necessary to make them into pork.

"They don't waste anything here," said the guide, and then he laughed and added a witticism, which he was pleased that his unsophisticated friends should take to be his own: "They use everything about the hog except the squeal." In front of Brown's General Office building there grows a tiny plot of grass, and this, you may learn, is the only bit of green thing in Packingtown; likewise this jest about the hog and his squeal, the stock in trade of all the guides, is the one gleam of humor that you will find there.

After they had seen enough of the pens, the party went up the street, to the mass of buildings which occupy the centre of the yards. These buildings, made of brick and stained with innumerable layers of Packingtown smoke, were painted all over with advertising signs, from which the visitor realized suddenly that he had come to the home of many of the torments of his life. It was here that they made those products with the wonders of which they pestered him so—by placards that defaced the landscape when he traveled, and by staring advertisements in the newspapers and magazines—by silly little jingles that he could not get out of his mind, and gaudy pictures that lurked for him around every street corner. Here was where they made Brown's Imperial Hams and Bacon, Brown's Dressed Beef, Brown's Excelsior Sausages! Here was the headquarters of Durham's Pure Leaf Lard, of Durham's Breakfast Bacon, Durham's Canned Beef, Potted Ham, Deviled Chicken, Peerless Fertilizer!

Entering one of the Durham buildings, they found a number of other visitors waiting, and before long there came a guide, to escort them through the place. They make a great feature of showing strangers through the packing plants, for it is a good advertisement. But Ponas Jokubas whispered maliciously that the visitors did not see any more than the packers wanted them to.

They climbed a long series of stairways outside of the building, to the top of its five or six stories. Here were the chute, with its river of hogs, all patiently toiling upward; there was a place for them to rest to cool off, and then through another passageway they went into a room from which there is no returning for hogs.

It was a long, narrow room, with a gallery along it for visitors. At the head there was a great iron wheel, about twenty feet in circumference, with rings here and there along its edge. Upon both sides of this wheel there was a narrow space, into which came the hogs at the end of their journey; in the midst of them stood a great burly Negro, bare-armed and bare-chested. He was resting for the moment, for the wheel had stopped while men were cleaning up. In a minute or two, however, it began slowly to revolve, and then the men upon each side of it sprang to work. They had chains which they fastened about the leg of the nearest hog, and the other end of the chain they hooked into one of the rings upon the wheel. So, as the wheel turned, a hog was suddenly jerked off his feet and borne aloft.

At the same instant the ear was assailed by a most terrifying shriek; the visitors started in alarm, the women turned pale and shrank back. The shriek was followed by another, louder and yet more agonizing—for once started upon that journey, the hog never came back; at the top of the wheel he was shunted off upon a trolley, and went sailing down the room. And meantime another was swung up, and then another, and another, until there was a double line of them, each dangling by a foot and kicking in frenzy—and squealing. The uproar was appalling, perilous to the ear-drums; one feared there was too much sound for the room to hold—that the walls must give way or the ceiling crack. There were high squeals and low squeals, grunts, and wails of agony; there would come a momentary lull, and then a fresh outburst, louder than ever, surging up to a deafening climax. It was too much for some of the visitors—the men would look at each other, laughing nervously, and the women would stand with hands clenched, and the blood rushing to their faces, and the tears starting in their eyes.

Meantime, heedless of all these things, the men upon the floor were going about their work. Neither squeals of hogs nor tears of visitors made any difference to them; one by one they hooked up the hogs, and one by one with a swift stroke they slit their throats. There was a long line of hogs, with squeals and life-blood ebbing away together, until at last each started again, and vanished with a splash into a huge vat of boiling water.

It was all so very businesslike that one watched it fascinated. It was pork-making by machinery, pork-making by applied mathematics. And yet somehow the most matter-of-fact person could not help thinking of the hogs; they were so innocent, they came so very trustingly; and they were so very human in their protests—and so perfectly within their rights! They had done nothing to deserve it, and it was adding insult to injury, as the thing was done here, swinging them up in this cold-blooded, imper-sonal way, without a pretence at apology, without the homage of a tear. Now and then a visitor wept, to be sure; but this slaughtering machine ran on, visitors or no visitors. It was like some horrible crime committed in a dungeon, all unseen and unheeded, buried out of sight and of memory.

One could not stand and watch very long without becoming philosophical, without beginning to deal in symbols and similes, and to hear the hog-squeal of the universe. Was it permitted to believe that there was nowhere upon the earth, or above the earth, a heaven for hogs, where they were requited for all this suffering? Each one of these hogs was a separate creature. Some were white hogs, some were black; some were brown, some were spotted; some were old, some were young; some were long and lean, some were monstrous. And each of them had an individuality of his own, a will of his own, a hope and a heart's desire; each was full of self-confidence, of self-importance, and a sense of dignity. And trusting and strong in faith he had gone about his business, the while a black shadow hung over him and horrid Fate waited in his pathway. Now suddenly it had swooped upon him, and had seized him by the leg. Relentless, remorseless, it was; all his protests, his screams, were nothing to it—it did its cruel will with him, as if his wishes, his feelings, had simply no existence at all; it cut his throat and watched him gasp out his life. And now was one to believe that there was nowhere a god of hogs, to whom this hog-personality was precious, to whom these hog-squeals and agonies had a meaning? Who would take this hog into his arms and comfort him, reward him for his work well done, and show him the meaning of his sacrifice? Perhaps some glimpse of all this was in the thoughts of our humble-minded Jurgis, as he turned to go on with the rest of the party, and muttered, "*Dieve*—but I'm glad I'm not a hog!"

The carcass hog was scooped out of the vat by machinery, and then it fell to the second floor, passing on the way through a wonderful machine with numerous scrapers, which adjusted themselves to the size and shape of the animal, and sent it out at the other end with nearly all of its bristles removed. It was then again strung up by machinery, and sent upon another trolley ride; this time passing between two lines of men, who sat upon a raised platform, each doing a certain single thing to the carcass as it came to him. One scraped the outside of a leg; another scraped the inside of the same leg. One with a swift stroke cut the throat; another with two swift strokes severed the head, which fell to the floor and vanished through a hole. Another made a slit down the body; a second opened the body wider;

a third with a saw cut the breastbone; a fourth loosened the entrails; a fifth pulled them out—and they also slid through a hole in the floor. There were men to scrape each side and men to scrape the back; there were men to clean the carcass inside, to trim it and wash it. Looking down this room, one saw, creeping slowly, a line of dangling hogs a hundred yards in length; and for every yard there was a man, working as if a demon were after him. At the end of this hog's progress every inch of the carcass had been gone over several times, and then it was rolled into the chilling room, where it stayed for twenty-four hours, and where a stranger might lose himself in a forest of freezing hogs.

Before the carcass was admitted here, however, it had to pass a government inspector, who sat in the doorway and felt of the glands in the neck for tuberculosis. This government inspector did not have the manner of a man who was worked to death; he was apparently not haunted by a fear that the hog might get by him before he had finished his testing. If you were a sociable person, he was quite willing to enter into conversation with you, and to explain to you the deadly nature of the ptomaines which are found in tubercular pork; and while he was talking with you, you could hardly be so ungrateful as to notice that a dozen carcasses were passing him untouched. This inspector wore an imposing silver badge, and he gave an atmosphere of authority to the scene, and, as it were, put the stamp of official approval upon the things which were done in Durham's.

Jurgis went down the line with the rest of the visitors, staring open-mouthed, lost in wonder. He had dressed hogs himself in the forest of Lithuania; but he had never expected to live to see one hog dressed by several hundred men. It was like a wonderful poem to him, and he took it all in guilelessly—even to the conspicuous signs demanding immaculate cleanliness of the employees. Jurgis was vexed when the cynical Jokubas translated these signs with sarcastic comments, offering to take them to the secret rooms where the spoiled meats went to be doctored.

The party descended to the next floor, where the various waste materials were treated. Here came the entrails, to be scraped and washed clean for sausage casings; men and women worked here in the midst of a sickening stench, which caused the visitors to hasten by, gasping. To another room came all the scraps to be "tanked," which meant boiling and pumping off the grease to make soap and lard; below they took out the refuse, and this, too, was a region in which the visitors did not linger. In still other places men were engaged in cutting up the carcasses that had been through the chilling rooms. First there were the "splitters," the most expert workmen in the plant, who earned as high as fifty cents an hour, and did not a thing all day except chop hogs down the middle. Then there were "cleaver men," great giants with muscles of iron; each had two men to attend him—to slide the half carcass in front of him on the table, and hold it while he chopped it, and then turn each piece so that he might chop it once more. His cleaver had a blade about two feet long, and he never made but one cut; he made it so neatly, too, that his implement did not smite through and dull itself—there was just enough force for a perfect cut, and no more. So through various yawning holes there slipped to the floor below—to one room hams, to another forequarters, to another sides of pork. One might go down to this floor and see the pickling rooms, where the hams were put into vats, and the great smoke rooms, with their airtight iron doors. In other rooms they prepared salt pork—there were whole cellars full of it, built up in great towers to the ceiling. In yet other rooms they were putting up meat in boxes and barrels, and wrapping hams and bacon in oiled paper, sealing and labeling and sewing them. From the doors of these rooms went men with loaded trucks, to the platform where freight cars were waiting to be filled; and one went out there and realized with a start that he had come at last to the ground floor of this enormous building.

Then the party went across the street to where they did the killing of beef—where every hour they turned four or five hundred cattle into meat. Unlike the place they had left, all this work was done on one floor, and instead of there being one line of carcasses which moved to the workmen, there were fifteen or twenty lines, and the men moved from one to another of these. This made a scene of intense activity, a picture of human power wonderful to watch. It was all in one great room, like a circus amphitheater, with a gallery for visitors running over the center.

Along one side of the room ran a narrow gallery, a few feet from the floor, into which gallery the cattle were driven by men with goads which gave them electric shocks. Once crowded in here, the creatures were prisoned, each in a separate pen, by gates that shut, leaving them no room to turn around, and while they stood bellowing and plunging, over the top of the pen there leaned one of the "knockers," armed with a sledge hammer, and watching for a chance to deal a blow. The room echoed with the thuds in quick succession, and the stamping and kicking of the steers. The instant the animal had fallen, the "knocker" passed on to another, while a second man raised a lever, and the side of the pen was raised, and the animal, still kicking and struggling, slid out to the "killing bed." Here a man put shackles about one leg, and pressed another lever, and the body was jerked up into the air. There were fifteen or twenty such pens, and it was a matter of only a couple of minutes to knock fifteen or twenty cattle and roll them out. Then once more the gates were opened, and another lot rushed in; and so out of each pen there rolled a steady stream of carcasses, which the men upon the killing beds had to get out of the way.

The manner in which they did this was something to be seen and never forgotten. They worked with furious intensity, literally upon the run—at a pace with which there is nothing to be compared except a football game. It was all highly specialized labor, each man having his task to do; generally this would consist of only two or three specific cuts, and he would pass down the line of fifteen or twenty carcasses, making these cuts upon each. First there came the "butcher," to bleed them; this meant one swift stroke, so swift that you could not see it—only the flash of the knife; and before you could realize it, the man had darted on to the next line, and a stream of bright red was pouring out upon the floor. This floor was half an inch deep with blood, in spite of the best efforts of men who kept shoveling it through holes; it must have made the floor slippery, but no one could have guessed this by watching the men at work.

The carcass hung for a few minutes to bleed; there was no time lost, however, for there were several hanging in each line, and one was always ready. It was let down to the ground, and there came the "headsman," whose task it was to sever the head, with two or three swift strokes. Then came the "floorsman," to make the first cut in the skin; and then another to finish ripping the skin down the center; and then half a dozen more in swift succession, to finish the skinning. After they were through, the carcass was again swung up, and while a man with a stick examined the skin, to make sure that it had not been cut, and another rolled it up and tumbled it through one of the inevitable holes in the floor, the beef proceeded on its journey. There were men to cut it, and men to split it, and men to gut it and scrape it clean inside. There were some with hoses which threw jets of boiling water upon it, and others who removed the feet and added the final touches. In the end, as with the hogs, the finished beef was run into the chilling room, to hang its appointed time.

The visitors were taken there and shown them, all neatly hung in rows, labelled conspicuously with the tags of the government inspectors—and some, which had been killed by a special process, marked with the sign of the "kosher" rabbi, certifying that it was fit for sale to the orthodox. And then the visitors were taken to the other parts of the building, to see what became of each particle of the waste material that had vanished through the floor; and to the pickling rooms, and the salting rooms, the canning rooms, and the packing rooms, where choice meat was prepared for shipping in refrigerator cars, destined to be eaten in all the four corners of civilization. Afterward they went outside, wandering about among the mazes of buildings in which was done the work auxiliary to this great industry. There was scarcely a thing needed in the business that Durham and Company did not make for themselves. There was a great steam power plant and an electricity plant. There was a barrel factory, and a boiler repair shop. There was a building to which the grease was piped, and made into soap and lard, and then there was a factory for making lard cans, and another for making soap boxes. There was a building in which the bristles were cleaned and dried, for the making of hair cushions and such things; there was a building where the skins were dried and tanned, there was another where heads and feet were made into glue, and another w[h]ere bones were made into fertilizer. No tiniest particle of organic matter was wasted in Durham's. Out of the horns of the cattle they made combs, buttons, hairpins, and imitation ivory; out of the shin bones and other big bones they cut knife and tooth brush handles, and mouthpieces for pipes; out of the hoofs they cut hairpins and buttons, before they made the rest into glue. From such things as feet, knuckles, hide clippings, and sinews came such strange and unlikely products as gelatin, isinglass, and phosphorus, bone black, shoe blackening, and bone oil. They had curled-hair works for the cattle tails, and a "wool pullery" for the sheep skins; they made pepsin from the stomachs of the pigs, and albumen from the blood, and violin strings from the ill-smelling entrails. When there was nothing else to be done with a thing, they first put it into a tank and got out of it all the tallow and grease, and then they made it into fertilizer. All these industries were gathered into buildings near by, connected by galleries and railroads with the main establishment, and it was estimated that they had handled nearly a quarter of a billion of animals since the founding of the plant by the elder Durham a generation and more ago. If you counted with it the other big plants—and they were now really all one—it was, so Jokubas informed them, the greatest aggregation of labor and capital ever gathered in one place. It employed thirty thousand men; it supported directly two hundred and fifty thousand people in its neighborhood, and indirectly it supported half a million. It sent its products to every country in the civilized world, and it furnished the food for no less than thirty million people!

This was the first time in his life that he had ever really worked, it seemed to Jurgis; it was the first time that he had ever had anything to do which took all he had in him. Jurgis had stood with the rest up in the gallery and watched the men on the killing beds, marveling at their speed and power as if they had been wonderful machines; it somehow never occurred to one to think of the flesh-and-blood side of it—that is, not until he actually got down into the pit and took off his coat. Then he saw things in a different light, he got at the inside of them. The pace they set here, it was one that called for every faculty of a man—from the instant the first steer fell till the sounding of the noon whistle, and again from half-past twelve till heaven only knew what hour in the late afternoon or evening, there was never one instant's rest for a man, for his hand or his eye or his brain. Jurgis saw how they managed it; there were portions of the work which determined the pace for the rest, and for these they had picked men whom they paid high wages, and whom they changed frequently. You might easily pick out these pacemakers, for they worked under the eye of the bosses, and they worked like men possessed. This was called "speeding up the gang," and if any man could not keep up with the pace, there were hundreds outside begging to try.

Yet Jurgis did not mind it; he rather enjoyed it. It saved him the necessity of flinging his arms about and fidgeting as he did in most work. He would laugh to himself as he ran down the line, darting a glance now and then at the man ahead of him. It was not the pleasantest work one could think of, but it was necessary work, and what more had a man the right to ask than a chance to do something useful, and to get good pay for doing it?

So Jurgis thought, and so he spoke, in his bold, free way; very much to his surprise, he found that it had a tendency to get him into trouble. For most of the men here took a fearfully different view of the thing. He was quite dismayed when he first began to find it out—that most of the men hated their work. It seemed strange, it was even terrible, when you came to find out the universality of the sentiment; but it was certainly the fact—they hated their work. They hated the bosses and they hated the owners; they hated the whole place, the whole neighborhood—even the whole city, with an all-inclusive hatred, bitter and fierce. Women and little children would fall to cursing about it; it was rotten, rotten as hell—everything was rotten. When Jurgis would ask them what they meant, they would begin to get suspicious, and content themselves with saying, "Never mind, you stay here and see for yourself."

One of the first problems that Jurgis ran upon was that of the unions. He had had no experience with unions, and he had to have it explained to him that the men were banded together for the purpose of fighting for their rights. Jurgis asked them what they meant by their rights, a question in which he was quite sincere, for he had not any idea of any rights that he had, except the right to hunt for a job, and do as he was told when he got it. Generally, however, this harmless question would only make his fellow working-men lose their tempers and call him a fool. There was a delegate of the butcher-helpers' union who came to see Jurgis to enroll him; and when Jurgis found that this meant that he would have to part with some of his money, he froze up directly, and the delegate, who was an Irishman and only knew a few words of Lithuanian, lost his temper and began to threaten him. In the end Jurgis got into a fine rage, and made it sufficiently plain that it would take more than one Irishman to scare him into a union. Little by little he gathered that the main thing the men wanted was to put a stop to the habit of "speeding up"; they were trying their best to force a lessening of the pace, for there were some, they said, who could not keep up with it, whom it was killing. But Jurgis had no sympathy with such ideas as this—he could do the work himself, and so could the rest of them, he declared, if they were good for anything. If they couldn't do it, let them go somewhere else. Jurgis had not studied the books, and he would not have known how to pronounce "laissez faire"; but he had been around the world enough to know that a man has to shift for himself in it, and that if he gets the worst of it, there is nobody to listen to him holler . . .

One curious thing he had noticed, the very first day, in his profession of shoveler of guts; which was the sharp trick of the floor bosses whenever there chanced to come a "slunk" calf. Any man who knows anything about butchering knows that the flesh of a cow that is about to calve, or has just calved, is not fit for food. A good many of these came every day to the packing houses—and, of course, if they had chosen, it would have been an easy matter for the packers to keep them till they were fit for food. But for the saving of time and fodder, it was the law that cows of that sort came along with the others, and whoever noticed it would tell the boss, and the boss would start up a conversation with the government inspector, and the two would stroll away. So in a trice the carcass of the cow would be cleaned out, and the entrails would have vanished; it was Jurgis's task to slide them into the trap, calves and all, and on the floor below they took out these "slunk" calves, and butchered them for meat, and used even the skins of them.

One day a man slipped and hurt his leg; and that afternoon, when the last of the cattle had been disposed of, and the men were leaving, Jurgis was ordered to remain and do some special work which this injured man had usually done. It was late, almost dark, and the government inspectors had all gone, and there were only a dozen or two of men on the floor. That day they had killed about four thousand cattle, and these cattle had come in freight trains from far states, and some of them had got hurt. There were some with broken legs, and some with gored sides; there were some that had died, from what cause no one could say; and they were all to be disposed of, here in darkness and silence. "Downers," the men called them; and the packing house had a special elevator upon which they were raised to the killing beds, where the gang proceeded to handle them, with an air of businesslike nonchalance which said plainer than any words that it was a matter of everyday routine. It took a couple of hours to get them out of the way, and in the end Jurgis saw them go into the chilling rooms with the rest of the meat, being carefully scattered here and there so that they could not be identified. When he came home that night he was in a very somber mood, having begun to see at last how those might be right who had laughed at him for his faith in America.

Source: Upton Sinclair, *The Jungle* (New York: Doubleday, Page & Company, 1906).

DOCUMENT 8
Samuel McClure Launches the Muckraking Era (1903)

*With the January 1903 edition of his magazine, Samuel McClure launched his
publication into the field of investigative journalism. His magazine set the standard
for this genre and became an important weapon and inspiration for the Progressive
movement. What follows is McClure's editorial that accompanied that edition.*

How many of those who have read through this number of the magazine
noticed that it contains three articles on one subject? We did not plan it
so; it is a coincidence that the January McClure's is such an arraignment
of American character as should make every one of us stop and think.
How many noticed that? The leading article, "The Shame of Minneapolis," might have been called "The American Contempt of Law." That title
could well have served for the current chapter of Miss Tarbell's History of
Standard Oil. Audit would have fitted perfectly Mr. Baker's "The Right to
Work." All together, these articles come pretty near showing how universal is this dangerous trait of ours. Miss Tarbell has our capitalists conspiring
among themselves, deliberately, shrewdly, upon legal advice, to break the
law so far as it restrained them, and to misuse it to restrain others who were
in their way. Mr. Baker shows labor, the ancient enemy of capital, and the
chief complainant of the trusts' unlawful acts, itself committing and excus-
ing crimes. And in "The Shame of Minneapolis" we see the administration
of a city employing criminals to commit crimes for the profit of the elected
officials, while the citizens—Americans of good stock and more than average culture, and honest, healthy Scandinavians—stood by complacent and
not alarmed. Capitalists, workingmen, politicians, citizens—all breaking
the law, or letting it be broken. Who is left to uphold it? The lawyers?
Some of the best lawyers in this country are hired, not to go into court to
defend cases, but to advise corporations and business firms how they can
get around the law without too great a risk of punishment. The judges?
Too many of them so respect the laws that for some "error" or quibble they
restore to office and liberty men convicted on evidence overwhelmingly
convincing to common sense. The churches? We know of one, an ancient
and wealthy establishment, which had to be compelled by a Tammany
hold-over health officer to put its tenements in sanitary condition. The
colleges? They do not understand. There is no one left; none but all of

us. Capital is learning (with indignation at labor s unlawful acts) that its rival's contempt of law is a menace to property. Labor has shrieked the belief that the illegal power of capital is a menace to the worker. These two are drawing together. Last November when a strike was threatened by the yard-men on all the railroads centering in Chicago, the men got together and settled by raising wages, and raising freight rates too. They made the public pay. We all are doing our worst and making the public pay. The public is the people. We forget that we all are the people; that while each of us in his group can shove off on the rest the bill of to-day, the debt is only postponed; the rest are passing it on back to us. We have to pay in the end, every one of us. And in the end the sum total of the debt will be our liberty.

Source: McClure's Magazine 1 (January 1903): 336.

DOCUMENT 9
Lincoln Steffens, *Shame of the Cities* (1904)

One of the most powerful of the investigative reporters of the Progressive Era was Lincoln Steffens. Among his most influential work was his exposé of corruption in city government, which provided both evidence and inspiration for urban reformers. Following is an excerpt from the introduction to his book Shame of the Cities *(1904), which comprised of a series of articles first published in* McClure's Magazine.

Because politics is business. That's what the matter with it is. Make politics a sport, as they do in England, or a profession, as they do in Germany, and we'll have well, something else than we have now if we want it, which is another question. But don't try to reform politics with the banker, the lawyer, and the dry-goods merchant, for these are business men and there are two great hindrances to their achievement of reform: one is that they are different from, but no better than, the politicians; the other is that politics is not "their line" . . .

The commercial spirit is the spirit of profit, not patriotism; of credit, not honor; of individual gain, not national prosperity; of trade and dickering, not principle. "My business is sacred," says the businessman in his heart. "Whatever prospers my business, is good; it must be. Whatever hinders it, is wrong; it must be. A bribe is bad, that is, it is a bad thing to take; but it is not so bad to give one, not if it is necessary to my business"

"Business is business" is not a political sentiment, but our politician has caught it. He takes essentially the same view of the bribe, only he saves his self-respect by piling all his contempt upon the bribe. And he has the great advantage of candor. "It is wrong, maybe," he says, "but if a rich merchant can afford to do business with me for the sake of a convenience or to increase his already ample wealth, I can afford, for the sake of a living, to meet him half way. I make no pretensions to virtue, not even on Sunday. And as for giving bad government or good, how about the merchant who gives bad goods or good goods, according to the demand?"

... The corruption that shocks us in public affairs we practice ourselves in our private concerns. There is no essential difference between the pull that gets your wife into society or and that which gets a heeler into office, a thief out of jail, and a rich man's son on the board of directors of a corporation; none between the corruption of a labor union, a bank, and a political machine.

... We are responsible, not our leaders, since we follow them. We let them divert our loyalty from the United States to some "party"; we let them boss the party and turn our democracies into autocracies and our republican nation into a plutocracy. We cheat our government and let our leaders loot it, and we let them trade and bribe our sovereignty from us.

Source: Lincoln Steffens, *The Shame of the Cities* (New York: McClure and Phillips and Co., 1904).

DOCUMENT 10
Cary Nation: Crusader for Temperance (1909)

Established in 1872, the Woman's Christian Temperance Union comprised of a group of feminists, who by the turn of the century had taken their political commitment to the streets. In their crusade to make the prohibition of alcohol the law of the land, members picketed bars and saloons. They prayed for the souls of the bar patrons. They also tried to block the entryways of establishments that sold liquor. All of these demonstrations paled, however, in the face of their most vociferous member Cary Nation, Dressed in her trademark black dress and bonnet with a Bible in one hand and a hatchet in the other, she waged a personal war against the purveyors of "demon rum." The following piece is an eyewitness report by Lindsey Williams, who described one of her "demonstrations."

Cary took the train to Wichita and spent the first day searching for an appropriate victim. She had not intended to make herself known just yet, but lost her composure in the Hotel Carey bar room.

A large, risqué painting of *Cleopatra At Her Bath* caught her eye. She marched up to the bartender and shook her quivering forefinger at him. "Young man," she thundered, "what are you doing in this hellhole?"

"I'm sorry, madam," replied the bartender, "but we do not serve ladies."

"Serve me?" she screamed. "Do you think I'd drink your hellish poison?" Pointing to Cleopatra, she demanded, "Take down that filthy thing, and close this murder mill."

With this she snatched a bottle from the bar and smashed it to the floor. Cary marched out of the bar room amidst incredulous stares of the many imbibers.

Returning to her room she withdrew a heavy wooden club and an iron bar from her suitcase and bound them into a formidable weapon.

In the morning she returned to the Hotel Carey, concealing her club and a supply of stones under the black cape that became her trademark. Without a word, she began her labors by demolishing *Cleopatra At Her Bath.* "Glory to God, peace on earth and goodwill to men," she shouted as she flailed against mirrors, bottles, chairs, tables and sundry accessories. Whiskey flowed in rivers across the floor.

The hotel detective found Mrs. Nation beating furiously on the long, curving bar with a brass spittoon. "Madam," he said sternly, "I must arrest you for defacing property."

"Defacing?" she screamed. "I am destroying!"

Source: Joseph R. Gusfield, *Symbolic Crusade: Status Politics and the American Temperance Movement* (Urbana, IL: University of Illinois Press, 1986); and http://www2.potsdam.edu/alcohol/Controversies/Womans-Christian-Temperance-Union.html-8.

DOCUMENT 11
Walter Rauschenbusch Calls for a New Age
of Christianity (1916)

Walter Rauschenbusch, the great theologian of the Social Gospel, called for a reawakening of the social conscience in Christianity. Following is an excerpt from his book entitled The Social Principles of Jesus *(1916).*

Other reformers have condemned religious practices because they were departures from the holy Book or from primitive custom. Jesus, too, pointed out that some of these regulations were recent innovations. But the real standard by which he judged current religious questions was not ancient authority but the present good of men. The spiritual center on which he took his stand and from which he judged all things, was the Kingdom of God, the perfect social order. Even the ordinances of religion must justify themselves by making an effective contribution to the Kingdom of God. The Sabbath was made for man, and its observance must meet the test of service to man's welfare. It must function wholesomely. The candle must give light, or what is the use of it? The salt must be salty and preserve from decay, or it will be thrown out and trodden under foot. If the fig tree bears no fruit, why is it allowed to use up space and crowd better plants off the soil? This, then, is Christ's test in matters of institutional religion. The Church and all its doings must serve the Kingdom of God.

II

The social efficiency of religion is a permanent social problem. What is the annual expense of maintaining the churches in the United States? How much capital is invested in the church buildings? (See U.S. Census Bulletin No.103 of 1906) How much care and interest and loving free-will labor does an average village community bestow on religion as compared with other objects? All men feel instinctively that religion exerts a profound and subtle influence on the springs of conduct. Even those who denounce it, acknowledge at least its power for harm. Most of us know it as a power for good. But all history shows that this great spiritual force easily deteriorates. *Corruptio optimi pessima.*

Religion may develop an elaborate social apparatus of its own, wheels within wheels, and instead of being a dynamic of righteousness in the natural social relations of men, its energies may be consumed in driving its own machinery. Instead of being the power-house supplying the Kingdom of God among men with power and light, the Church may exist for its own sake. It then may become an expensive consumer of social wealth, a conservative clog, and a real hindrance of social progress.

Live religion gives proof of its value by the sense of freedom, peace, and elation which it creates. We feel we are right with the holy Power which is behind, and beneath, and above all things. It gives a satisfying interpretation of life and of our own place in it. It moves our aims higher up, draws our fellow-men closer, and invigorates our will.

But our growth sets a problem for our religion. The religion of childhood will not satisfy adolescent youth, and the religion of youth ought not to satisfy a mature man or woman. Our soul must build statelier mansions for itself. Religion must continue to answer all our present needs and inspire all our present functions. A person who has failed to adjust his religion to his growing powers and his intellectual horizon, has failed in one of the most important functions of growth, just as if his cranium failed to expand and to give room to his brain. Being microcephalous is a misfortune, and nothing to boast of.

Precisely the same problem arises when society passes through eras of growth. Religion must keep pace. The Church must pass the burning torch of religious experience from age to age, transmitting the faith of the fathers to the children, and not allowing any spiritual values to perish. But it must allow and aid religion to adjust itself. Its inspiring teaching must meet the new social problems so effectively that no evil can last long or grow beyond remedy. In every new age religion must stand the test of social efficiency. Is it passing that test in Western civilization?

Religion is a bond of social coherence. It creates loyalty. But it may teach loyalty to antiquated observances or a dwarfed system of truth. Have you ever seen believers rallying around a lost cause in religion? Yet these relics were once a live issue, and full of thrilling religious vitality.

Source: Walter Rauschenbusch, *The Social Principles of Jesus* (New York: Grosset & Dunlap, 1916), 140–42.

DOCUMENT 12
John Muir on the National Parks (1901)

John Muir, naturalist and advocate of forest and wildlife preservation, organized the Sierra Club, which inspired and prodded Progressives to include protecting the natural environment in their litany of social concerns. Following is an excerpt from his book, Our National Parks (1901), *which argued for the preservation and expansion of the national park system.*

The tendency nowadays to wander in wildernesses is delightful to see. Thousands of tired, nerve-shaken, over-civilized people are beginning to find out that going to the mountains is going home; that wildness is a necessity; and that mountain parks and reservations are useful not only as fountains of timber and irrigating rivers, but as fountains of life. Awakening from the stupefying effects of the vice of over-industry and the deadly apathy of luxury, they are trying as best they can to mix and enrich their own little ongoings with those of Nature, and to get rid of rust and disease. Briskly venturing and roaming, some are washing off sins and cobweb cares of the devil's spinning in all-day storms on mountains; sauntering in rosiny pinewoods or in gentian meadows, brushing through chaparral, bending down and parting sweet, flowery sprays; tracing rivers to their sources, getting in touch with the nerves of Mother Earth; jumping from rock to rock, feeling the life of them, learning the songs of them, panting in whole-souled exercise, and rejoicing in deep, long-drawn breaths of pure wildness. This is fine and natural and full of promise. So also is the growing interest in the care and preservation of forests and wild places in general, and in the half wild parks and gardens of towns. Even the scenery habit in its most artificial forms, mixed with spectacles, silliness, and kodaks; its devotees arrayed more gorgeously than scarlet tanagers, frightening the wild game with red umbrellas,—even this is encouraging, and may well be regarded as a hopeful sign of the times.

All the Western mountains are still rich in wildness, and by means of good roads are being brought nearer civilization every year. To the sane and free it will hardly seem necessary to cross the continent in search of wild beauty, however easy the way, for they find it in abundance wherever they chance to be. Like Thoreau they see forests in orchards and patches of huckleberry brush, and oceans in ponds and drops of dew. Few in these hot, dim, strenuous times are quite sane or free; choked with care like clocks full of dust, laboriously doing so much good and making so much money,—or so little,—they are no longer good for themselves.

When, like a merchant taking a list of his goods, we take stock of our wildness, we are glad to see how much of even the most destructible kind is still unspoiled. Looking at our continent as scenery when it was all wild, lying between beautiful seas, the starry sky above it, the starry rocks beneath it, to compare its sides, the East and the West, would be like comparing the sides of a rainbow. But it is no longer equally beautiful. The rainbows of to-day are, I suppose, as bright as those that first spanned the sky; and some of our landscapes are growing more beautiful from year to year, notwithstanding the clearing, trampling work of civilization. New plants and animals are enriching woods and gardens, and many landscapes wholly new, with divine sculpture and architecture, are just now coming to the light of day as the mantling folds of creative glaciers are being withdrawn, and life in a thousand cheerful, beautiful forms is pushing into them, and new-born rivers are beginning to sing and shine in them. The old rivers, too, are growing longer, like healthy trees, gaining new branches and lakes as the residual glaciers at their highest sources on the mountains recede, while the rootlike branches in the flat deltas are at same time spreading farther and wider into the seas and making new lands.

Source: John Muir, *Our National Parks* (New York: Houghton, Mifflin and Company, 1901).

DOCUMENT 13
Teddy Roosevelt on Trusts (1901)

In his first address to Congress as president of the United States, Theodore Roosevelt defined his attitude regarding trusts. He acknowledged the public's wariness of these new structures but accepted trusts as an economic reality of the new century. At the same time he also accepted the challenge of the federal government to regulate and supervise the actions of these trusts.

There is a widespread conviction in the minds of the American people that the great corporations known as trusts are in certain of their features and tendencies hurtful to the general welfare. This springs from no spirit of envy or charitableness, nor lack of pride in the great industrial achievements that have placed this country at the head of the nations struggling for commercial supremacy. It does not rest upon a lack of intelligent appreciation of the necessity of meeting changing and changed conditions of trade with new methods, nor upon ignorance of the fact that combination of capital in the effort to accomplish great things is necessary when the world's progress demands that great things be done. It is based upon sincere conviction that combination and concentration should be, not prohibited, but supervised and within reasonable limits controlled; and in my judgment this conviction is right.

It is no limitation upon property rights or freedom of contract to require that when men receive from Government the privilege of doing business under corporate form, which frees them from individual responsibility, and enables them to call into their enterprises the capital of the public, they shall do so upon absolutely truthful representations as to the value of the property in which the capital is to be invested. Corporations engaged in interstate commerce should be regulated if they are found to exercise a license working to the public injury. It should be as much the aim of those who seek for social-betterment to rid the business world of crimes of cunning as to rid the entire body politic of crimes of violence. Great corporations exist only because they are created and safeguarded by our institutions; and it is therefore our right and our duty to see that they work in harmony with these institutions.

The first essential in determining how to deal with the great industrial combinations is knowledge of the facts—publicity. In the interest of the public, the Government should have the right to inspect and examine the workings of the great corporations engaged in interstate business. Publicity is the only sure remedy which we can now invoke. What further remedies are needed in the way of governmental regulation, or taxation, can only be determined after publicity has been obtained, by process of law, and in the course of administration. The first requisite is knowledge, full and complete—knowledge which may be made public to the world.

Artificial bodies, such as corporations and joint stock or other associations, depending upon any statutory law for their existence or privileges, should be subject to proper governmental supervision, and full and accurate information as to their operations should be made public regularly at reasonable intervals.

When the Constitution was adopted, at the end of the eighteenth century, no human wisdom could foretell the sweeping changes, alike in industrial and political conditions, which were to take place by the beginning of the twentieth century. At that time it was accepted as a matter of course that the several States were the proper authorities to regulate, so far as was then necessary, the comparatively insignificant and strictly localized corporate bodies of the day. The conditions are now wholly different and wholly different action is called for. I believe that a law can be framed which will enable the National Government to exercise control along the lines above indicated; profiting by the experience gained through the passage and administration of the Interstate-Commerce Act. If, however, the judgment of the Congress is that it lacks the constitutional power to pass such an act, then a constitutional amendment should be submitted to confer the power.

Source: Theodore Roosevelt: "First Annual Message," December 3, 1901. Online by Gerhard Peters and John T.

DOCUMENT 14
Triangle Shirtwaist Factory Fire (1911)

On March 25, 1911, a fire broke out at the Triangle Shirtwaist Factory in New York City, resulting in a major industrial accident that took the lives of 146 workers. The blaze was indicative of poor working conditions in early twentieth-century American industry, which was fraught with hazards such as poor ventilation and overcrowding. The Triangle Shirtwaist incident, described in the following New York Times article, exposed the unsafe working conditions that existed in many city sweatshops and led to legislation improving the safety conditions in factories to protect workers.

Men and Girls Die in Waist Factory Fire; Trapped High Up in Washington Place Building; Street Strewn with Bodies; Piles of Dead Inside

Three stories of a ten-floor building at the corner of Greene Street and Washington Place were burned yesterday, and while the fire was going on 141 young men and women at least 125 of them mere girls were burned to death or killed by jumping to the pavement below. The building was fireproof. It shows now hardly any signs of the disaster that overtook it. The walls are as good as ever[;] so are the floors, nothing is the worse for the fire except the furniture and 141 of the 600 men and girls that were employed in its upper three stories. Most of the victims were suffocated or burned to death within the building, but some who fought their way to the windows and leaped met death as surely, but perhaps more quickly, on the pavements below.

All Over in Half an Hour

Nothing like it has been seen in New York since the burning of the General Slocum. The fire was practically all over in half an hour. It was confined to three floors the eighth, ninth, and tenth of the building. But it was the most murderous fire that New York had seen in many years. The victims who are now lying at the Morgue waiting for some one to identify them by a tooth or the remains of a burned shoe were mostly girls from 16 to 23 years of age. They were employed at making shirtwaist[s] by the Triangle Waist Company, the principal owners of which are Isaac Harris and Max Blanck. Most of them could barely speak English. Many of them came from Brooklyn. Almost all were the main support of their hard-working families. There is just one fire escape in the building. That one is an interior fire escape. In Greene Street, where the terrified unfortunates crowded before they began to make their mad leaps to death, the whole big front of the building is guiltless of one. Nor is there a fire escape in the back. The building was fireproof and the owners had put their trust in that. In fact, after the flames had done their worst last night, the building hardly showed a sign. Only the stock within it and the girl employees were burned. A heap of corpses lay on the sidewalk for more than an hour. The firemen were too busy dealing with the fire to pay any attention to people whom they supposed beyond their aid. When the excitement had subsided to such an extent that some of the firemen and policemen could pay attention to this mass of the supposedly dead they found about half way down in the pack a girl who was still breathing. She died two minutes after she was found.

The Triangle Waist Company was the only sufferer by the disaster. There are other concerns in the building, but it was Saturday and the other companies had let their people go home. Messrs. Harris and Blanck, how-ever, were busy and their girls and some stayed.

Leaped Out of the Flames

At 4:40 o'clock, after the employees in the rest of the factory had gone home, the fire broke out. The one little fire escape in the interior was resorted to by many of the doomed victims. Some of them escaped by run-ning down the stairs, but in a moment or two this avenue was cut off by flame. The girls rushed to the windows and looked down at Greene Street, 100 feet below them. Then one poor, little creature jumped. There was a plate glass protection over part of the sidewalk, but she crashed through it, wrecking it and breaking her body into a thousand pieces. Then they all began to drop. The crowd yelled "Don't jump!" but it was jump or be burned the proof of which is found in the fact that fifty burned bodies were taken from the ninth floor alone. They jumped, the[y] crashed through broken glass, they crushed themselves to death on the sidewalk. Of those who stayed behind it is better to say nothing except what a veteran police-man said as he gazed at a headless and charred trunk on the Greene Street sidewalk hours after the worst cases had been taken out: "I saw the Slocum disaster, but it was nothing to this." "Is it a man or a woman?" asked the reporter. "It's human, that's all you can tell," answered the policeman.

It was just a mass of ashes, with blood congealed on what had probably been the neck. Messrs. Harris and Blanck were in the building, but the[y] escaped. They carried with the[m] Mr. Blanck's children and a governess, and they fled over the roofs. Their employees did not know the way, because they had been in the habit of using the two freight elevators, and one of these elevators was not in service when the fire broke out.

Found Alive After the Fire

The first living victim, Hyman Meshel of 322 East Fifteenth Street, was taken from the ruins four hours after the fire was discovered. He was found paralyzed with fear and whimpering like a wounded animal in the base-ment, immersed in water to his neck, crouched on the top of a cable drum and with his head just below the floor of the elevator. Meantime the remains of the dead[—]it is hardly possible to call them bodies, because that would suggest something human, and there was nothing human about most of these[—]were being taken in a steady stream to the Morgue for identification. First Avenue was lined with the usual curious east side crowd. Twenty-sixth Street was impassable. But in the Morgue they received the charred remnants with no more emotion than they ever display over anything. Back in Greene Street there was another crowd. At midnight it had not decreased in the least. The police were holding it back to the fire lines, and discussing the tragedy in a tone which those seasoned witnesses of death seldom use. "It's the worst thing I ever saw," said one old policeman. Chief Croker said it was an outrage. He spoke bitterly of the way in which the Manufacturers' Association had called a meeting in Wall Street to take measures against his proposal for enforcing better methods of protection for employees in cases of fire.

No Chance to Save Victims

Four alarms were rung in fifteen minutes. The first five girls who jumped did so before the first engine could respond. That fact may not convey much of a picture to the mind of an unimaginative man, but anybody who has ever seen a fire can get from it some idea of the terrific rapidity with which the flames spread. It may convey some idea too, to say that thirty bodies clogged the elevator shaft. These dead were all girls. They had made their rush there blindly when they discovered that there was no chance to get out by the fire escape. Then they found that the elevator was as hopeless as anything else, and they fell there in their tracks and died. The Triangle Waist Company employed about 600 women and less than 100 men. One of the saddest features of the thing is the fact that they had almost finished for the day. In five minutes more, if the fire had started then, probably not a life would have been lost. Last night District Attorney Whitman started an investigation not of this disaster alone but of the whole condition which makes it possible for a firetrap of such a kind to exist. Mr. Whitman's intention is to find out if the present laws cover such cases, and if they do not to frame laws that will.

Girls Jump To Sure Death. Fire Nets Prove Useless. Firemen Helpless to Save Life

The fire[,] which was first discovered at 4:40 o'clock on the eighth floor of the ten-story building at the corner of Washington Place and Greene

Street, leaped through the three upper stories occupied by the Triangle Waist Company with a sudden rush that left the Fire Department helpless. How the fire started no one knows. On the three upper floors of the building were 600 employees of the waist company, 500 of whom were girls. The victims mostly Italians, Russians, Hungarians, and Germans were girls and men who had been employed by the firm of Harris & Blanck, owners of the Triangle Waist Company, after the strike in which the Jewish girls, formerly employed, had been become unionized and had demanded better working conditions. The building had experienced four recent fires and had been reported by the Fire Department to the Building Department as unsafe in account of the insufficiency of its exits. The building itself was of the most modern construction and classed as fireproof. What burned so quickly and disastrously for the victims were shirtwaists, hanging on lines above tiers of workers, sewing machines placed so closely together that there was hardly aisle room for the girls between them, and shirtwaist trimmings and cuttings which littered the floors above the eighth and ninth stories. Girls had begun leaping from the eighth story windows before firemen arrived. The firemen had trouble bringing their apparatus into position because of the bodies which strewed the pavement and sidewalks. While more bodies crashed down among them, they worked with desperation to run their ladders into position and to spread firenets. One fireman running ahead of a hose wagon, which halted to avoid running over a body spread a firenet, and two more seized hold of it. A girl's body, coming end over end, struck on the side of it, and there was hope that she would be the first one of the score who had jumped to be saved. Thousands of people who had crushed in from Broadway and Washington Square and were screaming with horror at what they saw watched closely the work with the firenet. Three other girls who had leaped for it a moment after the first one, struck it on top of her, and all four rolled out and lay still upon the pavement. Five girls who stood together at a window close to the Greene Street corner held their place while a fire ladder was worked toward them, but which stopped at its full length two stories lower down. They leaped together, clinging to each other, with fire streaming back from their hair and dresses. They struck a glass sidewalk cover and it [fell] to the basement. There was no time to aid them. With water pouring in upon them from a dozen hose nozzles the bodies lay for two hours where they struck, as did the many others who leaped to their deaths. One girl, who waved a handkerchief at the crowd, leaped from a window adjoining the New York University Building on the westward. Her dress caught on a wire, and the crowd watched her hang there till her dress burned free and she came toppling down. Many jumped whom the firemen believe they could have saved. A girl who saw the glass roof of a sidewalk cover at the first-story level of the New York University Building leaped for it, and her body crashed through to the sidewalk. On Greene Street, running along the eastern face of the building more people leaped to the pavement than on Washington Place to the south. Fire nets proved just as useless to catch them and the ladders to reach them. None waited for the firemen to attempt to reach them with the scaling ladders.

All Would Soon Have Been Out

Strewn about as the firemen worked, the bodies indicated clearly the preponderance of women workers. Here and there was a man, but almost always they were women. One wore furs and a muff, and had a purse hanging from her arm. Nearly all were dressed for the street. The fire had flashed through their workroom just as they were expecting the signal to leave the building. In ten minutes more all would have been out, as many had stopped work in advance of the signal and had started to put on their wraps. What happened inside there were few who could tell with any definiteness. All that those escaped seemed to remember was that there was a flash of flames, leaping first among the girls in the southeast corner of the eighth floor and then suddenly over the entire room, spreading through the linens and cottons with which the girls were working. The girls on the ninth floor caught sight of the flames through the window up the stairway, and up the elevator shaft. On the tenth floor they got them a moment later, but most of those on that floor escaped by rushing to the roof and then on to the roof of the New York University Building, with the assistance of 100 university students who had been dismissed from a tenth story classroom. There were in the building, according to the estimate of Fire Chief Croker, about 600 girls and 100 men.

Source: New York Times (March 26, 1911), 1.

DOCUMENT 15
Jane Addams on Suffrage (1909)

Jane Addams, born in Cedarville, Illinois, was one of the eight children, the daughter of a prosperous miller. In 1881 she graduated from Rockville Female Seminary, and at the age of 27 on a trip to London with her friend Ellen Starr she visited a settlement house, where she discovered her life's ambition. When she returned to Illinois, she and her friend opened a similar house in Chicago, though one developed on a distinctly American model. Situated in a poor immigrant section of Chicago in a house rented from Charles Hull, the center became famous as a refuge for the underprivileged, and educational institution teaching lessons in all manner of subjects from hygiene to democracy, a model of middle-class values, and more, and Jane Addams became internationally recognized a leader in social service advocacy. Addams was also a strong suffragist and believed that women needed to raise their political voice in order to alleviate the conditions in which so many women and children suffered. Men, she points out, vote on political issues from either a military or an industrial point of view. She is advocating a third alternative—human welfare—which while unfamiliar to men would be quite compatible with a women's perspective.

"The Modern City and the Municipal Franchise for Women"

Modern cities fear no enemies from without. Unsanitary housing poisonous sewage, contaminated water, infant mortality, the spread of contagion, adulterated food, impure milk, smoke-laden air, ill-ventilated factories, dangerous occupations, juvenile crime, unwholesome crowding, prostitution, and drunkenness are the enemies which modern cities must face and overcome, would they survive. Logically, their electorate should be made up of those who can bear a valiant part in this arduous contest, those who in the past have at least attempted to care for children, to clean houses, to prepare foods, to isolate the family from moral dangers; those who have traditionally taken care of that side of life which inevitably becomes the subject of municipal consideration and control as soon as the population is congested. To test the elector's fitness to deal with this situation by his ability to bear arms is absurd. These problems must be solved, if they are solved at all, not from the military point of view, not even from the industrial point of view, but from a third, which is rapidly developing in all the great cities of the world the human-welfare point of view. A city is in many respects a great business corporation, but in other respects it is enlarged housekeeping. May we not say that city housekeeping has failed partly because women, the traditional housekeepers, have not been consulted as to its manifold activities?

Source: Miller NAWSA Suffrage Scrapbooks, 1897–1911; Scrapbook 7; page 141. Library of Congress, Rare Book and Special Collections Division, Washington, D.C. 20540.

DOCUMENT 16
President Woodrow Wilson's Joint Address to Congress, Leading to a Declaration of War against Germany (1917)

On April 14, 1917, President Wilson asked Congress for a declaration of war against Germany. Many scholars believe the war brought an end to the Progressive movement or at least put it on hold for over a decade. What follows are excerpts from that speech.

Gentlemen of the Congress:

I have called the Congress into extraordinary session because there are serious, very serious, choices of policy to be made, and made immediately, which it was neither right nor constitutionally permissible that I should assume the responsibility of making.

It is a war against all nations. American ships have been sunk, American lives taken, in ways which it has stirred us very deeply to learn of, but the ships and people of other neutral and friendly nations have been sunk and overwhelmed in the waters in the same way. There has been no discrimination. The challenge is to all mankind. Each nation must decide for itself how it will meet it. The choice we make for ourselves must be made with a moderation of counsel and a temperateness of judgment befitting our character and our motives as a nation. We must put excited feeling away. Our motive will not be revenge or the victorious assertion of the physical might of the nation, but only the vindication of right, of human right, of which we are only a single champion.

With a profound sense of the solemn and even tragical character of the step I am taking and of the grave responsibilities which it involves, but in unhesitating obedience to what I deem my constitutional duty, I advise that the Congress declare the recent course of the Imperial German Government to be in fact nothing less than war against the government and people of the United States; that it formally accept the status of belligerent which has thus been thrust upon it, and that it take immediate steps not only to put the country in a more thorough state of defense but also to exert all its power and employ all its resources to bring the Government of the German Empire to terms and end the war . . .

We have no quarrel with the German people. We have no feeling towards them but one of sympathy and friendship. It was not upon their impulse that their government acted in entering this war. It was not with their previous knowledge or approval. It was a war determined upon as wars used to be determined upon in the old, unhappy days when peoples were nowhere consulted by their rulers and wars were provoked and waged in the interest of dynasties or of little groups of ambitious men who were accustomed to use their fellow men as pawns and tools.

It is a distressing and oppressive duty, Gentlemen of the Congress, which I have performed in thus addressing you. There are, it may be many months of fiery trial and sacrifice ahead of us. It is a fearful thing to lead this great peaceful people into war, into the most terrible and disastrous of all wars, civilization itself seeming to be in the balance . . .

But the right is more precious than peace, and we shall fight for the things which we have always carried nearest our hearts, for democracy, for the right of those who submit to authority to have a voice in their own Governments, for the rights and liberties of small nations, for a universal dominion of right by such a concert of free peoples as shall bring peace and safety to all nations and make the world itself at last free. To such a task we can dedicate our Eves and our fortunes, every thing that we are and everything that we have, with the pride of those who know that the day has come when America is privileged to spend her blood and her might for the principles that gave her birth and happiness and the peace which she has treasured. God helping her, she can do no other.

Source: Woodrow Wilson, *War Messages*, 65th Cong., 1st Sess. Senate Doc. No. 5, Serial No. 7264, Washington, D.C., 1917; pp. 3–8, *passim.*

DOCUMENT 17
Eugene V. Debs Defends Freedom of Speech and the Working Class (1918)

Eugene V. Debs, union organizer and presidential candidate on the Social Party ticket five times, was found guilty in 1918 of sedition for speaking out against World War I. Before sentencing Debs was given permission to address the court, and he spoke out forcefully in favor of the working class and free speech.

Your Honor, years ago I recognized my kinship with all living beings, and I made up my mind that I was not one bit better than the meanest on earth. I said then, and I say now, that while there is a lower class, I am in it, and while there is a criminal element I am of it, and while there is a soul in prison, I am not free.

I listened to all that was said in this court in support and justification of this prosecution, but my mind remains unchanged. I look upon the Espionage Law as a despotic enactment in flagrant conflict with democratic principles and with the spirit of free institutions ...

Your Honor, I have stated in this court that I am opposed to the social system in which we live; that I believe in a fundamental change—but if possible by peaceable and orderly means.

Standing here this morning, I recall my boyhood. At fourteen I went to work in a railroad shop; at sixteen I was firing a freight engine on a railroad. I remember all the hardships and privations of that earlier day, and from that time until now my heart has been with the working class. I could have been in Congress long ago. I have preferred to go to prison ... I am thinking this morning of the men in the mills and the factories; of the men in the mines and on the railroads. I am thinking of the women who for a paltry wage are compelled to work out their barren lives; of the little children who in this system are robbed of their childhood and in their tender years are seized in the remorseless grasp of Mammon and forced into the industrial dungeons, there to feed the monster machines while they themselves are being starved and stunted, body and soul. I see them dwarfed and diseased and their little lives broken and blasted because in this high noon of Christian civilization money is still so much more important than the flesh and blood of childhood. In very truth gold is god today and rules with pitiless sway in the affairs of men.

In this country—the most favored beneath the bending skies—we have vast areas of the richest and most fertile soil, material resources in inexhaustible abundance, the most marvelous productive machinery on earth, and millions of eager workers ready to apply their labor to that machinery to produce in abundance for every man, woman, and child—and if there are still vast numbers of our people who are the victims of poverty and whose lives are an unceasing struggle all the way from youth to old age, until at last death comes to their rescue and lulls these hapless victims to dreamless sleep, it is not the fault of the Almighty: it cannot be charged to nature, but it is due entirely to the outgrown social system in which we live that ought to be abolished not only in the interest of the toiling masses but in the higher interest of all humanity ...

I believe, Your Honor, in common with all Socialists, that this nation ought to own and control its own industries. I believe, as all Socialists do, that all things that are jointly needed and used ought to be jointly owned—that industry, the basis of our social life, instead of being the private property of a few and operated for their enrichment, ought to be the common property of all, democratically administered in the interest of all ...

I am opposing a social order in which it is possible for one man who does absolutely nothing that is useful to amass a fortune of hundreds of millions of dollars, while millions of men and women who work all the days of their lives secure barely enough for a wretched existence.

This order of things cannot always endure. I have registered my protest against it. I recognize the feebleness of my effort, but, fortunately, I am not alone. There are multiplied thousands of others who, like myself, have come to realize that before we may truly enjoy the blessings of civilized life, we must reorganize society upon a mutual and cooperative basis; and to this end we have organized a great economic and political movement that spreads over the face of all the earth.

There are today upwards of sixty millions of Socialists, loyal, devoted adherents to this cause, regardless of nationality, race, creed, color, or sex. They are all making common cause. They are spreading with tireless energy the propaganda of the new social order. They are waiting, watching, and working hopefully through all the hours of the day and the night.

They are still in a minority. But they have learned how to be patient and to bide their time. The feel—they know, indeed—that the time is coming, in spite of all opposition, all persecution, when this emancipating gospel will spread among all the peoples, and when this minority will become the triumphant majority and, sweeping into power, inaugurate the greatest social and economic change in history.

In that day we shall have the universal commonwealth—the harmonious cooperation of every nation with every other nation on earth.

Your Honor, I ask no mercy and I plead for no immunity. I realize that finally the right must prevail. I never so clearly comprehended as now the great struggle between the powers of greed and exploitation on the one hand and upon the other the rising hosts of industrial freedom and social justice.

I can see the dawn of the better day for humanity. The people are awakening. In due time they will and must come to their own.

When the mariner, sailing over tropic seas, looks for relief from his weary watch, he turns his eyes toward the southern cross, burning luridly above the tempest-vexed ocean. As the midnight approaches, the southern cross begins to bend, the whirling worlds change their places, and with starry finger-points the Almighty marks the passage of time upon the dial of the universe, and though no bell may beat the glad tidings, the lookout knows that the midnight is passing and that relief and rest are close at hand. Let the people everywhere take heart of hope, for the cross is bending, the midnight is passing, and joy cometh with the morning.

I am now prepared to receive your sentence.

Source: Eugene Debs, Statement to the District Court of the Northern District of Ohio, September 18, 1918. *United States vs. Eugene V. Debs*, Criminal Case. Number 4057, Record Group 21, Records of the U.S. District Court, Northern District of Ohio. National Archives, Central Plains Region (Kansas City), Record Group 21, Records of the District Courts of the United States.

ANNOTATED BIBLIOGRAPHY

Abbot, Karen. 2009. *Sin in the Second City*. New York: Random House.

Abbot's story of the Eveleigh sisters, Chicago's most famous madams, is an entertaining and informative read that explores the intersections between the underworld of Chicago—including its corrupt politicians—and its more respectable society at the turn of the century. This story also gives ample attention to the religious and civic reformers who joined forces to end legal prostitution in Chicago.

Adams, Henry. 1918. *The Education of Henry Adams*. Boston and New York: Houghton & Mifflin Company.

These reflections on the politics and society of his time by the country's pre-eminent historian, whose friends and associates included the leading public officials of his era, are fundamental reading for anyone interested in late nineteenth- and early twentieth-century America.

Addams, Jane. 1902. *Social Ethics and Democracy*. New York: The Macmillan Company. Political reflections by America's premier social worker of the time.

Addams, Jane. 1912. *Twenty Years at Hull-House with Autobiographical Notes*. New York: The Macmillan Company.

An insider's view of the settlement house and the neighborhood it served by the founder of the settlement movement in this country.

Akin, Edward N. 1991. *Flagler: Rockefeller Partner and Florida Baron*. Gainesville, FL: University Press of Florida.

Biography of the developer of Florida's east coast that gives insight into the Progressive mentality of one of the era's most successful entrepreneurs.

Blum, John C. 1956. *Woodrow Wilson and the Politics of Morality*. Boston: Little Brown and Co.

This short biography of Wilson concentrates on childhood influences that gave him a strict ethical code that provided him with a moral certitude that determined his path regardless of opposing opinion.

Blumin, Stuart. 1989. *The Emergence of the Middle Class: Social Experience in the American City, 1760–1900*. New York: Cambridge University Press.
The Progressive movement has often been described as a "middle class" movement. Blumin traces the emergence of a recognizable and self-aware "middle class" from the time of the American Revolution up to the beginning of the Progressive Era.

Boyer, Paul. 1992. *Urban Masses and Moral Order in America, 1820–1920*. Cambridge: Harvard University Press.
In examining urban reform in the Progressive Era, Boyer describes two sharply divergent trends in thinking about urban planning and social control. Many held views rooted in religious tradition that had a bleak view of humanity and argued for coercive strategies, and others argued for reform methods based on the new social sciences that emphasized the importance of environmental betterment as a means of urban moral control.

Brinkley, Douglas. 2009. *The Wilderness Warrior*. New York: HarperCollins.
This biography of Theodore Roosevelt centers on the president's experiences as naturalist, frontiersmen, and hunter, and the critical role these experiences had in the formation Roosevelt's political agenda.

Cashman S. D. 1988. *America in the Gilded Age*. Albany: State University of New York Press.
Cashman provides a good overview of the era. He argues that the Progressive movement did not begin with Theodore Roosevelt but rather he rode the wave of Progressivism to national prominence.

Croly, Herbert. 1912. *Marcus Alonzo Hanna; His Life and Work*. New York: Macmillan and Company.
While providing a good biography of the Ohio political boss who made McKinley president, the book also offers insight into the mind of Herbert Croly, one of the chief architects of Theodore Roosevelt's views on government regulation of big business.

Davis, Deborah. 2012. *Guest of Honor: Booker T. Washington, Theodore Roosevelt, and the White House Dinner That Shocked a Nation*. New York: Simon and Schuster.
This very readable book paints a clear and accurate picture of the social and political context in which Roosevelt's famous dinner with Booker T. Washington occurred.

Degler, Carl. 1980. *At Odds: Women and Family in America from the Revolution to the Present*. New York: Oxford University Press.
  A pioneer work in women's studies, this book traces the evolution of women's role in society from the eighteenth through the twentieth century and places the tension between the struggle for women's equality and the women's role in the home into historic context.

Du Bois, W. E. B. (1903) 2005. *The Souls of Black Folk*. New York: Simon and Schuster.
  A seminal study of race relations in the South at the beginning of the twentieth century by the era's preeminent sociologist.

Fisher, James T. 2000. *Communion of Immigrants: Catholics in America*. New York: Oxford University Press.
  Beginning with one of the first Spanish expeditions to Florida, in 1528, this book traces Catholicism's growth from a suppressed and persecuted foreign religion to the largest and most ethnically diverse denomination in the country.

Ginger, Ray. 1963. *Age of Excess*. New York: MacMillan.
  Although published a half century ago, Ginger's book remains one of the most popular interpretations of the era. The book covers social, political, economic, and cultural history from the end of Reconstruction through the Progressive age and ties the themes together by asserting that the insatiable desire for economic gain was the common theme of the era.

Glaab, Charles, and A. Theodore Brown. 1967. *A History of Urban America*. New York: MacMillan Co.
  A general history of the United States that uses the growth of the city as its organizing theme.

Glad, Paul. 1964. *McKinley Bryan and the People*. New York: Lippincott.
  The book discusses in detail the candidates' personalities, the economic issues and regional forces, the rise of the Populist Party, campaign strategy, and voting patterns.

Goldman, Emma. 1971. *Living My Life*. Minneola, NY: Dover Publications.
  Provides a direct view of some of the major labor-owner conflicts at the end of the nineteenth century from the perspective of one of the leading anarchists of the time.

Goldstone, Lawrence. 2011. *Inherently Unequal: The Betrayal of Equal Rights in the Supreme Court 1865–1903*. New York: Walker and Company.
  A well-written legal history that contextualizes and summarizes the key Supreme Court decisions that emasculated the Fourteenth and Fifteenth Amendments at the end of the nineteenth century.

Gorn, Elliot, and Warren Goldstein. 2004. *A Brief History of American Sports*. Chicago: University of Illinois Press.

A brief but well-written summary of American sports, which emphasizes the connection between sports and rise of urban life in America.

Kearns Goodwin, Doris. 2013. *The Bully Pulpit: Theodore Roosevelt, William Howard Taft, and the Golden Age of Journalism*. New York: Simon and Schuster.

This well-written and researched book uses biography to uncover the complex relationship between Theodore Roosevelt and William Howard Taft and its transformation from close political friends and allies to political contestants who divided their party in 1912. The book also provides great insights into the investigative journalists of the era and their interplay with Roosevelt and his administration.

Kessler-Harris, Alice. 2006. *Gendering Labor History*. Urbana and Chicago: University of Illinois Press.

In this seminal work, Kessler-Harris explains the impact of gender on American labor history. She argues that the gendering of male as well as female workers has impacted social class in America.

La Follette, Robert. (1911) 1913. *Robert La Follette's Autobiography: A Personal Narrative of Political Experiences*. Madison, WI: The Robert M. La Follette Co.

This personal history of Bob La Follette, Progressive governor of Wisconsin, provides insight into how Progressive politics functioned at the local and state level.

Link, Arthur. 1963. *Woodrow Wilson and the Progressive Era*. New York: Harper Torch.

Well organized and skillfully written, this book by the editor of the Wilson papers, is an in-depth authoritative study of the man, his politics, and his presidency.

Morris, Edmund. 2001. *Theodore Rex*. New York: Random House.

This book deals exclusively with the years of the Roosevelt presidency. Morris charts Roosevelt's accomplishments, including the acquisition of the Panama Canal and the Philippines, the creation of national parks and monuments, and the harnessing of the power of the corporations. Making ample use of TR's private and presidential papers as well as the archives of such associates as John Hay, William Howard Taft, Owen Wister, John Burroughs, and Henry Adams, Morris provides the reader with an insider's view into details of the dynamic presidency of Theodore Roosevelt.

Mott, Frank Luther. 1957. *A History of American Magazines*. Cambridge, MA: Belknap Press.

An excellent three-volume reference work that covers the major magazines published from colonial times to mid-twentieth century. In addition to details of the format, circulation, and content of magazines, the work includes insight into the social and political dynamics as seen through these publications.

Mowry, George. 1951. *The California Progressives*. Chicago: Quadrangle Paperbacks.

This book describes California Progressives as a group of closely allied businessmen who formed a political coalition that opposed big business as well as labor when they saw their own interests threatened. It traces the brief life of this group from its origins in 1906 to its demise in 1912.

Nugent, Walter T. K. 2009. *Progressivism: A Very Short Introduction*. New York: Oxford University Press.

Written in the aftermath of the election of President Obama, this very brief history covers the essential details of the Progressive Era while trying to draw parallels with current events.

Okrent, Daniel. 2010. *Last Call: The Rise and Fall of Prohibition*. New York: Scribner, 2010.

A well-written and detailed story of the creation of the "dry" political coalition—including women, religious reformers, and professional politicians—and the strategy they used to make Prohibition the law of the land. More than a history of Prohibition, it is an excellent study of grassroots political strategy.

Opdycke, Sandra. 1999. *No One Was Turned Away: The Role of Public Hospitals in New York City Since 1900*. New York: Oxford University Press.

This book traces the history of two major urban hospitals—one public, one private—and their strategies to survive in an age when hospitals changed from simple charitable establishments designed to give hospice to poor sick people to the complex scientifically sophisticated enterprises they became in the twentieth century.

Painter, Nell. 2013. *Standing at Armageddon*. New York: Norton and Company.

Written as a "people's history," the author argues that the strong pressures of the agricultural and industrial laborers forced the passage of Progressive reforms in the early twentieth century.

Rauschenbusch, Walter. 1907. *Christianity and the Social Crisis*. New York: Macmillan & Co.

Thoroughly readable treatise by the person considered the theologian of the Social Gospel movement.

Reiss, Steven. 1991. *City Games: The Evolution of American Urban Society and the Rise of Sports.* Chicago: University of Chicago Press.
This very well-written and researched book discusses the development of sports and its relation to the changing political social and economic realities of urban America.

Riis, Jacob. 1890. *How the Other Half Lives: Studies among the Tenements of New York by Jacob A. Riis with Illustrations Chiefly from Photographs Taken by the Author.* New York: Charles Scribner's Sons.
An early and telling example of photographic journalism, this important work provided a persuasive argument for those who advocated government assistance in poor urban neighborhoods. The book also presents a colorful and lively—if somewhat racist—view of immigrant urban communities.

Riordan, William L. (1905) 1963. *Plunkitt of Tammany Hall.* Reprint, New York: E. P. Dutton.
Story of an urban political leader in the gilded age into the early twentieth century in his own words.

Schlesinger, Arthur M. 1933. *The Rise of the City, 1878–1898.* New York: Macmillan and Co.
Seminal work in urban history by one of the first historians to put the rise of the urban boss into historic perspective.

Sinclair, Upton. 1906. *The Jungle.* New York: Doubleday.
The book that persuaded Congress to pass the Pure Food and Drug Act.

Smith, Erin A. 2000. *Hard-Boiled: Working-Class Readers and Pulp Magazines.* Philadelphia: Temple University Press.
Well-researched and well-written history of the pulp magazine industry and those who read them. This book also provides insight onto the male working-class culture of urban America in the first decades of the twentieth century.

Spear, Alan. 1967. *Black Chicago: The Making of a Ghetto.* Chicago: University of Chicago Press.
This book traces events that led to the development of the black ghetto on the south side of Chicago from the end of the nineteenth century and treats them as a series of events that led to the great Chicago race riot of 1919.

Stulman Dennet, Andrea. 1997. *Weird & Wonderful: The Dime Store Museum in America.* New York: New York University Press.

This book presents the dime store museum as a unique institution that combined many forms of entertainment under one roof for one price. The book also provides insight into urban entertainment and lifestyle at the turn of the century.

Sullivan, Mark. 1933. *Our Times: The United States 1900–1925*. New York: Charles Scribner's Sons.
Seminal and still significant social history of the United States in the first two decades of the twentieth century.

Thelen, David. 1976. *Robert M. La Follette and the Insurgent Spirit*. Boston: Little Brown and Co.
Well-researched biography of Wisconsin's Progressive governor provides good insights into the Progressive politics at the state and local level.

Vann Woodward, C. 1974. *The Origins of the New South, 1877–1913*. Baton Rouge: Louisiana State University Press.
Seminal work on Southern history provides good insights into the dynamics of the Populist movement in the South.

Wells, Ida B. 1892. *Southern Horrors: Lynch Law in All Its Phases*. http://www.digitalhistory.uh.edu/disp_textbook.cfm?smtid=3&psid=3614
Wells detailed and gave graphic descriptions of lynching's in the South.

WEBSITES

American Memory.gov
Association of Religious Data Archives *ARDA; http://www.thearda.com
Duke University Libraries; http://www.scriptorium.lib.duke.edu
The Gilder Lehrman Center for the Study of Slavery, Resistance and Abolition, Yale University; http://www.yale.edu/glc/archive/1152.htm
Historymatters.org
History of Chicago; http://www.encyclopedia.chicagohistory.org
Pbs.org/wgbh/americanexperience
University of Pennsylvania Archives online; http://www.archives.upenn.edu/home/archives.html
U.S. Census Bureau Data Base; http://www.census.gov/data.html#

ARTICLES

Arnesen, Eric. 1994. "Like Banquo's Ghost, It Will Not Down: The Race Question and the American Railroad Brotherhoods, 1880–1920." *The American Historical Review* 99(5) (December): 1601–33.

This article discusses the impediments to organization created by racial tensions in the labor movement.

Baker, Ray Stannard. 1903. "The Right to Work: The Story of the Non-Striking Miners." *McClure's Magazine* 20(3) (January): 323–35.
Expose of worker relations in the aftermath of the great Anthracite coal strike.

Barrett, James R. 1992. "Americanization from the Bottom Up: Immigration and the Remaking of the Working Class in the United States, 1880–1930." *The Journal of American History*, 79(3), Discovering America: A Special Issue (December): 996–1020.
Argues that Americanization was not exclusively a middle class campaign, but was also embraced by workers groups.

Bates, J. Leonard. 1957. "Fulfilling American Democracy: The Conservation Movement, 1907 to 1921." *The Mississippi Valley Historical Review* 44(1) (June): 29–57.
Discusses the politics that drove the conservation movement.

Bendroth, Margaret. 2004. "Why Women Loved Billy Sunday: Urban Revivalism and Popular Entertainment in Early Twentieth-Century American Culture." *Religion and American Culture: A Journal of Interpretation* 14(2) (Summer): 251–71.
Describes the strategy and attraction of Billy Sunday. Evangelist Billy Sunday (1862–1935) is well known for an aggressively masculine platform style that was clearly aimed at attracting a male audience to his urban revival campaigns. Less recognized but equally important are Sunday's meetings for "women only," in which the handsome, athletic evangelist preached passionate, explicit sermons on sexual vice to an audience that had been purged of all male interlopers.

Beringause, A. F. 1957. "The Double Martyrdom of Randolph Bourne." *Journal of the History of Ideas* 18(4) (October): 594–603.
Documents the trials and alienation faced by Bourne as he insisted on remaining opposed to the World War I.

Brown, David. 2003. "Redefining American History: Ethnicity, Progressive Historiography and the Making of Richard Hofstadter." *The History Teacher* 36(4) (August): 527–48.
Good bibliographic essay on Progressive movement.

Carnegie, Andrew. 1889. "Wealth." *North American Review* 148(391) (June): 653.
Andrew Carnegie explains his Gospel of Wealth.

Cohen, Sol. 1969. "Urban School Reform." *History of Education Quarterly* 9(3) (Autumn): 298–304.

Outlines goals and strategies of urban Progressive educators.

Destler, Chester McA. 1941. "Consummation of a Labor-Populist Alliance in Illinois, 1894." *The Mississippi Valley Historical Review* 27(4) (March): 589–602.

Provides insights into strategies used by Populists to attract urban workers to the Populist Party.

Diamond, William. 1941. "Urban and Rural Voting in 1896." *The American Historical Review* 46(2) (January): 281–305.

Provides insights into the urban working-class vote that contributed significantly to McKinley's victory.

Diffee, Christopher. 2005. "Sex and the City: The White Slavery Scare and Social Governance in the Progressive Era." *American Quarterly* 57(2) (June): 411–37.

Provides insights into the role of woman and religious groups in urban reform movements.

Durden, Robert F. 1963. "The 'Cow-bird' Grounded: The Populist Nomination of Bryan and Tom Watson in 1896." *The Mississippi Valley Historical Review* 50 (3) (December): 397–423.

Discusses political strategy and debate among Populists when Democrats nominated William Jennings Bryan.

Flanagan, Maureen A. "Gender and Urban Political Reform: The City Club and the Women's City Club of Chicago in the Progressive Era." *The American Historical Review* 95, no. 4 (October 1990): 1032–50.

Flanagan examines women's participation in Chicago politics and argues that Progressive concerns and tactics were determined by gender.

Frese, Stephen J. 2003. "Aldo Leopold: An American Prophet." *The History Teacher* 37(1), Special Feature Issue: Environmental History and National History Day 2003 Prize Essays (November): 99–118.

Good biographic sketch of an important conservationist.

Gilmore, Al-Tony. 1973. "Jack Johnson and White Women: The National Impact." *The Journal of Negro History* 58(1) (January): 18–38.

Discussion of race in the Progressive Era.

Gloege, Timothy E. 2013. "Faith Healing, Medical Regulation, and Public Religion in Progressive Era Chicago." *Religion and American Culture: A Journal of Interpretation* 23(2) (Summer): 185–231.

This essay examines a six-year campaign against the radical faith healer John Alexander Dowie mounted in the 1890s by Chicago doctors, public health officials, and their "respectable" middle-class allies. It helped grant medical professionals the right to oversee the public body just as elite Protestants superintended its soul.

Gratton, Brian, and Jon Moen. 2004. "Immigration, Culture, and Child Labor in the United States, 1880–1920." *The Journal of Interdisciplinary History* 34(3) (Winter): 355–91.

Alarmed by child labor in factories and mills, Progressive Era reformers criticized immigrants and immigrant cultures for sanctioning exploitation of their young. This article argues that higher male earnings, technological shifts, and changes in law and culture compelled children to become students instead of wage earners.

Hendricks, Rickey L. 1982. "The Conservation Movement: A Critique of Historical Sources." *The History Teacher* 16(1) (November): 77–104.

Good bibliographic essay on Progressive Conservation movement.

Holmes, William F. 1975. "The Demise of the Colored Farmers' Alliance." *The Journal of Southern History* 41(2) (May): 187–200.

Describes the accomplishments of the Colored Farmers' Alliance and also the violence used by white southerners to destroy the alliance.

Johnson, Joan Marie. 2000. "Drill into us . . . the Rebel Tradition: The Contest over Southern Identity in Black and White Women's Clubs, South Carolina, 1898–1930." *The Journal of Southern History* 66(3) (August): 525–62.

The formation of women reform movements in the South.

Jones, Beverly W. 1982. "Mary Church Terrell and the National Association of Colored Women, 1896 to 1901." *The Journal of Negro History* 67(1) (Spring): 20–33.

Reform movements begun by black women.

Kaplan, Sidney. 1956. "Social Engineers as Saviors: Effects of World War I on Some American Liberals." *Journal of the History of Ideas* 17(3) (June): 347–69.

Describes the demise of liberal idealism in the aftermath of World War I.

Kelley, Robin D. G. 1993. "We Are Not What We Seem: Rethinking Black Working-Class Opposition in the Jim Crow South." *The Journal of American History* 80(1) (June): 75–112.

Discusses black labor monument in the South in the Progressive Era.

Leuchtenburg, William E. 1952. "Progressivism and Imperialism: The Progressive Movement and American Foreign Policy, 1898–1916." *The Mississippi Valley Historical Review* 39(3) (December): 483–504.
Discusses the forces—including commercial and racist—that drove American Imperialism in the Progressive Era.

Lodge, Henry Cabot. 1904. "A Million Immigrants a Year: Efforts to Restrict Undesirable Immigrants." *Century Magazine* 67(5) (January) 466–469.
Provides insight into Progressive attitudes on race.

Mandel, Bernard. 1955. "Samuel Gompers and the Negro Workers, 1886–1914." *The Journal of Negro History* 40(1) (January): 34–60.
Discusses the union movement and race.

Moehling, Carolyn M. 2002. "Broken Homes: The 'Missing' Children of the 1910 Census." *The Journal of Interdisciplinary History* 33(2) (Autumn): 205–33.
Progressive Era activists claimed that poverty led to broken homes: Impoverished parents—particularly single mothers—were compelled to place children in the care of relatives or institutions. Consequently, the 1910 census reported numerous "missing children" in the data, especially among single immigrant and black mothers.

O'Neill, William L. 1965. "Divorce in the Progressive Era." *American Quarterly* 17 (2) (Summer), Part 1: 203–17.
Describes the divorce debate in the Progressive movement. It was one of the issues that divided Progressives.

Peavler, David J. 2008. "African Americans in Omaha and the 1898 Trans-Mississippi and International Exposition." *The Journal of African American History* 93(3) (Summer): 337–61.
Describes the changes in collective memory that created the popular conception of the idyllic plantation of the antebellum era.

Perry, Elisabeth I. 1985. " 'The General Motherhood of the Commonwealth': Dance Hall Reform in the Progressive Era." *American Quarterly* 37(5) (Winter): 719–33.
Provides insights into women's participation in the Progressive movement.

Schultz, Stanley K. 1965. "The Morality of Politics: The Muckrakers' Vision of Democracy." *The Journal of American History* 52(3) (December): 527–47.
Discusses investigative reporters and the sense of mission that drove their work.

Smith, Willard H. 1966. "William Jennings Bryan and the Social Gospel." *The Journal of American History* 53(1) (June): 41–60.

Uses quotes from Bryan to explain the interplay between Bryan's Fundamentalism and his support for the Social Gospel movement and how Bryan negotiated the seemingly contradictory positions of fundamentalism and Progressivism.

Tyler-McGraw, Marie. 1991. "Parlor to Politics: Women and Reform, 1890–1925." *The Journal of American History* 78(1) (June): 260–64.

Discusses the influence of women's reform movements on Progressive politics.

Urban, Wayne. 1976. "Organized Teachers and Educational Reform During the Progressive Era: 1890–1920." *History of Education Quarterly* 16(1) (Spring): 35–52.

Discusses the goals of educational reformers in the Progressive Era.

Wilson, Christopher P. 1996. "Stephen Crane and the Police." *American Quarterly* 48(2) (June): 273–315.

This discussion of police activity also provides insights into daily life in turn of the century urban America.

INDEX

About the Author

Francis J. Sicius, PhD, is professor of history at St. Thomas University, Miami, Florida. His published works include an award-winning biography of Peter Maurin, cofounder of the Catholic Worker Movement; *The Greenwood Encyclopedia of Daily Life in America, Volume 3, 1900–1940*; and ABC-CLIO's *Daily Life through American History in Primary Documents, 1860–1920*.